Underdogs and Newshounds

Chris Skudder

PROJECTIS PUBLISHING

LONDON

First published in paperback in 2022
by **PROJECTIS PUBLISHING** (UK)
a subdivision of PROJECTIS CONSULTANTS Ltd.

© Chris Skudder & PROJECTIS PUBLISHING 2022

Typeset in Calibri by PROJECTIS PUBLISHING
Printed in the United Kingdom by PODWW, 9 Culley Court, Orton Southgate, Peterborough, PE2 6XD. PODWW is FSC certified.

British Cataloguing in Publication Data.
A catalogue record for this book is available
from the British Library.

Chris Skudder, 2022
Underdogs & Newshounds
PROJECTIS PUBLISHING, London.
Projectispublishing.com

ISBN 978-1-913984-09-0

First edition (2022)
The text of this book has been put on the blockchain by PROJECTIS CONSULTANTS Ltd. and its CEO Dr Christian de Vartavan to protect its IP.

Keywords: Sports, reporting, travelling
Disclaimer: The opinions expressed in this book are not necessarily those of the publisher.

From 1966 through to Qatar, England's World Cups have lifted us up, and battered us down.

Broadcaster Chris Skudder has lived them all, from sketchy technicolour on his neighbour's telly in the glory days, to escapades all over the globe through seven tournaments with his TV crews.

'Underdogs and Newshounds' doesn't hold back. More than an eye witness account, Chris reveals the stories you rarely hear or can never be fully told on television. You get the feeling you're travelling with him, getting close to fans, players, managers, undercover cops, the press pack and host nations along the way.

And as a lifelong Birmingham City fan, Chris continues to live the lows and lowers that any struggling club or England supporter knows only too well.

This is a book for any fan who ever hit the road for the big international tournaments, or harbours a dream of doing so. But there's more here than for just sports fans, from someone who saw the bigger picture. It hones in on the people and the places, littered with wry humour, punctuated by dark tales from the road.

Chris Skudder is one of the most travelled and experienced sports correspondents in British broadcasting. He was one of the original wave of broadcasters from the satellite revolution of the early 90's when Sky News shook up the establishment - one of the pioneers of rolling news and sports news. Recognised by sports fans the world over, Chris also earned a place in history as the first person to commit the words 'Sky Sports' to tape, a voiceover for the original commercial tender from the days when the idea of a dedicated sports channel was first in play.

Eye witness to seven football World Cups, he is known for being in the thick of the action - interviewing everyone from die hard fans to undercover officers and some of the biggest names in sport. With a career spanning more than 35 years - 25 of them with Sky News and Sky Sports News, he now works for ITV News among others. He is also a podcaster, gig goer and music fan. Each of the chapters of his debut book, Underdogs and Newshounds, hits the right note with a musical reference tied to the storytelling.

Chris is the newshound who always roots for the underdog. As a lifelong follower of his original hometown club - perennial underachievers Birmingham City - he is the first to admit, it keeps him grounded!

CONTENTS

Foreword : 1

While football's the backdrop to this book, it's not about the football, or at least, the stories you already know. There are libraries full of them and you've heard it all before. This is a document from the road, an incident packed trail through seven unforgettable World Cups; USA, France, Japan, Germany, South Africa, Brazil and Russia, viewed through the lens of a television correspondent who was there, and the club 'education' that paved the way for me as a fan. It was never about groin strains and 4-4-2s for me. It was the people, the places and the events, capturing the essence of the occasion. I was lucky enough to be a fan with a camera and microphone, and tried to tell stories for the person shouting questions (or abuse) from the other side of the screen. 'Take me there' was my mantra, for the people who couldn't be. But many of the stories here were the ones you didn't hear, or that I couldn't fully tell on television.

When you follow the most chronically underachieving football team (Birmingham City, but frankly, any number of hapless clubs can compete for that title - well, maybe not quite), emotional scarring is the price you pay. I've lost count of the 'f***ed-off-with-this-lot' moments and promises never to return. But like A New Year's resolution blurted out nine pints down on the final night of December they usually last about a week.

Some clubs just got lucky with money. I've often asked fans of Manchester City and Chelsea, let's face it pre-windfall also rans, how they got their heads around suddenly being serial winners. Either way, the 'one-eighty' about turn in fortunes at Stamford Bridge led me to an unforgettable meeting with Roman Abramovich whose alleged 'dirty' Russian cash became a game changer, before it all rebounded on him so spectacularly during Russia's war with Ukraine. Believe me, it was quite an experience being the only journalist on Chelsea's open top bus parade when they won their first title under the media-shy oligarch. Having been warned off, meeting one of the world's most darkly mysterious, richest men eye to eye at the top of the stairs of a 'two bob' double decker has me sweating at the memory all over again! Read on!

England's recurring failures, when they probably should have been winning things only compounded everything I've just said above. Indeed, as I write this we're only just over the near miss at the Euros in summer 2021. I watched it from afar, lying in a Tokyo hotel bed at four in the morning after a sleepless night cursing my mobile phone while the signal froze at the crucial moments. You always knew something would go wrong when the pressure was on. I called it from as early as the group stage. England would lose in the Final. It's what we do. But wait! You sense the narrative is changing and the stories here might just prove to be the prelude to a less painful future. Might. England will, er, win something soon (wide eyes emoji). If I'm wrong, just blame a negative (over cautious) coach or the over-hyped expectation that naysayers would (justifiably) call entitlement. Never a good look.

Following a basket case club (and country) does shape you as a person and depending on how deep the scarring, makes you either bitter and twisted or all the more rounded for it ('character forming' always sounds so laboured). As the years go by, youthful anger usually gives way to a gallows humour that makes all the catastrophes a bit more bearable. I got there decades ago. Brummies are good at it, and never take themselves too seriously (at least the ones from the blue side of the city). It's probably where my tongue-in-cheek irreverence across these pages comes from. Just keep the default bar low, and everything beyond that's a bonus.

Much of this was written during the pandemic lockdown of 2021 when we really came to understand how football is nothing without fans. We'd never realised just how much they were missed until they were gone. I hope these stories illuminate their essential place in the people's game. They're also a celebration of the underdog spirit that's part of the British DNA. I'm a natural outsider myself and have always been drawn to people with the confidence (or defiance) to follow their star and be themselves, whether that be through sport, music, or just life itself.

You'll notice music references also punctuate this book. Quite apart from some of the specific stories here and my penchant for outsider music (leftfield, underground, indie, alternative, whatever you want to call it) the chapter titles just felt appropriate in the context of the storytelling. Bring me an underdog all day long whether it's on the sports field or an artist trying to make a mark against the odds. The ones who never got the attention they deserved and whose work remains hidden to all bar those who are rewarded by going looking for lost gems. There was a song playing on 6 Music just now as I write, 'The Mauritian Badminton Doubles Champion,

1973' by Scottish songwriting outsider Hamish Hawk. Now, that's what I call a song title. 'Like Common People sung by Christopher Wren' as the lyric goes, while sounding like Scott Walker doing (Suede's) Brett Anderson. Oceans away from the mainstream.

I once went to review a gig for Sky Arts by that late, great British institution Mark E Smith and his unique, cult band The Fall at a smallish venue in Oxford. The maverick outsider, who once barked out the BBC football results like they'd never been read before. But once I got there and met some of the diehards, contrarians and oddballs in the crowd it became less about the music and more about them. Frank Skinner was there too, eulogising even more than he does about West Brom, and a quiet bloke in a raincoat who declared that he didn't really like music, 'only Mahler and The Fall'. He was the kind of underdog I'm talking about. Beautifully contradictory and perfectly random.

Joining Sky in the very early 90s felt like a natural fit. The satellite newcomer was the underdog to the BBC's establishment and a fearless spirit in those early years of growth made it a great place to be. I always tried to be honest and occasionally that drifted closer than intended to in-house boundaries. But at a time when the lines between journalism and PR have become ever more blurred, I could never regret wanting to 'tell it like it is'.

I've recently watched the BBC's 'Fever Pitch' documentary, on the 90s rise of the Premier League and almost choked on my tea when I popped up in a cameo stumbling over some words from Arsène Wenger's first day at Arsenal in '96. Lest we forget, for the purpose of the narrative in this book, at that time, England (and Gareth Southgate) had also just blown their Euros penalty shootout against the Germans at Wembley. If not England's, these were Sky's pioneering glory days, the outsiders against the big boys, the early years when Sky Sports News was but a twinkle in Rupert Murdoch's eye and all the sport was on Sky News at '20 past the hour'. Those were the days. Bizarrely, as you'll read later, I was the first person to ever record the words 'Sky Sports' to tape, before the channel even existed. But as the company grew into a giant I left because of it too. Huge outlays on the price of screening our great game meant cutting costs and when I left suddenly after more than 25 years, never one for a fuss, I said nothing, even after they'd managed to send me someone else's severance contract! Only in posterity do we make sense of everything and if leaving wasn't easy, what a journey we had along the way...

Chapter 1
Let England Shake
1966 and 1970

"The gorillas have shot down a helicopter..." Bob Dougall just said it on the news. Must be true. Gorillas! Blimey. Apes versus mankind in the Vietnam War. What was their beef? I remember it like yesterday, standing transfixed in front of the television in the living room of our Victorian Birmingham home with its net curtains and mushy pea green carpet. They showed the wreckage on the newsreel report, black and white pictures of men crouching down with bazookas on their shoulders. But no sign of the gorillas. I felt a little let down but was already siding with the animals. It must have been the matinée memory of Fay Wray being plucked from a New York skyscraper by King Kong, and a chopper being swatted out of the sky by the giant beast. That, and a vivid imagination. Well, that's my excuse, anyway. It would take a few more years for aural doppelgängers like 'guerillas' to enter my vocabulary. And anyway, I was only too happy to see the underdog fighting back.

It was 1970 and my early attempts at making sense of the news hadn't yet distinguished fact from childhood fantasy. It was still a monochrome world in our house. Man walking on the moon for the first time, Churchill's funeral, Bobby Kennedy being shot dead on television and England winning the '66 World Cup had all passed by in black and white. In the window of Rediffusion on Kings Heath High Street, Birmingham the old test card suddenly came to life. The girl with the balloon playing noughts and crosses blossomed from grey to glorious colour. Nothing would be the same again.

But colour TV still seemed a pipe dream in the Skudder house, so the return of the World Cup would have to be played away from home. Next door to be precise. Mexico '70 at the Shinglers' house. They had a new colour telly, so we went round to watch England trying to retain the Jules Rimet Trophy. Donald was a television producer for ATV (then Midlands regional ITV) in Birmingham. So he was famous in my world. A larger than life barrel-like man with horn rimmed glasses, clipped beard and a bellowing laugh that frightened the children. His wife Liz was an English eccentric, prone to walking round the house naked while us boys took a mattress to the top of the stairs and rode it wildly down like a rollercoaster before ending up in a heap at the bottom. She was what we'd now call bohemian, the manager of the Ian Campbell folk group, a local musician who lived just down our road.

Then there were the Campbell kids, Ali and Robin. Ali I remember well, a little red-headed lad who came round to the Shingler house to play football or look for his dad. Fairly unremarkable at the time, until years later after we'd left Brum and I turned on Top Of The Pops. There was Ali with his distinctive voice, propelled along by that unmistakable 'ching-ching' reggae rhythm: 'Ivor-y madonna, dying in the dust......' Food For Thought, indeed. UB40 and the Campbell brothers were well on their way from the modest suburbs of Birmingham to conquering the world.

I don't think it was just my age, just turning 11, but the 1970 World Cup held a magic that still gives me a tingle more than half a century later. England, world champions, defending our pride far away in exotic Mexico, and from where live broadcasts barely looked possible. Live television football in those days was restricted to pretty much one game a season, the FA Cup Final. So to have a window on the World Cup, match after match from the other side of the globe was a thing of wonder. The picture wasn't great, the product of early, straining satellite technology with narrow lines across the screen and a fuzzy distortion on the commentators' microphones that made them sound as far away as Neil Armstrong on the moon the year before. But like then, it was live, and it came with a sense of pioneering magic.

By then, bespoke World Cup songs had caught on and ours was what I'd probably regard now as a crime against music, but it did the job. 'Back Home, there'll be thinking about us, when we are far away...' awkwardly bellowed out by a bunch of tone deaf footballers. But it captured the hearts of the nation as we sent them on their way.

Then there were the collectible plastic 'World Cup Coins' that you'd pick up in a little blue packet from the local petrol station every time your dad filled up. There was a powder blue collecting board into which you'd insert all the coins embossed with a likeness of the England squad's faces. For some reason I distinctly remember Everton's Brian Labone, long since forgotten by just about all bar the Merseyside faithful. Perhaps he was the one I needed to complete the set, but either way, I had the lot, all snapped neatly into place before the tournament had even started. Mine eventually vanished amid a pile of domestic junk in the growing up period that followed. But my heart soared when I found an original set staring out at me from a glass cabinet in the National Football Museum in Manchester a few years ago. The exact shade of blue and Brian Labone had been just as I remembered and treasured all those decades earlier.

England had been drawn in the same group as the favourites Brazil, and that meant a showdown with the world's greatest player, Pelé. A national 'event' and we all trooped round to the Shinglers' next door to watch. I can still remember the nerves, the excitement as England goalkeeper Gordon Banks pulled off his gravity defying 'save of the century' from Pelé's perfect header, and the disappointment when the jinking Jairzinho thundered the only goal of the game into the England net. Bobby Moore had also made one of the most celebrated, beautifully timed tackles ever, on the great man Pelé.

But even back then my curiosity for the news story had been piqued; how the cards had been stacked against England when the captain was accused of stealing a gold bracelet from a jeweller's store in Bogota, Colombia in the build up to the tournament. It was headline news all over the world, the talk of the playground and the England camp was under siege. Nothing was ever proved but the pressure didn't help, along with conspiracy theories that England's defence of the trophy was being sabotaged. Years later I'd be sitting alongside Bobby commentating for Capital Radio, pinching myself I was working with one of my boyhood heroes, while all this ran through my head. What a story! Of course I never raised it with him, but still chuckle when I remember the Capital football phone-in and Bobby being ambushed by a rogue caller: 'Oh, and by the way, Bobby...what DID you do with that bracelet?!' Cue, a startled silence, then, a sharpish "I never 'ad it in the first place, mate'. Straight in, like that perfectly timed tackle.

But back to that World Cup. Although the Brazilians had got the better of England, we still got through the group and were on collision course for the West Germans, who had revenge on their minds after the '66 Final. It was the quarter finals and the nation came to a standstill. Not for us the monochrome, black and white television experience, but new, glorious technicolour, well, sort of, in the Shinglers' front room where the tension was tight as a drum. I couldn't eat. Too nervous. England wore crimson red, just as they did on that glorious day at Wembley four summers earlier. Leon, Mexico was the venue and we prayed for a victory. It started like a dream. Alan Mullery, another who I'd later work with as a pundit on Sky News, finished expertly in the first half and England were ahead in scorching heat.

Then it looked all over when '66 hero Martin Peters made it 2-0 just after half time. I can still see him running off to celebrate waving both hands in 'Hallelujah!' fashion just like the boot polish faced minstrels singing 'Well, Hello Mamma!' on the cringeworthy Black and White Minstrel Show' that (shockingly) characterised the times. Two goals up! Donald Shingler didn't know much about football, but I seem to remember him proclaiming that it was all over with a bellowing laugh. My tension was starting to fall away when Franz Beckenbauer, who I'd later interview as boss of the German 2006 World Cup bid, snaked one through a crowd of players and into the corner. 2-1. Uh-oh. Instantly my heart began to rise back towards my fast drying mouth. Bobby Charlton, a man for a crisis, was inexplicably taken off by Sir Alf Ramsey. But worse than that, England's imperious goalkeeper Gordon Banks had not even made the match after going down with a stomach upset. Poisoned! Sabotaged! were high up the conspiracy theories that surfaced in the following years, but whatever the truth, England had Chelsea's Peter 'The Cat' Bonetti standing in between the sticks, and he was having a nightmare.

Still, we sat on the edge of our seats as time ticked away agonisingly slowly. I can still remember that tension 50 years on. Just hang on! Then it happened. A long cross to the back post and the smallest man on the pitch, Uwe Seeler (who I interviewed years later at the Germany World Cup, still looking just the same, short, plump and balding) sent a skewed, looping header back over his own shoulder, arching over the keeper and into the net. 2-2. We were throwing this away.

Somehow England survived the final few minutes but we were locking into extra time with a dodgy keeper, no Bobby Charlton, crippling heat and a rejuvenated West Germany raring to go. At this point I could not watch. Of all the half century plus of going through the wringer watching football around the world since then, this was the only time I couldn't bear it. I got off my seat, walked into the garden, found a half inflated leather ball and nervously prodded it round the grass like a diner feeling sick and pushing peas around the plate.

Ten minutes of fresh air with a few deep breaths and I was back in, just in time to see the inevitable. Cross to the far post, knocked back across the six yard box and the arch predator Gerd Muller (RIP) gleefully hooking the ball past the hapless Bonetti (also RIP). I can still see it now. Crushing. 2-0 up, 3-2 down. Defeat snatched from the jaws of victory and a regular returning point for years to come when we saw fit to vent our spleen or bemoan the disillusioning downs of football fandom.

Brazil of course went on to win it in the Final against Italy, Pelé's glorious header and quite probably the greatest goal ever scored, a perfectly worked move finished off with devastating efficiency by full back Carlos Alberto. So good, it was almost poetic. Pelé was the king, so when he came to Birmingham a year or two later for a friendly with his club Santos against Villa, it felt like the whole city descended on Villa Park. I was there, aged 12, along with nearly 55,000 others, crammed into a corner of Villa's vast Holte End terrace. Never mind that it was enemy territory, Pelé was in town. Half of Birmingham's burgeoning West Indian community, not regularly seen at the football in those days also decided to join the party. My memory was not so much of the floodlights failing, which they did, halfway through, leaving the great man wondering around in the dark, but more of the giant West Indian standing right in front of me wearing one of those oversized woolly hats keeping a few yards of dreadlocks in place. I didn't see much, but got my first smell of a reefer. The air around me was sweet that night, only turned sour by the fact that Villa won 2-1. Local tribalism had long kicked in by then and any self-respecting Birmingham City fan despised that lot from across the city. At least that's what my Dad taught me.

Pelé meanwhile was entering the twilight years of his career. If anyone had ever told me that night at Villa Park that decades later I'd be sitting face to face with the great man at more than one World Cup, I'd have said you'd been smoking half the ganja in the Holte End. But happen it did. And he was charming. But then again he was the face of Mastercard, whose logo was never far away on an advertising board behind him. Be careful of excessive 'product placement' was always the warning from our television news executives, but hey, it was Pelé, and he was corporate gold. I loved the Brazilians and their carefree approach.

Working the sports news beat also got me close to Carlos Alberto, scorer of that iconic goal in Mexico City. By the noughties the man who had lifted that record third Jules Rimet World Cup trophy in Mexico was now an international coach with Azerbaijan. England had been drawn in the same qualifying group as the Azeris for the 2006 World Cup and played them home and away. The away game was first, in the same week that Northern Ireland also played in Baku. I covered both and by the end of the week felt I knew Carlos Alberto like an old friend. I'd wandered up to him in training one day, told him I worked for Sky and in minutes we were locked into a personal reminiscence of that summer of 1970. He talked me through that goal, of the casual pass by the incomparable Pelé as he rolled the ball into his path, then that fully unloaded flourish from the full back as he lashed the ball like an arrow across the scorched grass and into the billowing net. I was 11 all over again, and humbled to be hearing it first hand. His passing a decade later in 2016 brought worldwide reflection and admiration for possibly the greatest team in World Cup history. Life's short, I mused. Enjoy it while you can and take your chances.

Azerbaijan. A nation that England fans should forever be thankful for. There was only one thing that crossed my mind when I heard England had been paired with them in that World Cup qualifying group and I would be out there to cover it for Sky. I'll get on to my memories of 1966 shortly, but ever since that fateful day on July 30th of that year, we'd always been told that it was the 'Russian' linesman who had confirmed that Geoff Hurst's hat trick goal in the Final had crossed the line. The swivel, the flashing shot that smashed against the underside of the bar when the match was on a knife edge at 2-2 in extra time. And then, in a flurry too quick for the camera frame rates of that time, the ball bouncing down onto the goalline and out back into play while England's players celebrated (hopefully, pleadingly in some cases) in front of the match officials. In my opinion, it was never a goal, however many times you look at it. About half over the line I reckon, when it has to be fully over for the goal to stand. But then again, I can't help it. I've always pulled for the underdog, the outsider, and even though this was my country, I can still see the argument from the German side on this one. As we'll come to later in this book, there's an old football adage that the game has a habit of 'even-ing itself out' when it comes to luck and Frank Lampard's 2010 goal that clearly crossed the line against the Germans in South Africa but wasn't given, probably settled a very old score, even though I was fuming about the injustice at the time. More on that later.

The linesman, Tofiq Bahramov was England's saviour that day in '66 at Wembley. Though he wasn't Russian, he was from Azerbaijan. But that's how the public came to remember him (no doubt led by the tabloid media). Anyone from the communist Soviet bloc was identified as 'Russian'. Ridiculous really, as Russia didn't even formally play their first World Cup under their own flag until 1994 in the US, and the men from behind the Iron Curtain came to England in '66 with the Soviet 'CCCP' emblazoned across their red shirts.

But anyway the man with the flag that day was a national hero in Baku. Azerbaijan had become independent following the fall of the Soviet Union in 1991 and two years later after Bahramov's death at the age of 68, the national stadium was named after him. Not bad, considering it bore the name of Bolshevik revolutionary hero Lenin until then.

As soon as it became known that England would be playing in that very stadium, a statue went up outside in his honour, and England fan groups, eager to project positive stories after years of violence at home and abroad fixed up a small ceremony in which Geoff Hurst would turn out at the statue to honour the man who helped him become immortal as the only player to ever score a hat-trick in a World Cup Final. At that time, Mark Perryman, official 'England Fans' spokesman and a one man army when it came to organising this kind of thing, put me in touch with Bahramov's son, Bahram Bahramov. Great name. I'm not sure I've ever come across a Robert Roberts, William Williams or Thomas Thomas but where there's a Neville Neville anything's possible. Mind you, I did have a great grandfather by the name of Sil Sill, Silvester if you want the whole thing, but a name that his family loved so much that it was passed on to the first son for FIVE successive generations.

I arranged to meet Bahram at the old family home in the backstreets of Baku with camera crew in tow. I don't know what I expected at the home of a national celebrity but there was something oddly familiar about it. A gloomy red brick terrace on a busy main road that might have come out of any Victorian city back home. It was dark and dingy with net curtains in every window suppressing the light, and intricate lace doilies laid out on dark antique sideboards. The slightly musty smell reminded me of visiting old relatives in the terraced backstreets of Sparkbrook in Birmingham as a young boy. But in the small front room was a lifetime of memorabilia marking the Bahramov journey through football as player, referee and fatefully, linesman. Medals, trophies, ribbons, old photos, scrapbooks and more clips and cuttings than you could take in. There was even a surprise for me. A medal from refereeing a European club Final, the UEFA Cup in 1972 when Wolves had played Spurs in an all English affair at Molineux. I'd been there that night, crammed into the bottom of the Wolves 'Southbank' terrace along with a class of fellow 12 year olds who'd made the trip over with one of our teachers from Brum. I'd had no idea that the man who'd helped England win the World Cup six years earlier was the man in the middle as we strained for a view of the action on that heaving terrace. Now here I was in his old front room in the backwaters of Baku wading through a treasure trove of memories.

They loved him there, even more than English fans did. 'Now that Azerbaijan is independent it's very right for him to be remembered as a member of the Azeri nation' it says on his Wikipedia page. "People like Tofiq Bahramov are only born once in a hundred years".

July 30th 1966. I'd remembered it myself, very clearly, even though it was only a couple of weeks after my seventh birthday. Villa Park had staged some of the group games and I have visceral memories of my father coming back from Argentina's bad tempered game against West Germany and cursing the cynical South Americans. No goals but a sending off, bad blood and general consensus that Argentina were dirty, very dirty. It all came to a head in the Wembley quarter final against England when the Argentina captain Rattin was sent off but refused to leave the field while chaos reigned for more than ten minutes. England manager Sir Alf Ramsey called them 'Animals'. I knew nothing of the media then but remember that headline to this day. More so than the semi when England saw off Eusebio's Portugal.

The final was an event in our house. I'd gone to Kings Heath village in the morning and came home with a board game called 'Take The Test', loosely involving passing your driving test by moving a car around the board, attached to some kind of stick shift. A game to keep the kids quiet while the football was on, that kind of thing. I placed the board on the living room carpet floor about four feet in front of the television screen and half played it with one eye on the screen, looking up and down, prompted by the 'oohs and aahs' of the assembled adults behind me. Mum and Dad, Grandad and Granny, from my Dad's side with decidedly more working class roots and a leaning towards Blues more than Villa. That generation weren't quite so tribal. I think it was the tension that made me recall it so vividly. For all the drama of the 'did it cross the line?' Russian linesman incident there are two images seared onto my memory from that match that I can still visualize to this day. The last minute of normal time, England 2-1 up and seconds away from becoming world champions. Agitated calls across the room of 'c'mon ref, blow yer whistle!!!!' By this time I was up on my knees inches in front of the screen. I can feel that tension, and still see what happened next, unfolding in a manifestation of real time that felt like slow motion. The ball falling loose at England's near post, the white-shirted West German Wolfgang Weber agonisingly getting there first and sliding the ball into the net. Noooo!! 2-2. Extra time.

The rest's a bit of blank until I see myself, standing this time in anticipation of the final whistle. 'Some people are on the pitch. They think it's all over! It is now!' The commentary line from the great Kenneth Wolstenholme by which we all define that moment when Geoff Hurst ran through to ram home the clinching goal in the dying seconds. Famous words that have gathered deep resonance with the passing of the years. For me though, it remains a visual sequence imprinted on my memory, almost frame by frame. The break, the space, the extravagant flourish from Hurst's left foot and the keeper, all in black, barely moving as the Wembley net billowed behind him. And that's it. Can't even remember the celebrations that followed, probably because I was already out in the front garden kicking a ragged old ball around and reliving the glory.

Not in a million years would I have thought that a few decades later I'd be interviewing all bar two of that team at different stages of my broadcasting journey. Sir Bobby Charlton always seemed to be around. Before he was sadly stricken by dementia, Bobby, whenever I met him was every inch the down to earth, humble statesman and deserved better as part of the FA's ill-fated delegation attempting to land the World Cups of 2006 and 2018. His brother Jack we'll come to later. USA '94 was eventful and hugely enjoyable while Ireland punched above their weight under Big Jack's leadership. Geoff Hurst, like Pelé, was corporate gold but one too many sights of the 'Arches', a 'McDonald's' board propped up behind him, and the 'M' word slipping into every other sentence was over-cooking it, and always risked the broadcast regulators Ofcom being unhappy over excessive product placement.

My fondest memories will remain with two of the team who died well before their time. Bobby Moore, as I mentioned earlier became a colleague during my short spell as a football commentator and reporter at Capital Gold in London. It was an absolute thrill to be sitting alongside him one night in early 1991 while Charlton Athletic played host to Oldham Athletic at Charlton's temporary adopted home of Selhurst Park. The mundanity of the fixture, at odds with the glamour of working alongside one of the most famous ex footballers in the world wasn't lost on me. I felt like a bit of a fraud. There was Bobby Moore, and here was me, sharing the same space. A true legend - and a fan with a microphone. I could barely hold it still. As it turns out, neither of us had our best night.

A player called Andy Peake was in the Oldham side that evening, and for some reason I called him Trevor Peake all night (same surname, different club). I felt a fool the next day, and got in a bit of trouble for it, but the thing was, Bobby hadn't noticed either, so I felt a bit better. But that's not why I remember that night so precisely. At the end of an anything-but-memorable game, Bobby, wearing an eye catching long, shiny black leather coat had said 'I'll give you a lift to the station'. So I took him up on the offer in his flashy jag, jumped out at the nearest tube and went on my way. Next morning I was in at Capital doing the breakfast sports bulletins during Tony Blackburn's show. The 'phone went. It was 'The Sun'. The conversation went something like this: 'We're hearing news that Bobby Moore has collapsed at home after last night's match' and could I tell them how he was when I left him a few hours earlier. In a bit of a panic I contacted Nick Wheeler, then in charge of the Capital news operation and he forbade me from giving them any quotes. So I didn't, though felt I wanted to.

A year or so earlier I'd made the front page of 'The Sun' with still one of my favourite ever stories. 'Boxing Mum KO's Fight' was the front page 'splash' headline. I'd been in the right place at the right time in Southampton when local fighter Steve McCarthy took on Tony Wilson in a British Middleweight title eliminator. Incredibly, with McCarthy cornering his man and on the verge of victory, Wilson's mother, a short West Indian woman wearing a floral dress and stiletto shoes stormed the ring. She clambered over my shoulder at ringside, slipped between the ropes, took off a shoe and assaulted McCarthy from behind, raining blows down on his head with the stiletto heel. Chaos followed, the fight was abandoned by a trembling referee and there was a riot in the hall. Someone was stabbed in the mayhem. 'The Sun' were all over it and shaky television pictures filmed from the back of the hall went round the world. It's still on YouTube.

But I digress. In the following days after taking that call, the tabloids told how England's World Cup winning captain was suffering from life threatening cancer. For the next couple of years, he was in and out of remission and rarely seen until one day in the Sky News newsroom I took a mid afternoon call from Vic Wakeling, Head of Sky Sports. Just two words, 'Bobby's died...' were all I remembered before rushing to piece together an obituary for the peak teatime bulletins. The memories of watching that '66 Final and his masterful showing against Brazil in 1970 all came flooding back.

Bobby Moore was mightily cool, somehow remote and detached like a screen idol, reflecting how he played the game. Alan Ball, on the other hand was the boy next door. The midfield dynamo, all bustle and enthusiasm. I'd been working on the south coast in my first full time radio role in the late 80's and Bally was manager at Portsmouth, just promoted to English football's top division. Pompey struggled and the gaffer was unpredictable.

Every week I would go to the manager's office in the upstairs room of the Victorian terraced house attached to the side of the main stand at Fratton Park. One day I entered for the usual chat, while three of Bally's assistants, former Chelsea great Peter Osgood, ex Norwich midfield maestro Graham Paddon, and youth team coach Dave Hurst sat around the office with their feet on the desks reading the racing papers. The boss was in a bad mood after another defeat in a relegation season and I soon found it out. 'Son' he said, 'if you keep asking me hard questions like that, you'll lose a friend'. I was intimidated and slid out of the office without protesting while the others looked over the top of their copies of The Sporting Life. Next thing I knew, Dave Hurst came running down the stairs, found me walking round the pitch and apologised, saying that the gaffer was 'out of order'. I was fine with it, because Alan Ball was box office. Another day he was in our Ocean Sound studios doing a non-football chat with one of the DJ's when he casually let me know that training had been disrupted that morning when the police turned up to speak to a couple of senior players over a bust-up the night before in a Portsmouth casino. Not the best bit of information to let slip in a newsroom. But that was Bally. You never knew what was coming next. When he was fired not long afterwards, my heart was in my mouth when I was instructed to go to his house and get the big interview. Not many managers would take too kindly to being 'doorstepped' in the hours after being axed, I reasoned. My heart was pounding when I dropped the knocker onto the front door. I wasn't expecting anyone to answer if I'm honest, but to my surprise the door swung open and there he was. 'Oh... er, hi... er, Alan, would you um... mind if we did a er... quick chat about um... what's happened?' I expected the door to slam in front of me. But instead - and to my surprise - he said 'Come in, son, I'll make a cup of tea.' I could hear his son Jimmy crying upstairs to add to the tension, but Bally was brilliant, utterly candid, open and emotional, and he gave me one of the most memorable interviews I ever did. After Bobby Moore, he was one of the first of the 66 heroes to die and I remember going on air at Sky News to break the news of his passing of a heart attack at the age of only 61.

Indeed, as I write this, most of that famous team is now gone. Jackie Charlton, Nobby Stiles, Gordon Banks, Ray Wilson, Roger Hunt and Martin Peters, plus Jimmy Greaves. A stark reminder that mortality is creeping ever closer for all of us. But with a clutch of memories too, some of which (for anyone like me with a leaning to schoolboy humour) will always banish the blues. Like the day one of my old Sky News colleagues Tom Skippings was doing a big walking, talking intro live from

Wembley which, for whatever reason, was to make reference to Martin Peters. We all had the same drill, concentrate on what you're saying, do the odd run through and try not to f*** it up. I personally hardly ever rehearsed for the simple reason that whenever I did, I'd make a pig's ear of it 'live' when it counted. The first take was usually the best so I rarely did run throughs. Not sure about 'Skips', but oh how we laughed when he walked out of the Wembley tunnel for the big 'gravitas' intro, tripped over his words and instantly referred to one of the heroes of '66 as 'Martin Penis'. It takes a pro to heroically hold it together after a cock-up like that but that's just what he did while we all rolled around the floor in hysterics back at base.

Moore? Charlton? I don't know who the 'Bobby' is in PJ Harvey's 'Let England Shake', certainly not a football reference, but once '66 and '70 had passed, 'England's dancing days are done' as the song goes, was about right. It would be an embarrassing 12 long years before the next World Cup appearance.

Chapter 2
Helplessness Blues

By the 1970 World Cup I was deep in the grip of football fandom. 1966 had shaken my world and drawn me deep under its spell. The weekend couldn't come soon enough.

Such was the fallout from winning the World Cup that we flocked to see club games. It's always irked me that I can't really remember what my first game was. Pre '66? I think so, though at six or seven years old it would have been occasional. But somewhere around this time it got very important to me. Midweek games on a school night were out of the question. I'd be in bed by half time so my mother would leave a note on my bedside table with the final score to be discovered first thing in the morning.

One such scrap of paper, torn off from an old envelope remains seared on to my memory. League Cup semi final second leg 1967, Birmingham City v Queens Park Rangers, Second Division v Third. We would be going to Wembley for the Final, obviously. Simple logic. Inferior teams didn't beat bigger ones in my world. Not even we (though my default expectation would soon come to correct itself), would mess this up. Nonetheless, we'd lost the first leg away 3-1 so there was some catching up to do. But we were at home and superior status would carry the day. Obviously. It didn't. The scrap of paper broke the bad news. In scribbled blue ballpoint pen it read: 'Blues 1 QPR 4'. Even my just-post-infants school maths could work out we'd lost on aggregate 7-2. Seven! To a third division team. Never mind that QPR went on to win the whole thing, I was inconsolable. But the underdog had driven a wedge into my psyche.

My father was a season ticket holder, front row of the old Main Stand that at the time of writing this in 2022 still remains. I've no idea whether he paid for me but I'd always squeeze through the turnstile in front of him, jammed between his overcoat and the cold metal bar, freed only by a loud metallic clunk that sprung me out into the concrete concourse. The smell still lingers more than half a century on. Cigar smoke, stale piss, boozy breath and Bovril.

Then there was the crowd. This was the key to the kingdom. Nothing will ever replace the overwhelming sense of awe and wonder at the first sight of that heaving, swaying mass on the terraces. Not the organised gathering of post Hillsborough all seated stadiums, but a living, breathing beast which I could barely take my eyes off and would later spend some of the greatest times of my youth immersed in. An epiphany that ignited my imagination. The sound, the smell. My father would later say I was transfixed and watched the crowd more than the game.

In the season starting just after that glorious summer of '66 I was a regular at St Andrew's. It never occurred to me that Birmingham City were less than outstanding, nor did I care. It gave me a reason to believe and sense of belonging that would never be shifted. As a Portsmouth fan once told me about his own fandom when I took that first radio job on his patch, it's a 'gut feeling'. And that about covers it. You took the rough with the smooth and the thin with the thinner. But it also made me an outsider. Not for me the win-most-weeks glory clubs, this was to be a lifelong affliction and probably a chip on the shoulder. But I was proud of it. And defiant to boot.

One game, in 1968 brought it all home. Birmingham City had drawn mighty Arsenal in the fifth round of the FA Cup. Blues were a division below the Gunners and big underdogs. I didn't hold out much hope even though we'd beaten them the season before in the same round in front of a packed house at St Andrew's. The round afterwards, the quarter finals, we'd got Spurs at home and held them to a 0-0 draw, Jimmy Greaves and all their stars. But what followed the next midweek in the replay was a stark taste of reality, just a few weeks after the QPR fiasco.

I'd been allowed to stay up and listen to the commentary on Radio 2, Peter Jones and Maurice Edelston and those greats of BBC broadcasting. It was a painful night and another early lesson that unconditional fandom has a habit of punching holes in your heart. We lost, nay, were thrashed, 6-0. Greavesie and co ran riot and I was deeply shocked. But I was already too far gone to back out now and when we got Arsenal again that following season I was up for more. I wasn't allowed to go to the original tie at Highbury in London on the Saturday. Too young for away matches, so we ended up instead watching Blues' Reserves at St Andrew's while listening to news of the big game with transistor radios glued to our ears. We went a goal down to the First Division giants and that appeared to be that. But late in the game, and against the odds, Geoff Vowden, a reliable journeyman, seemingly ever present in my early years, snatched an equaliser and Blues were heading for a glamorous fifth round replay against the big boys.

It would be a night game, and all logic told me that Mum would make it off limits on a school night. But I was eight now, going on nine and Dad felt he could squeeze me safely in to his seat on the front row. I was beside myself with excitement and fair to say, Birmingham had Cup fever too. To this day it remains the one game that meant there was no turning back. 43 years later I got to write about it in the 2011 Carling Cup Final official programme, also against Arsenal (who we beat as underdogs once again) because for me it captured the magic of those early years. For some reason, the match was not all ticket. But so many people tried to get in, that would all change thereafter with a ticket limit set at 52 and a half. The official crowd was recorded at 51,000 but the general consensus was that there were way more than that crushed together on the terraces, and reports of many thousands who left it too late coming up the hill towards the steaming floodlights locked out of the ground. It was the biggest night of my life.

As usual we parked the car in the same backstreet we always did on matchdays. Before we'd closed the doors behind us, a gaggle of kids had surrounded the vehicle. 'Mind your car, Mister?' Which wasn't a question, it was an order, unless you wanted to come back and find it minus wing mirrors or wilfully scratched from bumper to bonnet. We always agreed to pay. Usually somewhere between 'two bob' (two shillings or 10 new pence) and 'half a crown' (two shillings and sixpence, aka two and six or 12 and a half new pence post 1971 decimalisation) upon agreement to which, the kids would disappear inside their houses again and miraculously reappear five minutes after full time to collect their coins. It was inner city Brum, right behind the old Garrison pub made famous in recent years by the 'Peaky Blinders' television gangster series. St Andrew's was often a war zone on matchdays at the best of times as the hooligan years kicked in. I can even remember my Grandad, who would have been around at that time in pre World War One Birmingham telling me about these Peaky Blinders terrorising the very same streets many years before.

The atmosphere and sense of expectation under the lights were through the roof. I'd never seen so many people in one place before. Incredible is a word I've used many times over the years as hyperbole, but this really was. I could sense it in the old fellas chomping on their fags and cigars around me. Across the pitch on the Spion Kop terrace and behind the goal to my left I could see the crowds swaying and surging until they hit the metal stanchions that stopped the wave of bodies from crushing the fans lower down.

In the years that followed, and I got old enough to graduate from the safety of the seats to those very terraces, we all loved it when the surge started and we were carried off our feet down the terrace steps, usually after a goal or near miss. I remember one day losing a shoe, before someone further down passed it back over the bank of heads in front, and another when a mate ripped his trousers. It was life affirming stuff for a teenage boy, until the horror of the Heysel and Hillsborough disasters changed everything in the mid and late 80s.

I had always wondered whether it was better to stand in front of those metal barriers or behind? After all, they were Victorian relics crudely bolted into half crumbling concrete terraces and probably hadn't been safety tested for decades. In anticipation of the big surge, the roar and rumble that would signal a mass of bodies being flung forward, those standing behind the barriers would often brace themselves by locking elbows into the straight arm position to prevent the chest being crushed against the metal bar. It had happened to me a few times, resulting in a panicked attempt to force my hands in between to relieve the pressure. But what if you were in front and the whole thing came crashing forward? The immediate aftermath of Hillsborough brought the answer, horrific evidence of just how deadly those terraces were. A number of the metal barriers had given way under enormous pressure and some had simply twisted and buckled. Anyone trapped behind or in front never stood a chance. A sobering, shocking reality check for everyone who had ever experienced a terrace crush.

But in the late 60s, right through the 70s and much of the 80s before the crowds crashed under the onslaught of hooliganism, it was a weekly ritual. And on this night in early '68 it came wrapped in magic with an era defining goal. The ball was swung in from the right hand side, and there was Blues' Barry Bridges, hanging horizontal in mid air with his back to goal, then flashing his right foot and propelling the ball back over his head. In the blink of an eye, and I promise I can still see that freeze frame imprinted on my memory, the ball scorched into the corner of the net. Bob Wilson was in goal for Arsenal that night, a man who like me went on to broadcast, and who I came to know years later. He maintains it was the greatest goal ever scored against him. The only shame is that was that it wasn't filmed, nor even captured properly by the local newspaper photographers perched on their little stools either side of the goal. Descriptions of that magic moment were confined to an artist's impression in the local 'paper. The old boys in the Main Stand even talked about it for years afterwards. Bridges went on to score again, a winner after Arsenal had equalised, and our outsiders, our defiant underdogs roared on by that incredible crowd, pulled off a famous victory.

Sadly the crushes that night meant my Mum wouldn't allow me to go to the subsequent rounds. We beat Chelsea at home in the quarters 1-0 then met neighbours West Brom in the semi at Villa Park. I was confined to listening on the radio again and can remember that bereft, empty feeling after the 2-0 defeat that brought my world crashing down. A feeling I came to recognise only too well.

At my junior school, Colmore Road in Kings Heath, I saw myself as the biggest fan in the school. No idea if it was true but not many of my young classmates seemed to go to the matches. It was where I wrote my first ever football report, a school essay describing the Birmingham City striker Tony Hateley (father of future England international striker Mark) beating the opposition goalkeeper 'all ends up' in neatly joined up blue fountain pen ink. In half a century of reading match reports since, that expression is still used, and I still have absolutely no idea what it means. What 'ends'? And 'up' how? But when you were nine years old it sounded great, and showed how religiously I must have read the sports pages.

So imagine my disappointment when Mr Bretell, a short, wiry teacher with a prominent Adam's Apple that shot up and down when he talked, didn't pick me for the school team. We called him 'Bottleneck' and popular classroom opinion settled on him knowing little about football. I went to see our team play a rival school called Greet up on the school playing field, with its pronounced slope and square wooden goalposts that leaned back a few degrees too far. Their kit was a brilliant all yellow, shirt, shorts and socks and there was something about the sight of it that made them look invincible. They thrashed our lot, and the memory bank snapshot still shows itself again from time to time, one of those indefinable moments of childhood epiphany. The revelatory flashback that you can never quite pin down, prompted by a smell, sound or flash of colour. A fleeting whiff of childhood that makes the heart soar but then fades before the moment can be fully recaptured.

Anyway, I wasn't in the team and nor were a few others who thought they should be. The unofficial 'street' trials were always in the playground with goalposts painted onto the walls of the red brick air raid shelters that 25 or so years earlier were the last place of refuge when Birmingham came under nightly attack during the 'Blitz'. We'd play with any old object, a small block of wood or plastic wheel off a children's toy, but never a ball. A mother's worst nightmare when new school shoes were scuffed and ruined within a week. But for some reason, the best playground players weren't in the school team. 'Bottleneck' didn't seem to have a clue.

One day, one of the 'outsiders', a boorish bully called Steve had the nerve to ask Mr Bretell if his team could play the school. He agreed and I got to play for the rebels and live out my St Andrew's fantasies. We thrashed them 5-2 and I scored twice thanks to a bit of 'goalhanging'. I always loved that until one day a few years later after I'd moved to one of the grammar schools across the suburbs, Steve and his little gang from a rival school picked on me while I was walking home. They wanted me to fight the only girl in their gang, and when I refused, he punched me in the mouth. 'Put the boot in!' encouraged an older boy further back up the road when he saw what was happening. But I was blubbing by then and they'd all run off. One of Steve's lieutenants, a pathetic little weed came back and asked if I was 'gonna twit?' I didn't reply for sobbing but later wished I'd thrown him over the nearest hedge. I never saw Steve again. To make matters worse he supported Villa. Arse....

I don't know why being an outsider sat with me so comfortably. Maybe it's that inherently British DNA, to champion the underdog. But football felt like a perfect vehicle, and I would naturally gravitate towards it.

It wasn't just football either. Fuelled by teenage rebellion I wanted all the 'clobber'. It was a struggle trying to convince a conservative mother to let me wear the latest clothes. But 'Oxford Bags', the wide bottom trousers that had to be worn at half-mast above the ankles, 'penny round' collar Jaytex shirts, Doc Martens shoes (boots were for skinheads or bullies like that school boy Steve) and zip up cardigans and hooped socks in the colours of your football team that became a craze in the early 70's. Blue and white all the way. I can even remember going to the High Street and coming back with a brown pair of platform shoes with a broad yellow stripe right the middle from tongue to toe. Glam Rock was all the rage and we all wanted to look like Bowie or Brian Eno from Roxy Music. Except the cool grammar school kids who shunned anything that was remotely 'pop'.

I was still led by the single charts while some of the older boys or ones who had clued up older brothers would walk through the school yard clutching things like 'Deep Purple In Rock' or 'Dark Side Of The Moon'. Two of the lads from a couple of years higher up the school went on to form one of the great post-punk bands 'The Au Pairs' along with two girls from the Girls' school down the road. I can remember one lunchtime walking into Woolworth's just down the road from school (Kings Norton Boys' Grammar) and asking for a copy of Suzi Quatro's '48 Crash' while a huddle of cool kids leaned on the shop counter and burst out laughing. It probably had a lasting effect because by the time I'd hit my mid teens, my listening habits had taken a turn into leftfield and have never gone back! Maybe it was Peter Gabriel and Genesis whose foray into the charts in 1973 with 'I Know What I Like (In Your Wardrobe)' unlocked something magical in my wandering imagination. Either way, prog rock came calling along with a fascination for Bowie's otherworldliness and eventually the backwaters of indie. Maybe my musical tastes just caught up with my football habits and wider worldview. 'Outsider' music, the underdog artists who followed their star even if the mainstream crowd was listening to something safer and less interesting.

Watching football was the other graduation path, and from home games only, the road slowly opened up into endless possibility. Most at secondary school rarely went to away games, trips that brought their own kind of magic, mixed with terror.

My first ever trip was to Derby's Baseball Ground in the late 60's, pre segregation, when it was pretty much every man for himself and good luck if you were a boy trying to get a view of the game. My dad took us onto a cramped low-roofed terrace behind the goal, arriving late and missing kick-off. But that was only half of my worries. I would have been short even standing on a box, and as the crowd roared and hollered all round me my dad put me on the top of the rear wall at the back of the terrace, littered with bits of rubble and broken glass. Even then my view was precisely the far end penalty area only, and nothing else, bar the backs of bodies and heads and clouds of cigarette smoke. No idea what else went on, except that Derby scored at the near end of the pitch that I couldn't see, there was a mighty racket, and we lost 1-0. To cap a fast learning curve, as we walked out towards the street we were caught in a crush. Everyone was a giant in my small world and I could barely breathe. Tall men in stifling overcoats closed in all around my breathing space and my head was tilted right back looking skyward trying to gulp in some air.

As terrifying as that was, it still wasn't the coming of age that would mark out football away days. That was the first time you were allowed to go on your own, or in my case with my older brother Nick. But at 12 and 14 and a trip on the train to London, we weren't exactly veterans. October 1971, QPR away, and I wouldn't forget it. A 'Football Special' train, and more than a few lively characters on board, about four of them in our compartment.

Naturally, we followed the crowd through tube stations across London. And then we hit Shepherd's Bush. One of the leaders from our carriage compartment stopped everyone at the front of the group. All of a sudden he ordered a charge and we were swept up in the throng, hurtling down a flight of stairs before coming to a shuddering halt near the bottom at the ticket barrier. I remember the chant: 'Ooh! altogether! Ooh! altogether!' as the ringleaders urged the crowd to push harder. Suddenly, the barrier gave way and we were all catapulted through a gap until I felt a ticket inspector or transport police officer trying to grab my arm. In what seemed like half an hour but was probably a couple seconds I flailed wildly in panic while picturing arrest and shame, and was freed from his grasp. We spilled out into the street and instantly headed in the opposite direction to the mob. Later that afternoon, I spotted the man/youth who'd been prominent at the station being led around the side of the pitch with his arm up his back in the hands of a police officer. I would also come to recognise him again at the scene of later street and terrace disturbances.

My father's parents understood the football thing even though they never went to St Andrew's or Villa Park. We'd always go to their house on a Saturday morning and have fish'n'chips or a saveloy before heading off to the game. My grandad, Richard Henry Skudder, or Harry as he was known, was a real underdog. He'd had it tough, losing a toe to gangrene in later life, then a foot when they couldn't stop the spread of the infection, then his whole lower leg from the knee down when it spread even further. But that was nothing. In 1915 he'd fought at Gallipoli and it was only by a miracle that the whole family line wasn't severed during that desperate summer. A freak twist of fate came to the rescue. From a young age I knew he'd been shot but it was only when we sat and chatted during one pre-match lunch that I got the whole story. I can picture him now, fighting back emotion (it seemed to me), or at least being very reluctant to recall the memory of what happened on that August day.

He was a horseman in the Worcestershire Yeomanry, a Lance Corporal I think: 'We were at the top of the hill, and the horses were at the bottom', I remember him saying. He rolled back the neck of his shirt to the left, revealing a round scar, about the size of a modern ten pence piece just below the collarbone. A Turkish sniper had picked him out on that hill (possibly Chocolate Hill near Suvla Bay, where the Brits had recently landed after being shipped in from Alexandria in Egypt). What followed got more sobering as the years passed and I could comprehend the consequences, because frankly, it was a miracle. The sniper shot him in the middle of the chest, 99 times out of a hundred a kill. But by a freak stroke of luck the bullet struck his British Army issue tunic flush on one of its metal buttons. Half an inch left or right, and he was a dead man. Miraculously, the bullet ricochet'd upwards, shattered his jaw and landed in his shoulder. His war was over. I remember his eyes, the suppressed emotion, and can now guess the thought process in the telling of the story which must have gone something like 'I'm lucky to be here, and therefore, so are you'.

I was too young to really understand then, but have thought about it many times since. In his front spare bedroom upstairs there was an old Turkish sword in its sheath. I often played with it as a child and always wondered afterwards how he'd come to get it. In 2015 I attended the relatives' hundredth anniversary of Gallipoli with my son Henry, a proud day as we marched down Whitehall past the Cenotaph war memorial, with recollections of that childhood chat running through my mind. Survival against the odds, like a true underdog.

On my mother's side, my grandmother Dorothy was another who would have to fight back from adversity. But her background was quite different. She knew nothing of football, for a start! She'd grown up in rural Worcestershire in a privileged Victorian middle class bubble, home schooled by a governess in a household which also contained, in her own words, 'servants'.

Her side of the family threw up another intriguing story that spanned the generations. Her grandfather, my great-great-grandfather, a prominent local man called James Cox had been Mayor of Stratford-upon-Avon in the early 1880s, in the days when such people rode around in a horse and carriage. He and his father had founded a revolutionary steam engine powered sawmill business that went on to furnish many of Stratford's Victorian buildings in the then building boom. It's an historic site now, known as 'Cox's Yard', having been converted into an entertainment complex with a bar and theatre performance space in the 1990s. James was a big local player. He had a religious conversion and like a good Catholic had a football team sized family (including substitutes), an astonishing brood of fourteen kids!

But that's not the crux of the story. His youngest, Laura Cox, my great grandmother, met and fell in love in the 1880s with a then struggling musician and local music teacher. His name was Edward Elgar. Just an ordinary young man back then, whose father ran a music shop in Worcester, struggling to make a living from what he'd learned there, doing some speculative composing, and playing at local concerts where Laura was a promising young soprano. Elgar even wrote a minor composition for his sweetheart, a short interlude called 'Laura Valse' or Laura's Waltz. The original manuscript was knocking around the family for decades until it was given away by one of my great aunts sparking a family dispute. A bit of a whodunnit only partially solved to this day. It was auctioned off, retrieved at one stage, then 'lost' again and hasn't been seen since. But I digress. For Laura's father, Elgar wasn't a suitable match and the burgeoning relationship, described down the years in our clan as an 'engagement' was called off. One of Elgar's biographies describes how 'her family discouraged the attentions of an obscure musician, and the girl obeyed her family.'

By the time Laura had married and had four children with someone considered to have 'better prospects', Elgar, of course, had made it. Britain's greatest ever classical composer and a future 'Sir' to boot. 'Pomp and Circumstance', 'Enigma Variations', 'Land Of Hope and Glory', beautiful music, he wrote them all, though I doubt he'd have been too flattered by the latter classic being bastardised on the football terraces more than half a century later. 'We hate Nottingham Forest, we hate Albion too....' was the version we sang before going on to declare our hatred of Aston Villa. Quite apart from being bellowed by a bunch of lairy lads, it was no 'Land Of Hope and Glory, Mother of the Free'! But wait, it's well documented Elgar was also a late 19th century Wolves supporter (we all have our crosses to bear) and even composed what was possibly football's very first anthem for them, the clunkily titled 'He Banged The Leather For Goal'. So even if he had been part of the family line we would have fallen out in any case (winking emoji). I bet he'd have given his right arm to have composed 'Keep Right On To The End Of The Road'!

Not that life would have taken the same direction anyway of course, in the same way that we wouldn't have been around either if that bullet had missed my grandad's button at Gallipoli. Laura's more 'suitable' spouse, (the aforementioned) Silvester Sill had inherited a profitable grocery business from his late father when he was young and lived in the family's big house in the centre of Bidford-on-Avon. So you can see how James Cox might have thought this was the sort of chap his daughter should be getting involved with, rather than a penniless music man. Fascinating, and a bit of an 'own goal', given what Elgar went on to become, but it says something about middle class England and snobbery in the late 19th century.

According to the stories passed down through the generations Sill 'drank himself to death' years before his time (must have been a season ticket holder at Small Heath Alliance because we were rubbish then, too). Life started to unravel for the Laura clan and then got tougher when her own daughter's husband (the grandfather I never met), died even more prematurely. My mum was ten, the oldest of five young children when that happened, just before the Second World War. Fate had conspired against her side of the family in successive generations. But what it did do was breed strong resourceful women. I can remember the many visits to my granny's house in Birmingham in her twilight years. She was a force of nature even then, riding a bike until well into her eighties having brought up those five children decades earlier on her own. We heard stories of how she would drag them down the garden to an Anderson air-raid shelter during the terrifying nights of the 'Blitz' before they were all evacuated to a country school in Worcestershire when the bombing got too bad.

I, of course only knew her in old age. But I remember the hullabaloo when my brother and I saw fit one Sunday afternoon to scratch the letters 'BCFC' and 'BLUES' multiple times into her old antique brown leather armchairs. They'd probably once belonged to her mum Laura and for all I know the original manuscript of 'Laura Valse' was probably stuffed under one of the seat covers! Anyway, she went ballistic and my dad took us home with promises to administer a 'thrashing, to within an inch of your life!' which is how it was always threatened when we did something very naughty. Not that it ever happened, of course. Not even when we once kicked a football straight through the kitchen window and half the shattered glass landed in a bowl of stewed apples sitting on the table ready for tea.

Chapter 3
Kicking Television

My family had left Birmingham on Boxing Day 1973 to live in the wilds of Pembrokeshire, a huge change for a (then) city boy like me, especially one that followed an unfashionable football club. It was a big part of my early teenage life, and the thought of missing out on the Saturday ritual presented a conflict, though sweetened by the prospect of living by the seaside.

Like anywhere in far flung places, the make up of football fandom weighs heavily in favour of the big 'glory clubs'. In that part of West Wales it was the usual suspects and Leeds Utd, at that time all conquering, pulling in new, casual support. Then there were the other regulars; Man Utd, Liverpool, even Everton, though I guess their title win in the late 60s had something to do with that. Then there was the rebel youth in our village who for reasons best known to himself decided one night to visit the local bowling club and carve the legend 'Notts Forest are champs' into the beautifully manicured green with a spade. In six feet high letters. And he didn't even support them. The local council were not impressed, and the escapade made the neighbourhood newspaper, though I was more concerned with the abbreviated spelling aberration. Brian Clough would have taken him to one side with a stern, 'Young man, it's not Notts' and clipped him round the ear.

It's an oft overlooked fact that the round ball game is very well followed in Wales, with more playing the game than the national sport of rugby. But the wider rugby narrative swept over everyone on international weekends and half of my school seemed to disappear to Cardiff for ritual gatherings; tales of underage drinking bravado and 'how we beat the English' would be discussed in the playground and sixth form common room for weeks on end.

Pembrokeshire has actually long been known as 'Little England Beyond Wales' since the days of the Norman invasion and William The Conqueror who built a line of castles to keep the Welsh out. I reminded my peers about this whenever England lost, which was pretty much every time. Rugby, I always insisted, with defences going up higher than the battlements on a Norman castle, was not my game and I couldn't have cared less if the great Wales team of the early 70s had beaten England 30-0.

But after months of being mercilessly teased about the state of the England team my back was up and the outsider mentality kicked in hard. Give me an underdog all day long. I even played the odd game at school and revelled in some crash-tackling carnage. I didn't really know the rules but got the gist. If there's someone in front of you with the ball, take him out, even if that means hanging on round the neck or a 'straight arm' across the throat. It instilled a sense of defiance and a way of redressing the balance. They even told me my tackling was good but I wasn't a rugby man at heart and was too busy playing in the local grassroots football league.

Payback would also follow when Wales later went from all conquering champions to a hapless rabble and England routinely took them to the cleaners. My memory was long, and it brought some contrary satisfaction. But rugby, I discovered had more in common with my football education than I imagined. Unlike in England at that time where it was broadly seen as a grammar and public school game, in Wales it had a much more 'gut level' connection to the public with its working class roots and deeply entrenched place within local communities. Its source of local pride was no different to football and its rivalries across the border.

In my early days at Sky, I covered a Welsh Cup semi final when Swansea took on local rivals Llanelli, the famous 'Scarlets' at St Helen's, just off the seafront. So many people were trying to get in, they were climbing and scrambling over the outside walls and my cameraman and I were all over it. Great stuff. The people's game. You didn't get that at Harlequins. I could have been at St Andrew's on one of those big football nights. The only shame was that the Welsh Rugby Union then decided to trample all over their club histories and make some of them merge into regional clubs to benefit the national team. Neath was a hostile place to play for anyone, yet they gave up their status as one of Britain's strongest and most traditional clubs to merge with Swansea and form the Ospreys. That's where it was different to English football. Imagine Birmingham City and Aston Villa joining hands and forming a new club? Not in a million years.

If I wasn't playing the rival round ball game at the weekends I was heading back to Brum to watch Blues. My parents eventually ran a pub on the beach in one of the small coves on the coast path and aside from hordes of tourists, there was a strong clientele from the American Naval base at RAF Brawdy just around the bay. I took a couple of those American friends to matches, outsiders if ever I saw any. Kevin Quinnell was a lovely lad, first overseas tour with the US military, always ringing his folks with a loud and heartfelt 'I love you Mom!' and I took him up to Brum for the weekend. He had no idea what to expect and it was an empowering feeling to show him the magic of something new from an environment that I'd come to love, not dissimilar to later being out on the road at a World Cup with a camera and conveying what it was like to be there into people's lives back home.

American sports events were not like ours, well, at least not a day out at the football. Tailgating, American style might have happened at Twickenham, Wimbledon, Silverstone or on the heath at Royal Ascot, but at the football it was all about cramming into an adrenaline-fuelled pub, sinking a couple of beers, then spilling out into the streets and on to the terraces for a bit of one-eyed communion.

It turned into a day that he wouldn't forget in a hurry. FA Cup fifth round, Blues v West Ham who brought thousands of fans north at a time when their reputation for trouble was at its height. It was a raucous occasion, and I can still see Kevin's face beaming from ear to ear as the home crowd surged down from the back of the Spion Kop terrace time after time. They didn't get this sort of thing in American football. This was a blast! Blues were 3-0 up and the atmosphere was fantastic.

Then came the pitch invasions, several of them, and they weren't good natured. Hammers hooligans tried to stop the game and mayhem ensued all over the ground. Rival fans fought on the pitch. Kevin's jaw dropped: 'Why are they brawling?' he enquired innocently. Long story, Kevin, but after a few more beers and the invaders had left town, his chest was pushed out proudly like an underdog who'd just negotiated an unlikely initiation. On another occasion, Chuck Raines, an affable, laid back character from Knoxville, Tennessee also made the weekend trip, this time for a Villa - Blues derby at Villa Park. Same story, he'd never seen anything like it and came away even more bewildered than Kevin.

Mind you, we picked a shocking day, it rained sideways from morning til night and by the time we'd been crushed onto the Witton Lane terrace where the only means of getting to have a pee was to go where you stood and hope you didn't fill the next man's pocket, we were soaked to the skin. It was a notorious match too. The Battle Of Brum, 1983, a filthy game matching the weather, ending with Blues centre half Noel Blake dropping the nut on Villa's Steve McMahon at the final whistle and players seeking each other out in the changing room afterwards. To cap it off we lost 1-0.

Birmingham City's derbies with neighbours Aston Villa were rarely without incident. I usually went as a fan, but began to have my face recognised from television by the early 90s, not always with a comfortable outcome. The advent of policing with cameras around this time made any television reporter potentially persona non grata on the terraces, so it was generally 'keep your head down' or wear a hat.

I remember attending one Blues - Villa League Cup tie in '93 in the days when the gap between the two clubs was considerable and we usually lost. No, always lost. I'd gone with one of the young lads on the Sky News sports desk, Gary Hughes, a Villa fan, who would go on to become Sky's 'Head of Football' years later (as if David Cameron and Prince William wasn't enough). A drink in 'The Garrison', a good few years before the 'Peaky Blinders' phenomenon and then a walk, dodging the sporadic street warfare up the hill to St Andrew's.

It was one of those nights where you could barely move on the antiquated, crumbling terraces not long before the stadium was made all seater (sadly). Not being able to move freely meant a tricky trip to the gents at half time, especially with a post 'Garrison' bursting bladder. Not that most of the lads there were too fussy about where they relieved themselves. I recall giving up trying to get to the official cattle class urinals and had to settle for the corrugated sheeting that represented the wall at back of the Spion Kop. Oh well, better than nothing. Then the bloke next to me glanced sideways through rising steam from rivers of piss, looked a bit confused and enquired: 'Where the f*** do I know you from?! Chelmsley Wood?' I had arrived! We laughed about it for a long time afterwards. Even though my lot lost. Yet again.

Both at St Andrew's and on awaydays, trouble never seemed to be far away but it rarely bothered me and with a burgeoning journalistic inquisitiveness I wanted to know more. Sometimes it would catch you unawares. One day in the mid 90's I travelled to Maine Road to watch Blues play Manchester City, a fixture that had some 'history' attached to it. The 'Zulu Warriors', Birmingham's hooligan group had named themselves after a match at that very ground a decade and a half earlier. I was sitting in a home fans area and had no idea the 'Zulus' were out in force until the final few minutes when Man City scored the only goal of the game. Within moments all hell broke loose in the Blues section. A local policeman was badly beaten up and the culprit who assaulted him in the melee was caught on camera.

As we left the stadium, trouble spilled out into the rabbit run of Moss Side's Victorian terrace streets. I was suddenly caught right in the middle of it alongside a local lad and his girlfriend. Literally trapped. The three of us tried to melt back into one of the terraced house doorways while a gang of Birmingham fans fought running battles with the locals and police horses skidded around on the cobbles and tarmac trying to get amongst them. That was one of the few occasions when I felt genuinely unsafe. The following day I was on air at Sky News showing footage of the violence inside the stadium and the Manchester police officer having his nose broken by a known criminal. A man who had once been pointed out to me as dangerous by a police spotter contact I came to know well over the years. He once told me this man, now longer with us, slept with a knife under his pillow because he had so many enemies. He was jailed for the assault.

That was just one of many crowd disorder situations I'd come to witness at close quarters over the years (strictly non combat!) and after I joined Sky it unofficially became part of my brief on the road. Mainly because I knew a bit about it and was able to give it some context. Following England around the world for a decade I got to know the police officers who would work around the clock tracking the travelling risk groups of fans. We'll come to how that impacted the World Cups later, but just attending club matches often threw me into work mode when news events unfolded.

Not long after I'd been working at Sky in early '92 I was at a Birmingham Stoke game in the third tier when a full scale riot developed. Fans invaded the pitch, the referee was assaulted and the match abandoned before being completed behind closed doors later in the day. From casually watching the match on the terraces I ended up relaying the story on my mobile phone to the satellite viewers.

Like a policeman, in that respect you were never off duty. The same happened much later when the FA were sweating on winning the vote to stage the 2018 World Cup Finals. Scheduling Birmingham City's League Cup quarter final with bitter rivals Villa on the night before the vote in December 2010, when everyone concerned was desperate to project a positive image of English football, was probably not a good idea. Indeed, it was a terrible one as you'll hear later in the Russia 2018 chapter. What could possibly go wrong!? I was there as a fan, with a Greek friend from down south who'd seen most things as a Panathinaikos fan, but even he was shocked as the whole thing went pear-shaped. Once again, I was on my mobile phone relaying running commentary live onto Sky News.

I got to know many of football's movers and shakers including the owners at my club. I'd done a feature for Sky with Karren Brady when she'd first arrived, amid plenty of fanfare, or as many had seen it, a bit of a publicity stunt by David Sullivan. There were no 20-something-year-old women running high profile football clubs back then, so it was no surprise to see plenty of media attention. The well publicised quote about one of the players on the team bus saying 'I can see your tits from here', to be met by, 'well you won't be able to see them when I sell you to Crewe' was a good indicator of her resilient attitude in a male dominated environment.

David Gold I'd met one afternoon at the old Manor Ground in Oxford when Blues put seven goals past them. David loved a bit of media attention, was much more easy going and always very forthcoming. I got on well with him, well enough to be invited up from time to time to go in his personal executive box. I sat next to his late mum Rose at lunch in the boardroom once. She was old school, lived across the road from Upton Park and refused to leave the terraced home she'd lived in most of her life even though her son was one of the wealthiest men in England. Like a real life character from 'EastEnders' but without the cheese. On another occasion I filmed an interview with David while he flew his plane from the back garden of his Surrey home to Birmingham City's training ground on the outskirts of the city. It did cross my mind, I have to confess, when it was too late and I was up in the air, that flying alone with a 70-something man at the controls was probably not a good idea. I made a nervous quip about football's parachute payments, but the joke would have been on me and my cameraman if he'd keeled over at the controls.

Karren, in my opinion was not always the easiest to work with. In the mid 90's she'd been at the centre of a diplomatic incident after another riot broke out when Blues played Millwall at St Andrew's. The 'Zulus' had been front and centre causing serious trouble that day, including the shocking stabbing of a police horse, but Karren blamed Millwall. It didn't go down well. So come the return game at the New Den a few months later, the media were alerted for potential fireworks. I was there that night and the atmosphere was very moody. Shady men with arms folded provocatively standing on street corners waiting to orchestrate some kind of revenge after what had happened earlier in the season. I don't remember Brady even turning up. Brian Scovell, an old school journalist from the Daily Mail got the inside track that night. He'd been tipped off that the hardcore element from Brum had only got as far as Euston Station before being rounded up and sent straight back from where they came. Probably just as well.

I had a prickly relationship with Brady and it boiled over after the infamous Championship play off semi final between the same two clubs, Millwall and Birmingham in May 2002. The first leg had finished 1-1 so everything hinged on the second leg at The New Den. Millwall's traditional weapon on nights like these was their hostile crowd. For risk games like this most clubs would control who got hold of tickets, something like two each for every season ticket holder knowing that they would still easily sell out for such a huge fixture but at the same time have some control on keeping out potential troublemakers. Their chairman Theo Paphitis (the latter day guy from Dragon's Den) didn't see it that way. Not so much Dragon's Den, this was more Nest of Vipers. Every lunatic under the sun who wanted to make it as hostile as possible for the visitors was in the house that night. People could buy six tickets each.

I was there early, and had a ticket for a mate from Sky. He rang me to say that the Met Police had kept a large group of Blues fans at London Bridge to prevent any flashpoints before kickoff. By the time they all came off the train at South Bermondsey and were marched towards the ground, the match had already started. The game was tense and nothing much of note happened until the dying moments. With the game approaching extra time, Stern John knocked in the winning goal for Blues from point blank range. Our end erupted. We'd lost in the playoff semi finals for the previous three years in a row so you can imagine how wild it got as we celebrated heading towards the final at last and the chance of a place in the Premiership after 16 years away.

But what followed that night would lead the national news bulletins the following morning. A major riot on the streets of Bermondsey. The notoriously violent section of Millwall's support, bolstered by anyone it seemed with an axe to grind on the streets, turned against the police. We were kept in the stadium for something like two hours while violent anarchy raged outside. It was like a scene from Beirut in the 70s, cars torched and the air thick with flying rubble. Inside someone threw a stone up into our section. It pinged off the plastic seat directly in front of me and landed in my midriff. While the locals ran riot outside we were penned inside a holding area at the back of the stand and I was making calls to Sky to let them know what was going on outside. Some of the Blues section were intent on getting out into the streets, rocking a police van in the compound, looking for a confrontation, without knowing how serious the violence was. By the time we were let out, a news camera had been outside for about an hour prompted by my tip-off and captured some remarkable footage. One shot was framed to picture the sky which glowed orange from the flames of burning vehicles while planks of wood, bricks and anything the rioters could get their hands on sailed though the air like arrows raining down at the Battle of Hastings.

When we eventually got out, we were shocked to see such devastation. I bumped into the boxer Rob McCracken (later world heavyweight champion Anthony Joshua's trainer), a lifelong Blues fan who I'd met before through Sky and the football, with his fighting brother Spencer.

'Stick with us' said Rob, 'and you'll be fine'. If anyone could look after himself, it was him, and I duly followed within a couple paces while we crunched across rubble on the pavement. By then a moving wall of police vans was slowly driving alongside us, preventing contact with the remnants of Millwall's mob who had been chased off into the darkness of the side streets. A section of the Blues group tried to break away at the front but were held back by the police. My car was parked only a short distance away on the Old Kent Road, but despite my pleas to the Met officers escorting us away, I would have to go all the way back to London Bridge with everyone else, then come back and get my vehicle. Still, I was on a high with the result, and at one in the morning when I eventually got back to my car to drive home I was excitedly on the phone to David Gold. He was as thrilled as me.

I spent the next morning on Sky News and Sky Sports News relaying my eye witness account, and as luck would have it, that very afternoon, with events still high on the news agenda, Millwall's chairman Theo Paphitis happened to be attending an unconnected corporate event at St Andrew's. Sky arranged a live interview and I got to do it. In normal circumstances, professionalism kicks in and all is calm. But on this day I came close to losing it. Paphitis seemed unaware of the gravity of the night's events and out of touch. Voices were raised and I challenged him on what I considered the irresponsible distribution of tickets, six per person, and putting making a quick buck ahead of safety and security. 'Great telly' was the verdict from one of the Sky executives but I was on edge and wound up, so much so that I gave David Gold a hard time too. Some of the Birmingham City support I told him had been itching for a fight too. The following day one of the tabloids, probably in response to my eye witness account, quoted the senior police commander on the scene as saying that someone would have been killed if we had been let out onto the streets at the final whistle. It was no coincidence that soon after this incident a new penned in walkway was constructed between South Bermondsey station and Millwall's stadium, designed to prevent any contact between visiting supporters and the local crowd within the immediate area. It's largely worked well ever since.

If there's one journalistic quality that has to prevail, it's honesty; calling it as you see it. I've always done that, otherwise you fall into the PR trap; say nice things in return for some accommodating access. Gold diplomatically told me I'd been 'professional' in reporting the events as I saw them that night, but underneath I think he felt I'd let him down.

I know this, because a few weeks later we greeted each other outside the team hotel in Cardiff, the night before the playoff final against Norwich. 'Steve!' he called out, walking towards me in greeting, knowing full well that wasn't my name. That wasn't all. It was the St David's Hotel, down by the docks and as I stood at the bar with a friend having a beer, in walked Karren Brady with husband, former Blues player Paul Peschisolido. She threw me a look, and said, 'Have you been arrested yet?' while 'Pesch' smiled with embarrassment. I resisted the temptation to bite back despite what felt like a high two footed tackle right where it hurts!

I was sitting a few rows in front of Karren, 'Pesch' and Blues co-owner David Sullivan for the final which we won amid heart-stopping drama in a penalty shootout. Instinctively I ran up the steps to shake Sullivan's hand after teenager Darren Carter slotted home the winning penalty. He simply shot me a cold stare and did not smile. I think I'd p***** him off too! Maybe he should have saved that for a few years later when he sold our beloved club to a Chinese chancer who ended up in jail, and from whose ownership the club still hasn't recovered as I write this more than a decade later. While Sullivan saw the business opportunities of buying West Ham, culminating in that profitable but controversial move from the Hammers spiritual home at Upton Park to the Olympic stadium, for David Gold I felt it was a genuine 'coming home'. I'd really taken to his mum Rose when we met that day at Blues. A woman who lived and died on Green Street and had no intention of ever letting her East End roots go.

As fate would have it, Birmingham City and West Ham came together in the semi final of the Carling Cup not long after the switch in ownership, in the following round to the aforementioned fiasco against Villa which went so wrong off the field a few weeks previously. The disorder that night was still fresh in the memory, so the prospect of Blues and West Ham meeting in two major matches soon afterwards triggered a few alarm bells, especially given the two clubs' history of trouble in previous meetings. It wasn't lost on me either and I arranged to do some filming that night with undercover cameras, and no objection from the West

Midlands Police who were old hands, uncompromising old hands at times in dealing with high risk events at St Andrew's.

These things could often be speculative because you never knew what would happen and whether you'd be in the right place at the right time. The intention for me was never to compromise individuals involved in any disorder, simply to record events. It's news, not assistance in law enforcement, and I was never comfortable when police wanted to use footage that was caught on camera to identify individuals. It had happened a couple times, once at a Birmingham match at Wolves when a large street fight broke out in front of my cameraman in the late 90's, and then on a notorious occasion when England played Turkey in Sunderland. It was the return fixture for England's feared for match in Istanbul which we'll come to later, and not long after two Leeds United fans had been stabbed to death in the same city. A number of England fans appeared to want retribution. The result was a large, baying mob outside the Stadium Of Light and some unsavoury scenes that were bravely filmed by my cameraman Karl Coates. The pictures ran on Sky News and the police had used them to identify individuals. The first I knew about this was attending a police media briefing a week or two later and suddenly seeing pictures from my television report being used as reference material by the police. For that reason the life of a television news cameraman could be made difficult, a target for troublemakers. Some, like Karl who had filmed the trouble in Sunderland were fearless and made the storytelling so much easier. One Sky cameraman I later worked with, Mike Inglis, had been badly beaten up doing the same while working for ITV during Euro '92 in Sweden and was so traumatised he had to take sick leave for several months. Another I worked with for several years following England, Andy Brattan adopted a diplomatic approach. Try to be 'matey' with the crowds and hope that it was reciprocated. It didn't always work.

On this occasion I worked with an undercover reporter I'll call 'R' here. He knew some hardened former football hooligans and had operated in difficult filming environments over the years aimed at uncovering criminal behaviour. He had all the gear such as jackets with hidden cameras and microphones and he pitched up with a minder, about six feet four and not to be messed with! The plan was for 'R' and friend to mingle with the West Ham supporters and follow them from the city centre up to the stadium about a mile and a half away. The whisper was that this match would be used by West Ham as a 'reunion' of some of their older, semi retired hooligans who had been among the most active and notorious of the English hooligan 'firms' through the 1980s. The 'Inter City Firm' were arguably the most feared and respected of these groups during the height of 'casual culture' in the early 80s. So a reunion on such a big night of football had potential for serious disorder.

I also had my own hidden jacket camera, wore a hat and made my way through familiar territory to the streets around St Andrew's, never welcoming at the best of times. The first sign of the 'reunion' was like something from a 60s gangster flick. Two large, black vehicles, possibly Bentleys rolled down the Coventry Road hill a few hundred yards from the stadium and slewed off towards the pavement in an exaggerated stopping manoeuvre. The doors flew open on both and from each vehicle one man stepped out, both bald or shaven headed, in their late 50s or 60s, wearing long, dark coats, and by the looks of it, not appearing to like each other. They came face to face, or practically forehead to forehead, exchanged a few words, appeared to make up in a 'temporary tolerance' kind of way, got back in their cars, and drove off. Fascinating. Former rivals, possibly, but they appeared to be on the same side tonight. Shortly afterwards I saw one of them further up the hill not looking anything like as menacing. A slightly younger man, known to me as a West Ham 'face' was reassuring his companion who looked as though he wanted to be anywhere but there. The people around him, he was encouraged, were all 'West 'aaam'. But the older fella had one of those looks that said 'I'm too old for this kind of caper'.

The atmosphere was already tense and around 25 minutes before kick off the West Ham risk group suddenly arrived in unusual fashion, designed to avoid detection by the law. They had come by minibus and coaches and completely avoided the city centre. Arriving late and down backstreets close to the ground they would have the element of surprise. The air was thick with menace. I noticed people with bloodied faces from both sides. The Birmingham group had had the same idea of keeping away from the city centre and suddenly appeared in a large group further up the road adjacent to the stadium. A roar went up and the two sides clashed while riot police flailed wildly at anyone trying to get close. The police knew we were doing some filming but clearly no-one told the officer who ruthlessly knocked me flying with his shield, yelling 'Get back!' while I tried to explain I was 'TV'.

I moved into the stadium car park where individuals were trading insults and squaring up against another. 'Oi!' came a shout in my direction, while my tape was rolling. Three men approached, clearly from the West Ham side: 'You're gonna get it...' came a threat from the smallest one flanked by a couple of flat-capped sidekicks. Cloaked in menace and a boozy slur, there was even a look of surprise when I half strode in towards them for a better view. 'I'm gonna get it?' I enquired knowing that all three probably looked great on my rolling lapel camera. 'Yeah, you're gonna get it....unless you fack off'. I obliged with a knowing smile and repositioned for a better view. People were moving around the car park in search of one to one 'straighteners' out of sight of the police who already had their hands full. 'Oo wants it, 'nen?' came from somewhere. 'You fackin' mag!' (mug) from somewhere else and a 'Fookin' hit 'im!' in reply. That was the point of combustion. Another big roar, this time right in front of me and a mass fight in between the cars. Someone came flying towards me and landed on their back at my feet. Through the murk I could make out figures clambering on to the roofs of vehicles for space and bodies flying in all directions while riot police tried to restore order. It was a throwback to the routinely violent days of the past. I later attended the police debrief in the city centre and one breathless frontline officer spoke of how 'scary' it had been in the dimly lit battle zone.

'R' who'd been with the West Ham group in the city centre had missed most of the action. But there was a sting in the tail, for both of us. The West Ham fans melted away after the game, having dramatically lost the tie in extra time amid a feverish atmosphere. 'R' was standing with his minder in a group of tired, disillusioned Hammers fans waiting to be escorted back to the city centre when a pumped up Blues hooligan came bowling past, and with a provocative 'Come on then, Cockneys!' punched the minder full in the face before charging off down the hill with police in pursuit. He was too dazed to drive home.

To cap a bizarre night for me, the jacket camera footage I'd been in the right place for before the game was compromised by being badly framed (maybe when the police officer knocked me over), distorted and barely usable. The equipment had malfunctioned and we had to rely on a general camera whose images were less dramatic. The extra mile we'd gone to capture the story was in vain and all we had were a few shots of police using their batons and an interview with the head of the police operation, Steve Graham. Without hard pictures to back up a story, the standard newsroom procedure is to turn to the news agency 'wires', people who weren't there and who simply regurgitate second hand information. On this occasion the person back at Sky monitoring the 'wires' and making decisions on what runs and what doesn't in news bulletins the following morning decided that 17 arrests (which was the official figure) didn't merit a longer piece. But it really didn't tell the story and both I and the cameraman Tim Jones who'd worked long into the night weren't too amused they hadn't made more of what we'd worked hard, and with some risk, to capture.

Chapter 4
Great Gig in the Sky

Having a media profile from my gurning face on the box came with its advantages but also meant I had to have thick skin. I once came across something on the web apparently written by a well known DJ and music broadcaster from up north which went something like: 'What is it with that Chris Skudder on Sky News, LEERING at the viewers?' and generally mocking. Well, 'Pot, Kettle, Black' because I distinctly remember watching him on 'The Old Grey Whistle Test' years earlier giving me a silent lesson for the future on what not to do when you're live. He suddenly froze while doing a link (the autocue must have gone down) but instead of 'ad-libbing' like a pro just stood there in frozen panic like a rabbit caught in the headlights, struck dumb until the camera went off him. No offence, but that one's now off my chest!

I also remember bumping into the late agony aunt Claire Rayner one day in the corridor at Sky News where she was doing a guest spot. She stopped in her tracks and gave me a stare that suggested she'd just seen a serial killer. No idea what it was all about but it unnerved me for weeks! Probably just the gurning face. I was no oil painting on the television and must have scared her, as she did me (winking emoji).

Then there was the guy in the middle of nowhere at the Japan World Cup in 2002, confronting me about my on-screen demeanour. I remember it because it was so random, while I was watching a posse of Japanese kids playing baseball right down south in Miyazaki. He was from Sweden, presumably one of the unofficial overseas viewers that Sky accumulated over the years through the magic of the satellite footprint, and in broken English had an issue with me 'squinting' on camera (which I do, actually). Thick skin. Essential component.

Being recognised or considered fair game for hounding was not something I'd really considered outside of tribal football rivalries. On that score I would give as good as I got, though it's hard to even remember how that manifested itself in the days before social media. Probably just by face to face encounters while working in the field, as I never hid my affiliation with Birmingham City, who never had the best of reputations with other fans.

But in late 2010 something happened that brought home what it was like to be on the other side of the media fence. My wife was best friends with a woman, Jo Brown, who was killed by her estranged husband in the porch of their nearby home, while their two young children listened to the tragedy unfold in adjoining rooms. The story made national news across television and newspapers largely because he tried to get away with it by disposing of the body in a shallow grave which he'd prepared in advance. It was also adjacent to the Queen's estate, Windsor Great Park, and the body wasn't found for days until he eventually broke down and confessed after being played a witness recording of his own daughter's harrowing description of events. The tabloid newspapers reported on the story extensively including tweets from me in the days before the body had been located, accompanied by a stock photograph, captioned as Sky presenter being a 'pal' of the victim. I'd simply tweeted that the woman, a friend, was missing and that the children had been to our house in the interim.

With hindsight it was the wrong thing to do as numerous newspaper reporters gathered outside over a few days demanding a quote, one or two even shouting through the letterbox to get what they wanted. I was able to convince them that we all did the same job and I couldn't really say anything. It was a surreal experience, though nowhere near as shocking as the eventual outcome of the trial when the perpetrator, Rob Brown, who I'd known well for years, was convicted only of manslaughter, not murder, despite digging a grave in advance and making elaborate plans to cover his tracks. The judge, however, effectively overruled the jury and sentenced him to 26 years, though only half of those would be served. He's still inside at the time of writing. An extraordinary case.

Long before that incident, Sky was a progressive and exciting place to work in the 1990s when satellite television was the new big thing and the company pushed hard to make a mark against the established terrestrial news and sports outlets. Unexpectedly I had a part to play in the very early stages of the yet to be born Sky Sports and became the first person to ever record those two words to tape.

Before the channel had been launched, it was just Sky News and Sky One and the other fledgling, BSB, or British Satellite Broadcasting which had the square dish as opposed to the big round one. While I was still doing local radio I started doing some moonlighting with BSB who had the rights to Scottish football and ran the first British nightly sports news show which was presented by some of the future luminaries of British sports broadcasting like Jeff Stelling. Then, without warning in November 1990 the plug was pulled overnight. Sky and BSB merged to form British Sky Broadcasting and all existing BSB programming disappeared. But the next day I had a phone call from the secretary of Vic Wakeling who'd been the editor of the sports news show. Could I please come into the studios to do some recording for him. Strange, I thought, because the plug had already been pulled and no-one was left. So I duly turned up and was presented with a few short scripts to read. They ran something like: 'Sky Sports, the new home of live sport' with a few extra details of what 'Sky Sports' was. I had no idea at the time, though it felt like some kind of promotional content.

Months later it all made sense as the Sky Sports channel hit the airwaves for the first time and Scottish Football which had been part of the BSB merger deal was suddenly on Sky. Not that I knew it at the time but I'd had the privilege of voicing the original commercial tender for Sky Sports, designed to attract sponsors. Vic Wakeling who'd called me in for those recordings, went on to become hugely influential as the Head of Sky Sports. And the groundbreaking Premier League, which went on to transform the game in England followed about a year later.

I lost my local radio job to the soulless corporate trend towards regional stations but the timing was good to be freelance. Sky was growing fast, the new 'outsider', the underdog on the market and that suited me well, the perfect place to grow and make a mark. Local radio was the grounding, where you learned how to keep talking and it didn't matter what you looked like. But doing television was different and it took a bit of getting used to.

At that time Sky News was the only place you could get dedicated television sports news, 20 past the hour every hour with some half hour shows thrown in, and it felt good to be part of a changing landscape. We had a great team in those early 90s days, several years before the arrival of Sky Sports News which didn't come around until after the 1998 World Cup. Jeff Stelling was one of the original sports faces on

Sky News, along with Matthew Lorenzo, Paul Dempsey, Steve Bottomley and for a short time, Tessa Sanderson the Olympic javelin champion. As I didn't arrive at Sky until around May 1991, almost a couple of years after its launch, I never worked with Tessa who returned to athletics. But I always remembered a couple of classic gaffes when I was watching Sky News at home.

For me, reading scripts off autocue was an occupational hazard and I had a chronic urge to wander off piste, as you'll see below. But for others like Tessa it was more a case of reading every last word as they saw it scrolling up in front of them. You always had to be careful with words like 'Rankings', especially when there was a 'WTA' in front of it. Trust me, when the eyes casually scan a 'W' with 'ankings' an inch or two behind, you can easily get in a mess. On that score I never, ever read out the name 'Wankhede Stadium' for fear of 'corpsing' (bursting out laughing) on camera. Whenever it popped up in a script I hadn't written I'd just say 'the stadium in Mumbai'. Cowardly, eh? But better than a fit of sixth form giggles. Likewise, any goal by QPR's Danny Shittu was always avoided with a sheepish 'QPR took the lead' or 'Rangers edged in front' without any mention of the scorer. Thankfully though, they rarely scored at all so it didn't matter.

Tessa, God bless her, just ploughed right on. Golf was obviously not one of her strong points but there was something beautifully accurate about how Nick Faldo 'bog eyed' the fourth hole at some tournament or other. A perfectly descriptive way to describe a bogey, as it happens. Should've gone to Specsavers. Cricket wasn't one of Tessa's specialist sports either. I nearly choked on my tea when one day she told us (whichever batsman it was) had got himself out '1bw'. Egg before wicket.

Steve Bottomley was a great presenter in my opinion, one of the best sports news guys with an easy, laid back delivery that obviously helped get him to Sky in the first place. So his enforced departure came as a bit of a shock. It was the Sky News sports desk Christmas party in 1998 which we'd arranged for London's International Sportsman's Club, the place that was once run by Terry Venables. In those days we used numerous sportsmen as on air guests (or 'pundits') discussing the latest big sporting stories. That greatest of characters Henry Blofeld, for example on the cricket match fixing scandal or Alan Mullery, Ray Clemence, David

O'Leary, Neil Webb, Gary Stephens, Micky Quinn and John Gregory on the football, the latter three whom I'd worked with when they were all at Pompey in my radio days. On this occasion I remember the ever affable Clem being there along with Neil Webb and Phil Tufnell and many others. One of the tabloids had their own Christmas 'do' the same night and Steve Bottomley, who was, shall we say, 'worse for wear' argued with another journalist who did some Sky News sports punditry work, the late Steve Curry. It got heated, apparently over their shared passion for Manchester Utd, spilled over into further incidents and the evening ended with Steve being held down by Tuffers and others on the pavement outside the club. The story made the press and sadly Steve was suspended. He left Sky soon afterwards. A great shame, as he was a natural talent in my opinion. But rules are rules.

Working on the road was always the most rewarding for me but much of the time was spent presenting bulletins in the studio. I always found that to be something of a straitjacket. A sanitised studio environment where there was nothing to feed off and the endless repetition of stories, hour after hour could often be soul destroying. Maybe it was the influence of the freedom of radio, but I was a chronic 'ad-libber' and developed the aforementioned habit of wandering from prepared scripts on autocue. Quite apart from confusing the autocue operator it could land you in trouble. One night I was offered a filler piece at the end of a 'Sportsline' (sports news) half hour, a random story about the Iraqi national football team winning a big game and their fans celebrating in the streets. A man was seen walking between fleets of cars honking their horns in celebration, and appeared to be carrying a tray of food and drinks from which the drivers were readily helping themselves. Hard news it wasn't. But probably no excuse for me chiming in with a throwaway 'Better than having your hands chopped off!' The phone lines lit up and quite a few were not amused, bosses included!

The other challenging thing was trying to sound impartial when I had a vested interest in the story I was telling. Unflappable pro? Don't be ridiculous. Everyone knew I was a Birmingham City fan, to the extent that I always had to fight my corner in a company full of fans of the usual glory clubs. Villa too, far too many of them. In my latter years there, the Head of Sky Sports, Barney Francis, and the previously mentioned Head of Football, Gary Hughes. Both Villa. Nightmare!

I recall once being on air when Blues were promoted in the mid 90s at Huddersfield under Barry Fry, struggling to contain my excitement when the winning goal went in and my mic was live. But the one that everyone else remembers, and one of the rare big games I couldn't attend was the great escape from relegation at Bolton in 2014. There's nothing worse than having to tell a story about how your team failed miserably and then repeat it on air hour after hour. Guaranteed to leave you with a face like two slapped backsides and nowhere to hide.

On this day it was fast heading that way. 2-0 down at Bolton and needing at least a draw to stay up. All hope was fading fast and relegation to the third tier of English football for only the third time in our history looked inevitable. The jokes had already started and I really didn't feel like doing any more bulletins. But, wait! A goal back with 12 minutes to play and I was all over the screen on my desk while pretending to be doing some other work ready for the next live insert. Not a chance. The minutes ebbed away and with it went what appeared to be the last hope. Four minutes to on air, so I'd better be ready to step into the chair with the nightmare of having to confirm who's just gone down. Christ. Then it happened. The match was in stoppage time. Paul Caddis, the smallest man on the pitch, in what felt like suspended animation hung in the air and headed in an unbelievably dramatic equaliser. The relative quiet of the newsroom was shattered by a loud 'Yeeeeaaass!' and simultaneous bolt from my seat that almost knocked the computer off the table and alerted most of the building and floors below. I was off, on a near full lap of the building, pretty much in a simultaneous celebration charge to Blues manager Lee Clark, who was losing his sh** and sprinting down the touchline before diving into an army of delirious fans. Great pictures of that, by the way on the cover of Jon Berry's excellent 'Hugging Strangers'. I had no fans to dive into but was on air in a couple of minutes and could barely breathe. One of the more pleasurable evenings of talking into a camera followed. 'Now, let's just recap that story again!'

Having an allegiance wasn't always easy to disguise. I learned a hard lesson early on in my time at Sky, though this time it wasn't the football. Warwickshire County Cricket Club, Birmingham based and the team of choice for most Blues fans who tended to dominate vocally at matches, were the cream of England in the early to mid 90s and could boast one of the greatest batsman ever to grace the game. The West Indian Brian Charles Lara broke all records in the book in '94; the highest ever Test score of 375 against England (I can remember telling the breaking story on air, sitting alongside ice cool Selina Scott) - which he then broke again a decade later with a 400, and the highest ever First Class score of 501 for Warwickshire in a scarcely believable summer when nobody could get him out. Except a chap called Smith who played for Gloucestershire. The 'Bears' as Warwickshire are known went through the season winning everything bar one trophy, and even that was only a defeat in a Final. When Lara was out, it felt newsworthy on its own. And on this day against Gloucester, just a regular game with nothing riding on it, I was fully invested in my team winning every game they played.

I was on air on Sky News doing regular sports bulletins and Lara was in the mood to have some fun. Sky's cricket coverage was already very good, lots of analysis and all the replays dissecting the action. Lara smashed a ball into the air and for once it was slightly miscued. Smith, of Gloucestershire came running round and at full stretch took a fantastic catch. But the replays really did appear to show that he'd scooped the ball off the surface of the grass and therefore had not taken the catch cleanly. All in a fraction of a second of course, but I wasn't too happy, propelled probably by my personal investment, to see the umpire give Lara out. Then came my mistake, and it was a big learning curve. I told the audience that Smith had been 'less than honest' based on my perception of the video evidence in claiming the catch. My first and only brush with defamation and completely unintentional on my part.

My interest as a journalist was generally the people stories, the human interest tales that pulled in a wider audience. For me the 'sports' side was done to death everywhere else and 'team news' or 'groin strains' and '4-4-2s' were far less interesting than the bigger picture. It was remarkable to me that after nearly two decades in England, Chelsea's Russian oligarch former owner Roman Abramovich never gave an interview. Back in 2005 I had the opportunity to corner him. Chelsea had just won their first league title for 50 years, under Mourinho, and by luck I was the only television reporter, any reporter for that matter, on the open top bus parade around West London, from which I'd present live, rolling coverage for Sky Sports News. The only trouble was, as soon as I got anywhere near the bus, parked up outside Stamford Bridge I was collared by the Chelsea media team. 'Don't, whatever you do, point the camera at Mr Abramovich' was the polite instruction. I figured that Abramovich would be on cloud nine having seen his huge investment paying off so spectacularly and went for the 'play it by ear' approach. The streets were teeming with people outside the stadium confines and I felt like the classic outsider getting on to that bus full of Chelsea staff and players. I clambered up the stairs of the double decker, cameraman in tow, and as soon as I stepped out onto the open topped section, there he was, right in front of me. Abramovich and young son ready to take the ride round town. I instantly caught his eye, and there was a fixed, expressionless stare for a few seconds while he appeared to be computing 'Who the hell is this?'. It probably wasn't a standoff but my quickly spinning thought process went something like 'Oh Christ, I've upset him already.' This guy doesn't do ANY media and we're standing feet apart like gunslingers at the OK Corral. A little approval? Just to break the ice? He looked me up and down, paused a bit more and without smiling gave an exaggerated nod, head lifted back sharply then brought just as quickly down. Roughly translated, 'You're okay, welcome on board, but you're not getting an interview'. With that, he shuffled to the front of the bus and as we moved off along the crowded streets occasionally waved to the throng. He even smiled, but if he spoke to anyone on board for the whole trip, I didn't see it!

The mesmerising effect of World Cups on my childhood and adolescence made me want to experience football travel first hand and having the good fortune to have landed in a section of the media that was growing fast, I wanted to hit the road. Abramovich was still some years off moving to Stamford Bridge when Chelsea had some eventful European adventures in the 90s. Just before the '98 World Cup in France I'd been in Stockholm to see them win the Cup Winners' Cup, beating the Germans Stuttgart in the Final, 1-0. One memory abides from that night; the sight of a whole end of English fans with arms splayed out wide, swaying with a gentle rocking motion to a joyous vocal rendition of 'The Dambusters'. Anglo German football relations were still stuck in the post war time warp, perpetuated probably by Germany's audacity to have come to Wembley and beaten us on penalties in the Euro semi finals a couple of summers before!

That Chelsea European campaign had a happier outcome but less eventful journey than the one I also got to follow in the same competition in '95. I'd been at Wembley for the '94 FA Cup Final on a rain-lashed day when Chelsea were thumped 4-0 by Manchester Utd. I cornered Eric Cantona, who'd scored twice, in the tunnel afterwards and was struck by his odd, hunted demeanour. He pulled his head away from the microphone as if it was about to combust and looked down on me from his six feet two inches with what felt like a combination of suspicion and disdain. Truly a one off. As was the gaffer. It was so wet that day that I can remember standing in the tunnel after the game near the changing rooms and Sir Alex Ferguson's sons appearing in the small doorway at the exit point to the street. They were wearing black bin bags to keep dry and trying to get their old man's attention by yelling 'Daaaad!' endlessly up the tunnel. No prawn sandwich brigade in the Ferguson household.

I'd attended the wedding of Fergie's son Jason, then a Sky studio director, not long before through a mutual female friend and it couldn't have been more down to earth. Fergie's assistant Brian Kidd was the only football person there, and Alex (not yet a Sir) went out of his way to be warm and friendly. I met him numerous times over the years and found him, along with Arsène Wenger to be the most decent of people. The first time I'd encountered him in my early years at Sky was at Manchester Utd's old training ground 'The Cliff' in the days before Carrington. I'd caught him 'in character' after a training session off the back of one of Utd's less good days and he was sharp and prickly. The sort of mood that probably preceded the infamous flying boot episode that left David Beckham with a grazed eye. But outside of the work place I found him to be thoughtful, kind and with time for everyone. Anything but the fearsome character with a reputation for giving under performing players the 'hair-dryer' treatment. On one occasion I was at Cheltenham for the racing festival, standing in the parade ring before one of the big races when I noticed Sir Alex talking to some owners 20 or 30 yards away. When I looked up again from what I was doing he was striding towards me, hand outstretched in greeting. It was typical of what I saw of him socially, and he always remembered my name. An indication perhaps of how he was able to perfectly balance his management style, both garnering the respect of his players and at the same time knowing when to lay down the law.

Even though Chelsea had been destroyed in the just mentioned FA Cup Final they still got to make the following season's Cup Winners' Cup because Utd had also won the Premier League and therefore qualified for the Champions League instead. Chelsea made good progress and got as far as the semi finals where they came up against Zaragoza in Spain. It was a big occasion and in the days before convicted hooligans had to surrender passports before matches abroad, there were concerns that Chelsea's relatively small ticket allocation would attract large numbers of ticketless fans. Zaragoza, encouraged by UEFA stated unequivocally that tickets would not be sold to fans in Spain outside of the official Chelsea allocation. Clearly, the trip had lots of potential on the story front.

Zaragoza is a strange place. It looms out of the Spanish red-dirt interior like Las Vegas does from the wilderness in the Nevada desert. It just suddenly appears on the road from Madrid, ultra dry, then a bit of green as the city draws near and suddenly there it is. I was there two or three days before the game and knew exactly what would set the news agenda on the ground. My cameraman and I made straight for the stadium box office kiosks, rolled our tapes and in (embarrassingly) typical Englishman abroad 'I-can't-speak-another-language-so-I'm-just-expecting-you-to-understand' fashion, asked for two match tickets. The woman at the kiosk didn't hesitate in handing them over, and instantly we had our story. I relayed the news on Sky that Zaragoza were not practising what they preached regarding not selling to English fans, and with that, a section of Chelsea's notorious travelling support were already heading towards the airport.

We headed to the stadium to have a look inside and while filming were approached by a group of local 'ultras' who had somehow managed to gain entry. Security - and joined up thinking regarding ticket sales didn't appear to be high on the Spanish club's agenda. Naturally, as one of two of the group could speak some English I asked them what they thought about the prospect of Chelsea fans turning up without tickets, given their past reputation for misbehaviour. One of the youths in the group tilted back his head, pulled out his index finger, and drew it across his throat, cut-throat fashion. The gesture needed no translation and we had another story that again travelled fast back to the UK. These boys wanted to show off for the camera and I let them do it. But given what transpired in the coming days there would be a later inquest back at base on whether I had encouraged them and accelerated the disorder that followed on matchday. I took exception to this, naturally, and nothing came of it.

In the meantime, I was confronted by an English reporter from the Press Association, a character called Rob King, who felt his job was being made more difficult because, by the nature of 24-hour live television news in a fast developing media world, 'Sky sets the agenda' and then everyone else has to follow it. Correct. But how was that my fault? Stories break, so too bad if it brought on some extra work. At least he had the good grace to accept that the ticket sale exposé had been ahead of the game.

By match day the local police were on full alert, with very little appetite for tolerance. The English fans who gathered in the city squares and bars, including several hundred without tickets, were not treated with kid gloves. It was a scenario typical of whenever England or English clubs travelled abroad in the post Heysel ban years. A reputation goes before you, and many European police forces did not hesitate using force, some-times when it was not justified. On this occasion, the police were heavy handed and I witnessed angry fans, some with children, being the subject of unnecessary intimidation with batons.

There was particular interest in a vehicle full of exiled Chelsea fans who now lived in Spain. The 'Costa-del Crime', as some referred to areas of the south, and I witnessed a Spanish undercover police squad round up a small group as soon as they arrived in Zaragoza. I later discovered they had been tracked by intelligence all the way in. On the field, Chelsea lost the match hopelessly, 3-0 - but all the news was about disorder in the stands. Sure enough the fans who'd travelled without tickets had been able to buy them at the same kiosks that I had. They were placed into a section that even appeared to have been reserved for such a scenario, and it was from here that it all went wrong. An over zealous policing ope-ration, confronting a group of fans who needed no second invitation was never going to end well. Television images that night simply perpetuated the problem of the 'English disease', and the fallout from running battles in the stadium lingered for days.

Sky's 24 hour coverage of world events drew a hardcore following of 'news junkies' and in the 90s it felt like a groundbreaking place to work. The very nature of being live all the time of course brought 'accidents' from time to time. Hilarious for viewers, and, for much of the time for those involved too. You could usually see the funny side afterwards when the wrong guest was introduced live on air. Like the woman who was on just before one of my sports slots. Brought on to talk about some kind of financial issue in the corporate world, then looking dumbstruck after the first question and replying with a confused: '...I'm here to talk about the female condom!'.

One weekend night I'd been waiting to do my last bulletin and would normally wander through to the studio during the ad break and then pick up off the back of it. But as I pushed open the big metal studio door that always closed behind you with a reassuring heavy 'clunk', I noticed that the presenter, a weekend freelance called Gordon Radley was already talking. To the director, during the ad break I assumed. But no, all of a sudden, and with me just past the studio door, he decided to 'throw' to me, ie make the handover, while I was roughly ten yards away from my seat! 'Now, the sport, and here's....Chris'. I stopped in my tracks before realising he wasn't joking. Silence. Shuffling. Disbelief. To cap it all the studio director cut to a wide shot, and there I was in full view of the audience having to take what looked like a walk of shame form the door to my seat....and then put my microphone on...and then start presenting the bulletin live, with steam now coming out of my ears. How I got through it without having a blazing row I'll never know. But needless to say it wasn't the finest bit of television ever made. I had been made to look late, when I wasn't. They had come to me early and instead of 'filling' the airtime until I'd sat down, just made me look a fool. Not hard to do at the best of times, and I tended to be easy going when things went wrong, but this one was followed by an inquest of my instigation. I was fuming.

Internal politics could also be an issue, like in any company. Sky had a huge investment in Premier League coverage so unsavoury stories had to be handled carefully, presenting a potential issue if the 'news' operation which had a separate management structure to the 'sports' operation felt a story should be broadcast when it felt it was in the public interest.

One day one of the Sky Sports reporters Tim Abraham, who I'd known for years through local radio found himself at the centre of a great story at West Ham, but a politically tricky one. It was a routine West Ham training session in the days when Harry Redknapp was in charge and cameras were allowed in to film some of the action. Friction between teammates is an occupational hazard from time to time. Who could forget the occasion when Newcastle's Kieron Dyer and Lee Bowyer came to blows in the middle of the pitch at St James' Park after a difference of opinion.

This time, it was sparked by a training ground tackle from John Hartson on his Israeli teammate Eyal Berkovic, and by chance, (though probably not good luck for Tim given the 'hot potato' he was then presented with) the Sky Sports camera was rolling at exactly the right time. Berkovic theatrically hit the ground and responded to the tackle by instinctively throwing a semi 'punch' in his teammate's direction, catching him on the top of the leg. In a flash of temper Hartson, who was looming over the Israeli lashed out with his boot and caught Berkovic full in the face. They were shocking pictures, and Hartson was later full of apologies for what was a heated spur of the moment exchange. But at the time, only the Sky camera had proof it had happened. West Ham's media team urged them not to use it. The result? The pictures, which were spectacular, were kept off the television. But only temporarily. Inevitably in situations like this people in newsrooms get to see them, and some time later they were leaked, though no-one knew by whom. Stills of the incident, taken from the television footage appeared in one of the tabloid newspapers and the cat was out of the bag. Once that happened, and the story was out in the open from elsewhere, the internal politics shifted. Sky News, who may not have even known the pictures had existed previously, took the stance that they were in the public interest and put them to air.

The news versus sport dynamic often threw up conflicts, and even though I was able to skip between the two, sometimes the middle ground was unforgiving. It blew up spectacularly in early 2001 when Sven Goran Eriksson took over as England coach following the departure of Kevin Keegan. Sven was a big Sky News viewer, as was Kevin, and always stopped to chat. When it came to media, Keegan was probably the best of all the England coaches during the decade I followed England around the world. He would go out of his way to do something creative when he saw the camera. On more than one occasion when I was filming he would approach the camera and do a 'piece to camera' ,that is, a recorded sign-off: 'Kevin Keegan, Sky News, Budapest' (or wherever it was we were). He was a natural. Like on the bridge in the Hungarian capital, 'Buda...' he would say straight down the camera lens, gesturing to one side of the River Danube, then '...Pest' gesturing to the other side. It all helped the creative instincts. Alan Shearer and Kevin Phillips sitting on the bridge together, rival Newcastle and Sunderland strikers playing alongside each other for their country, allowing me to come up with something like '....bridging the Tyne-Wear divide across the Danube' in my script. Having a former television news person running the communications operations at the FA always helped these things and Paul Newman knew what we were looking for. He was around for Sven too, but Eriksson, for all his courtesy had nothing like Keegan's charisma or ability to woo the media. Not that that made him any less likeable.

Sven's first game was against Portugal at Villa Park and as usual when a new boss came in, especially one with Eriksson's reputation, his team selection was eagerly anticipated. I was on the ground doing the coverage for Sky News while my colleague Nick Collins did the same for Sky Sports News. Being first to break Eriksson's opening team selection would be a minor scoop, though no-one had told us that protocol should be that Sky Sports who were showing the game live that night would be the first to announce the line up at the top of the programme.

The newspapers were good at coming up with England line-ups on the morning of a game, either through a mole or very often by literally having a spy in the bushes for training sessions the day before! The ones in the bibs or vice versa indicated who would be playing alongside who. At the 2006 World Cup in Germany the media appeared to have a distinct advantage in spying on training sessions, simply because England's training base was set in a beautiful natural amphitheatre in Baden-Baden. It was surrounded by natural vantage points and lots of verdant cover. The FA it was rumoured had to sweep the hillsides to make sure no-one was secretly watching. Maybe there were foreign spies clandestinely watching practice penalty shootouts because we all know what happened when England made their usual exit from the tournament!

I was pitchside at Villa Park by early afternoon doing 'live' reports when I took a call from the Sky News newsroom to say we had had a tip-off from one of the player's agents on exactly how England would line up. It was genuine. Uncapped Charlton full back Chris Powell was the surprise choice at full back and immediately a graphic was made up of the team before I put it to air. It was a good scoop. But that's when the rows started. As the News team we had been using a Sky Sports camera on site for our live 'hits' so they were none too pleased to have the planned exclusive for the top of the live match programme already broken several hours earlier. Producer Tony Mills, sitting stone faced in one of the Outside Broadcast trucks threw up an angry hand when I put my head round the door to say hello.

An inquest followed as to how the information had leaked which involved the FA, though Sven made it clear that he had not given me any help. Feelings were running high and came to a head about an hour before kick-off. Geoff Shreeves, who'd graduated from being a floor manager when I first met him to doing the post match interviews, interrupted a chat with ITV commentator Clive Tyldesley to loudly tell me that I had now 'gone backwards at a hundred miles an hour'. Some of the press who got wind of the dispute did not disagree that I had got a rough deal. It made a number of the sports gossip columns and I appreciated the support. Shaun Custis, always affable and honest on the road wrote in his column that '...Skudder had only been doing his job.' That's exactly how I saw it.

Interestingly, within a month or two of this incident, for which I really was only the messenger, everyone who worked on sport at Sky News, and there were some good people, suddenly fell under the umbrella of Sky Sports. As it turned out this was to work in my favour. I had a dual role that nobody else really did, getting to present sport on Sky News and also hitting the road for Sky Sports News, the best of both worlds. By my experience it was a great combination. Having a studio profile, and a recognised face often opened doors when I was out and about, and it worked the other way too. Having been there in the thick of it on the road it was then a real bonus when it came to telling first hand stories with a bit of gravitas and credibility back in the studio. That is, you would often operate not just as the sports presenter but also as the in house correspondent or 'presenter's friend' as we called it, having to react to a breaking story sitting alongside the main news presenter. In the school of waffling away endlessly, if you'd been on the road it didn't half help!

I remember around this time Gary Newbon who I'd grown up watching on the old Midlands ITV (ATV as it was then) talking to me about what he considered the pitfalls of being a 'news hero' within the sports brief. I think some even saw me as a maverick when really I was always only focused on telling a story, without spin and as I saw it.

Euro 2004 in Portugal was a memorable tournament from that respect, notably because England were right in the mix and Sky were at the forefront of new digital broadcast technology. Up until then when doing a live report you would be tethered to an outside broadcast van with a dish on the roof by a fixed length of cable. But when the new 'digi-link' saw the light of day, the cable was redundant and you could wander hundreds of yards away from the truck and still broadcast live without any restrictions on movement. An absolute liberation if you wanted to try something creative or needed to be on the move. As luck would have it, I was one of the first to try the new technology. England versus France at the Stadium of Light in Lisbon, the game when teenage Wayne Rooney ripped Patrice Evra apart only to later become the first victim of England's 'curse of the metatarsal'. Before the game I'd been (literally) unleashed with the new roving live camera with the fans in the streets outside and, right on cue the perfect scenario for using the new tech unfolded.

UEFA (or the Portuguese hosts) had made a mess of getting fans safely into the stadium in good time before kick off and large queues of impatient England supporters were stuck in a labyrinth of fenced off corridors snaking around the periphery. With around 20 minutes until kick off and no sign of anyone moving, some fans decided to take the law into their owns hands and started pushing over the fences. Not an act of violence or hooliganism as we'd come to recognise in the past, more a build up of tension and anger that they'd miss the start of the game. Nonetheless the local riot police were in like a shot and physically forced the fans back from where they'd come. I was right behind them, with my cameraman Stuart Vickery alongside recording every move. We were beaming it all back live, warts and all to the Sky Sports News audience. Being in the thick of it, live, was what it was all about, a real adrenaline rush driven by a gut feeling, and essential viewing.

Inside the stadium the BBC or whoever had the rights were doing the standard studio pre-match pundits analysis, but we were in the best place and blowing them away. Tempers were raised and it was risky, but amid hundreds of England fans voicing their anger and frustration only one muffled expletive went to air. I was in my element and kept the narrative going for probably 15 minutes, feeding off the anger of the crowd. Back at base they had been gripped, and being so free and close to the axis of the story changed the landscape for live news broadcasts from the field thereafter. If only we'd had the same technology when Marseille exploded six years earlier, but we'll come to that in the France 98 World Cup chapter further on. This made a mark, though I was amused that the boss of Sky Sports News Andy Cairns, who'd given me the chance to go to the '94 World Cup in the USA a decade earlier for Sky News came up with this assessment: 'The best thing about Skuds,' he said, 'is that he has no idea what's going to happen next!' That was either a back-handed compliment or a veiled criticism, but ask the viewers what they want to see. What's happening in real time is, indeed, not to know what's coming next. Because it's live and all the better for it!

There was a period at Sky Sports News when I'm sure one or two in-house individuals thought I had an inside track on the football disorder scene, judging by some of the requests I received for information. I didn't have much option than to take that as a compliment, but it was certainly nothing more than keeping my nose to the ground. Because that was the job. Reporting is not about mutual back scratching, otherwise the brief skates too close to a public relations exercise.

If there's one thing that the internet has brought since the advent of the digital age when anyone can get involved, it's the inevitable surfacing of the truth somewhere. It always emerges. That just reinforces the need for traditional media to tell it like it is.

When it came to World Cups and Euros, Sky were never rights holders, so we were always the underdog and had to rely on being creative outside the usual sources of access. It's just the way it was. FIFA and UEFA had long term terrestrial broadcast partners and that left Sky not only without live match coverage for the major international tournaments but also with limited access to training sessions and media conferences.

Even watching the matches to report back from at World Cups was a challenge. FIFA would accommodate broadcast rights holders and major press outlets as a matter of course, but we were at the bottom of the list, and often had to rely on guest tickets provided by the FA or whatever national association it was to even gain entry to the stadiums on matchday. No matter that Sky was a major partner for club football around Europe, it held no sway for international tournaments. Even weekly regional newspapers were ahead of us in the queue. And a queue was often what it was, until the 'observer' match tickets had run out. Like Oliver Twist standing in line with a begging bowl, the allocation system felt farcical. Bangladesh Knitting Weekly would have been ahead of us in the queue for an England match, with all due respect to that particular country and practitioners in the art of crochet. It just meant we had to wheel and deal with occasional sympathetic officials from the game's governing body or downright flout the rules and get in by hook or by crook. Germany 2006, as you'll later discover, would be the celebration of that.

Being an outsider merely sharpened my appetite to beat the system and come up with creative coverage outside FIFA's limits. Beyond the venues and media conferences there was no shortage of content. The fans were a major source of that and everyone back home wanted to know what it was like to be there. What follows in the upcoming chapters is how it was at these World Cups and where the fun started.

Chapter 5
With or Without You
USA 1994

'With or Without You'? USA '94 was, of course, 'with' Ireland (and U2, as we'll get to), and very definitely 'without' England. Again. It really wasn't funny when England failed to qualify for the third time in six World Cups. It brought back the heartache and disasters of the 70s.

In the mid 2000s during Wembley's rebuilding phase, England's matches were played around the country. I was curious to meet a player whose life changed on the night the rot set in in late 1973. England had only needed to beat Poland at Wembley in their final qualifier for the '74 World Cup in West Germany and the job was done. Routine for any other 'big' nations. But they reckoned without the man that Brian Clough would come to call the 'clown', Polish goalkeeper Jan Tomaszewski. I'm not sure if it was luck or just one of those nights that goalkeepers have from time to time, but on a frantic night, whatever England threw at the immovable underdog he kept out with his arms, legs, body and backside. And as the gods of footballing fate conspired against us, at the other end, a young Peter Shilton let a relatively straightforward shot squirm underneath him for the goal that would ultimately stop us going to West Germany.

I was watching on our own colour telly by then, with my mind wandering back to that day three and a bit years earlier next door at The Shinglers when England had been knocked out of Mexico '70 by the West Germans themselves. I have another one of those images frozen onto my memory that night as England tried to batter down the Polish door. Derby's Kevin Hector, just on as a sub with the chance to save the day for England, only for Tomaszewski to defy gravity, splay his cartoon body in every direction and scramble the ball away yet again. It was more than thirty years later when he came to Manchester to do some punditry work for an England qualifier against the Poles but we all wanted to speak to the man who'd been dining out on his heroics for years. Just an ordinary bloke with a great story to tell. But I think he'd told it so many times he almost saw himself in the third person.

We only had ourselves to blame again for not making the following World Cup (Argentina '78). Indifferent results in the intervening years meant missing out on top seeding for qualifying. That led to landing in the same group as Italy with only one team going through and no play-offs. Tough gig. Losing to them in Rome early on then meant having to outscore them for the easier group games and by the time the return fixture came around at Wembley (which England won) they were already too far behind in the goals column to overtake them, and went out on goal difference. Hard to take, especially when Scotland had managed to make it for both of those missed World Cups. Though I have to admit I did support them both times, something which I could never bring myself to do at club level. Only defeat would ever be wished on the Villa which made their European Cup fluke (winking emoji) a few weeks before the '82 World Cup hard to swallow.

By the time the '82 tournament came round in Spain and England were half decent again, I wanted to be there. I decided this on New Year's Eve '81 while standing knee deep in the fountains of Trafalgar Square singing football songs and eventually stumbling face first into the drink. So drunk I never felt the cold. Trafalgar Square on the last night of the year was an incredible sight in those days. Both fountains (with the water pumps still switched on) would be submerged early in the evening by a pyramid of flailing human bodies trying to clamber over each other to the summit. But this was the last time it would ever pass off peacefully. The following New Year, in a tragic precursor of what was to come on the football terraces a few years later, a stampede and crush killed three people and injured 500 more. Sobering. The fountains were boarded up thereafter and it was never the same again. But that night 12 months previously, we were oblivious to the dangers. Fully submerged and soaked to the skin, I hankered for a World Cup baptism too. But it never happened. I had no money. Every last penny was wrung dry from the student grant and I ended up watching it in Wales at my parents' pub.

By the '86 World Cup I'd started my broadcast journey via hospital radio in Haverfordwest, the local Pembrokeshire paper and a crash course at the National Broadcasting School in London's Soho. I was now scratching around doing overnight graveyard shifts 'DJ-ing at Swansea Sound and reporting the sport on a Saturday afternoon. Still miles from being at a World Cup, and I can remember exactly where I was, slumped in a Swansea bedsit when the greatest player that ever lived, Maradona scored the 'Hand of God' goal that sent England home.

By Italia '90 I was getting closer. I'd secured a full time radio job down south on a great patch with Portsmouth and Southampton to cover and a yearning to make the next World Cup four years later in the USA, however unlikely that seemed. I'd seen Paul Gascoigne in his prime at this time, destroying Pompey single-handedly for Spurs in the Cup at Fratton Park. Two things stand out from that World Cup that England could so easily have won. Gary Lineker mouthing extravagantly to Bobby Robson to '…'ave a word!' with Gazza after he'd been booked in the semi final and was tearfully coming to terms with the realisation that he would miss the final if England got there. And then Jonathan Pearce, the commentator for the independent local radio network, with his dramatic description of Chris Waddle's 'moonshot' penalty in the ill-fated shootout with West Germany. Still rising when we last looked, heading for orbit.

I was soon working alongside Pearce at Capital in London (and the afore-mentioned role alongside Bobby Moore), but that lucky timing with Sky was looming and a 'round about' route that would take me to the first in a long line of World Cups. Sod's law would have it of course that England wouldn't be there. I was presenting in the Sky News studio the night it all went wrong in Rotterdam in the autumn of '93 when England lost to the Dutch and failed to qualify. It was the night of Graham Taylor and his infamous quote: 'Do I not like orange!'.

England got nothing from the referee and Ronald Koeman who should earlier have been sent off, scored a killer free kick to twist the knife. Steve Bottomley was the reporter out there for Sky News, and I can remember how much he wished he wasn't. England fans were causing trouble again, and Steve was trying to keep out of the way while I (unhelpfully) encouraged him to get in the middle of it to show us. He'd had a difficult time at the Euros in Sweden the year before where some of the media became targets. It wasn't long before our roles were reversed and I was the one taking the questions and running the gauntlet in the field. Just as I liked it.

While England were falling short again, I was out reporting in the thick of it the following month when Wales had their best chance of qualifying for the big event for the first time since 1958. Everything came down to their final qualifier against Romania at the old Cardiff Arms Park.

It turned into one of the longest nights and grimmest stories I ever had to tell. Wales' 2-1 defeat brought crushing disappointment for the 40,000 strong crowd but it was the tragedy that followed that captured the headlines. I can remember with pristine clarity what happened at the final whistle. From the media seats I saw what appeared to be some kind of firework, the sort of rocket you'd see everywhere on Bonfire Night, which had only recently passed, fired from the top tier of the opposite side of the stadium. It flashed across the field almost horizontally with a trail of smoke and roared at great speed over my left shoulder only a few feet away. I could smell the cordite and almost felt the velocity. That could have hit me, I thought, remembering childhood days in Brum when we'd fire rockets horizontally out of bottles down back alleys and see what happened when they scorched across the dirt before fizzing into a wall.

Instinctively I turned to see that this one had landed somewhere at the back of our stand. But in the following minutes it became clear there was a medical emergency. A group of a dozen or so spectators were in a huddle while one appeared to be waving frantically for help. Tragically, an elderly man, sitting quietly in his seat as the game ended had been struck in the throat by what turned out to be a marine distress flare. He was killed outright. The shocking news filtered through to the media before I'd left the stadium followed by a turn of events that would have me up all night assisting the police with their enquiries.

As I was leaving the Arms Park I told a passing supporter what had happened as, by then, most knew nothing about it. What he told me immediately tripped more than just the story radar alarm. He said he had been on that opposite side of the stadium and had seen someone in the row right in front of him set off what he also thought was a firework, intended, he assumed, to fly over the top of the stand. But not only that, he had taken photographs at the end of the match and was pretty sure that the person in question, the one who'd fired the flare, was caught on film. I told him he needed to go straight to the nearest police station and instinctively went with him, with the promise of an eye witness account of the incident when he'd passed on his information and was finished with the police.

Midnight passed. Half past...one o'clock, two, then three, and still no sign. He was still inside when I gave up waiting. But the police, it appeared had the evidence they needed and took hours to develop the film. Within a week or so two men from Wrexham had been identified and charged with manslaughter and were later jailed for three years. The victim was 67 year old grandfather John Hill who'd been at the match with his son of the same name, who I'd seen from below calling for help. He later described how the sound of the marine distress flare, 'a huge rushing noise' was like an aeroplane about to hit the stadium. What should have been a triumphant night for Wales ended in desperate tragedy.

That whole episode came flooding back 29 years later when Wales finally did manage to qualify for the World Cup in Qatar after 64 years of trying. But it wasn't the football I'll remember from that day in Cardiff either. It was the refugees I met from their opponents Ukraine whose lives had been turned upside down a few months earlier by the Russian invasion. I'd been thinking about the ferocity of that deadly flare in the context of how much more unimaginably terrifying it must have been for the Ukrainians before they fled. While doing some vox pops one of them casually told me that the district in Kyiv she'd recently left behind had been struck that morning by Russian rockets. That brought it home, like a ton of falling bricks. These were real people right in front of me telling stories with a matter-of-factness that belied their gravity. I'd had many casual conversations just like this with ordinary Russians at the 2018 World Cup. I'd warmed to them. But now this. It threw fresh light on my time there as you'll read later in the 'Red Army Blues' chapter. Many of them now rallied behind their country with what felt like barely a blurred line between shooting footballs or rounds from an assault rifle. Always on the side of the Motherland.

But back to '94, and of the British and Irish 'home' nations, Ireland under Jack Charlton showed everyone else how to do it by being the only country to qualify. A bloody good team with bags of character.

Sky News had a cult following across the Irish Sea. In the years before it became an official part of the Sky broadcast footprint, it still somehow had an army of viewers via the magic of the satellite dish or any old up-turned dustbin lid that could snag a signal. Whatever it took to get a picture! Maybe it was just human nature, wanting to know the British view of what was happening politically in their country. It was rarely off the news agenda. I often noted from my travels that people would want to know what you thought of their country and how they were doing in hosting whatever event it was. Israel was another good example. Sky has always been big there too, a country transfixed by 'watching-you-watching-us' syndrome, given its near constant status as a fixture on the international news agenda. When England went there in the noughties they wanted to know what we thought about them, along with the usual fascination with the English football scene. 'Who do you support? ….Who??!!.. Why? They're not very good….' It's a long story….' was usually the best way of dealing with that, although from time to time I'd convert a new international fan to the Blues cause!

The major English clubs have a huge following in Ireland and their fans devoured every last detail of our coverage. So when I heard I would be going to USA '94, embedded with the Ireland team I was beyond elated. Finally, my first World Cup and some fascinating group games made all the more intriguing by the venues. Italy in New York with its large Irish and Italian population, and Mexico in the summer sauna of Florida which promised to be a hothouse too far for a nation who'd long made fun of themselves as a pasty faced breed who could never stay out in the sun for more than five minutes. But all of this offset by a team who never knew when they were beaten and in manager Jack Charlton, a leader who knew how to get the best out of them.

We flew out to Miami on June 6th 1994, exactly 50 years on from one of the most momentous days of the 20th century. The clear view down from the left hand window of the Virgin jumbo was as it would have been for the US and British Airborne divisions on D-Day half a century before, had it not been one of the wettest days of that summer! What a sight it was. A mass of trailing wakes from scores of ships recreating the invasion of the Normandy beaches, like an artist's canvas with dashes of white set brightly against the dark backdrop of the English Channel.

Unlike England, whose World Cup base camps would always (post 80s, at least) be off limits to the media entourage, it wasn't like this with Ireland.

We were right there with them, a hotel just outside Orlando, and the team taking up the top two floors. All the reporters, not that there was anything like the number who follow England, were dotted around the rest of the hotel. It was a blast. The players got some reasonable freedoms under Big Jack, training in the morning just like the club sides back home, and then being allowed to wander around the hotel and mingle in the afternoon. Evenings, post meal, were off limits and generally no-one was allowed out, though as you'll discover later, it didn't quite work out like that! The atmosphere was generally genial, and the players enjoyed the banter. They even plotted to throw me in the pool one day while I was doing a live report for Sky News, and we all had a good laugh when Gary Newbon's room flooded one afternoon after a tropical downpour. Too much Newbon hot air must have brought on some internal precipitation (winking emoji).

Unlike England, Ireland didn't have the same kind of pressure and expectation on them and you could feel it. It was like a gang of mates on tour but with some top players and a fantastic team spirit capable of overcoming anyone. Paul McGrath, Roy Keane, John Sheridan, Andy Townsend, Jon Aldridge, Ronnie Whelan - it was a formidable squad. Keano was often pacing around the hotel and one afternoon I found myself in the outdoor swimming pool with Roy the only other person in it. He rarely said much at the best of times, especially in his younger days, a far cry from the outspoken pundit who would have the television audience eating out of his hand with those hilarious, withering put-downs of under performing players. In other words, he didn't suffer fools, and called a spade a spade.

So there was Keano, in his 'Speedos' swimming up and down the pool and me going the other way, but with far less grace. Every length, we'd pass. We had an interrupted conversation, a few words each up-and-down, and I mean VERY few words. 'All right, Roy?'....'Aye'.....'Looks like it might chuck it down in a minute'...'Yeah'....'How you getting on? ....'Ok'. After about ten lengths I thought I'd change tack and ask about Eric Cantona who was the most talked about player in the Premier League after his surprise move from then champions Leeds to Keane's Manchester Utd a couple of years before. The price was low for such a superb player, a modest 1.2 million pounds, and the rumour doing the rounds was that Leeds boss Howard Wilkinson had let him go after allegations he'd been having affairs with some of the Leeds players' wives. So as we passed up the pool for the umpteenth time I thought I'd casually throw it out there. 'What's Cantona like? Loads of rumours weren't there about his private life up at Leeds?' About as subtle as an air raid, with hindsight, and Keano's smooth breaststroke was broken with an abrupt, spluttered 'I don't know nothin'...' while I doggy-paddled past in the opposite direction. With that, he got to the end of his length, jumped out of the pool and headed inside sharpish, still dripping wet. I was just making small talk as it happened. But I think he thought I was trying to set him up and panicked at the thought of a big tabloid headline and Sir Alex Ferguson seeing red.

There was something about the Ireland campaign at USA '94 that didn't sit well with the media. With none of the home nations having qualified there was a feeling that the players, and the management were trying to cash in on their relative success. As soon as we got to Florida, we got word that if we wanted one to one interviews with the players at the hotel we would have to pay for them, via a players' 'pool', which they would presumably then share at the end of the tournament. It didn't go down well and had a mercenary tone that cheapened their presence. No one was used to doing this, especially at a World Cup where the competing nations were obliged to speak to the media every day anyway via an official FIFA media conference. In Ireland's case it was at the training base half an hour away where they'd have to put someone up at the end of training and generally say nothing of much interest. It was ever thus at major tournaments, whoever the competing nation was, bar Brazil whose attitude was always so open and relaxed. Their media days were a thing to behold. But generally World Cups are like Groundhog Day, there's nothing much to report most days and not a lot to talk about. But the media have column inches and television and radio bulletins to fill so need an agenda. And if there isn't anything of note to discuss, that could get pretty stretched and inventive!

Kevin Moran was the Ireland players' representative regarding the 'pool', and had to deal with the moans from the media. Kevin was very diplomatic and knew it wasn't really going to happen, so took it on the chin. But the downside was we didn't get the top players to talk to. They did grant us access but it was always their choice of 'victim', and nine times out of ten it always seemed to be the youngest player in the group, the whipping boy who wouldn't say no, and that was the 'green' Leeds full back Gary Kelly. Gary was terrific and played ball as best he could. But I did feel for him. One day we had to drive to the nearest local television station to record an interview which was a 15 minute ride away. As usual in Florida in summer, it lashes down with rain every day, almost like clockwork. Not just rain, monsoon rain, so that even with the wipers on full blast, you couldn't see the road in front of you. There was Gary, in the middle of nowhere, sitting in the passenger seat with biblical rain hammering down on the windows when suddenly he was (literally) thrown in at the deep end; he had to talk about something shocking that struck everyone in the camp like a bolt of lightning. We got word that the Colombian defender Andres Escobar who'd scored an unfortunate own goal that contributed to his country being knocked out of the tournament, had been shot dead by an assassin when the team returned home. It was thought a drugs or betting cartel may have been involved, and the story sent shock waves through the wider sporting world. Gary was pretty shaken up when he heard, as we all were. 'Football's not a matter of life and death, it's more important than that', Bill Shankly had once said. But that legendary anecdote could never have sounded more inappropriate.

It wasn't just the players who'd come up with the 'pool' idea for one to one interviews. Jack Charlton himself we were told wanted the same, and the sports agent John Givens (the brother of legendary Irish striker Don) who was part of Ireland's entourage, attempted to negotiate an agreement. But no-one was having it. If Charlton couldn't speak to the media from time to time at such a major event then it was a poor show. The general feeling was that Charlton would have to do it anyway on the day before matches according to FIFA rules. So his bluff was called and we waited for the official media conference to fill our boots, though it was a little prickly when he wasn't always forthcoming on the engagement front.

That came to a head before Ireland's second group game against Mexico in Orlando. The heat was utterly stifling that far south in the US in June and some of the Ireland players were really struggling, especially Steve Staunton, a redhead for whom staying out in the sun for long periods just wasn't an option. The problem was that someone at FIFA had the daft idea of scheduling the match against Mexico with a midday kickoff when the Florida heat was at its most fierce. This wasn't just about pale

Irishman needing a bit of shade, it was the safety of players hurtling around in the hottest part of the day.

Charlton insisted that his players should be allowed access to drinks and came up with the idea of throwing water bags on to the field to keep them hydrated. But FIFA, in the days when Sepp Blatter was still General Secretary, the hands on fixer of disputes, disagreed, and an unholy row erupted over player safety. The 1966 England World Cup winner was on the warpath and didn't mind who knew it. For the media, it was manna from heaven because Jack had no option but to do the pre-match media conference, and he was wound up on two fronts. The 'pool' and the water row. He kept it brief and was simmering with discontent, but we had a great story and it didn't cost a penny.

Not surprisingly the match against the Mexicans spilled over into animosity. We were sitting at the top of the open bowl on the side of the stadium, right above the Ireland contingent, and believe me, I've never attended a match in such heat. Lord knows what it was like to run around in for 90 minutes. FIFA had relented on the water bags issue and Jack was squirting bottles onto his players and launching the bags onto the field whenever he could. His temper wasn't helped by being 2-0 down against a Mexican team for whom this was probably the equivalent of a cool spring day in comparison. It then boiled over again. One of the FIFA officials stopped John Aldridge from coming on as a sub to replace one of his wilting teammates, and both sides lost it. Aldridge in full view and earshot of the camera called the official a 'f***ing tw*t' while Charlton grappled with the FIFA man in a tussle over a piece of paper confirming the substitution. It didn't end well. Jack was reprimanded by FIFA for losing control again and banned from the touchline. They lost the match too, 2-1. But it gave us a great story for the next few days.

Fortunately for Ireland they had some wriggle room in the group thanks to their sensational victory in the opening game against Italy in New York a few days earlier. Italy would go on to reach the final, but they had no answer to the legendary Irish spirit on another scorching day further north. As I mentioned earlier, just getting in at all to these matches was a challenge, being a Sky non rights holder. So we were reliant on the Football Association of Ireland to get us into matches and that meant doing deals with the management entourage in the hotel. We bought tickets as I recall, as many as we needed for our crew, without which we would have been stuck outside the venues.

Joe Delaney the FAI Treasurer was our 'go to' man for help with anything we needed and everything was met with an easy going Irish charm. However, two years after the tournament it was alleged that the FAI had been involved in a ticket swapping deal with other football associations that took them into murky waters. Touts, it emerged, had been buying and selling with the FAI and by the end of the tournament the Irish had been left with large numbers of unsold tickets. They were out of pocket to the tune of a six figure sum, revenue that had simply gone missing. Delaney later said he personally repaid the missing amount to the FAI but after an investigation resigned from his post. We had no idea about any of this at the time, but it was a precursor to the serious corruption that brought FIFA into disrepute years later, leading to the departure of President Sepp Blatter and numerous other delegates being thrown out of the organisation. The ticket fiasco also affected me personally at the Brazil World Cup in 2014, when I paid 650 dollars for a semi final seat that did not exist, as we'll come to later.

Back in '94 there were accusations that the Irish operation in major tournaments was a touch amateurish, probably because historically there just hadn't been any before the Euros in 1988, their first ever appearance at a major 'Finals'. It felt like that, in a genial 'boys on tour' kind of way, seeing the management team around the team base, revelling in being at the biggest tournament in the world. People were coming and going, having the 'craic' (fun) and match tickets seemed to be all over the place.

The alleged amateurish approach came to a head spectacularly at the 2002 World Cup in South Korea when Roy Keane sensationally walked out of the camp just before the tournament and came home, this time in a row over facilities at the team base in Saipan. He was a senior pro and serial winner by that stage in his career, and it caused a big scandal back in Ireland. But his no nonsense, deadly serious approach was clear to see even eight years earlier. Which made my encounter with his mum and dad on the eve of the huge match with Italy in New York so revealing. We'd gone out filming looking for fans, expecting the Irish bars to be busy and a good number of Italians to be in Little Italy. I thought it might be fairly equal on numbers but I was wrong. The Irish were everywhere. It's not hard to find a football crowd, and as we strolled through Manhattan, the sound of singing, 'Ole! Ole! Ole!' signalled that we'd found a crowd of Irish revellers. Stepping inside we got the impression they'd probably nearly emptied the place of Guinness, not to mention all of the Irish Whiskey and 'Jack Daniels' to boot.

There was a man on one of the tables having the time of his life. I couldn't work out what he was singing but it sounded like a good Irish sea shanty and he held the crowd in sway. 'Who's that?' I enquired to one of the throng who could barely stand. 'Ohhh, that's Mossie, Mossie Keane. He's from Cork'. And there he was, as luck would have it, Roy's dad, a shambling figure leading the community singing and by the look and sound of him a good way beyond 'half cut'. This was the guy who'd raised one of the best midfielder players in Europe. Sitting more sedately nearby was his missus, and yes, they both looked like their boy! As the years have passed I've come to appreciate Roy's dry humour as a pundit, but on this afternoon in New York, aside from the obvious facial similarities, you wouldn't really have put the deadly serious 'hard man' alongside the affable characters we'd just met.

I asked them if they'd come outside into the street and have a word. Far too noisy inside. 'Ohhhh,' said Mossie with a deeply lilting Cork accent 'ya know, I'd love to be in two places. I, I'll enjoy myself here, but.. I'd love to be back in Ireland, because the pubs in Ireland, the reaction will be just 'un-believ-i-bill'...the sing-song, the paaaarty, the 'craic', I want to be in two places at the one time, now, and I mean that!...' He blew out the words almost musically, like a ride up and down the holes of a flute. What a fantastic character, a few drinks down the line and ready to break out into full sing-song at any second. What I wouldn't have given to have Roy standing next to him at that moment, cringing with embarrassment and trying to usher him out of the way of the camera.

Game day at Meadowlands was a scorcher. And if the Swedish guy in Japan who accused me of being a serial squinter was watching, he would have had a field day. I was standing on top of a satellite news truck to do my live reports from the vast parking lot, and the American crew insisted on using a 'reflector', a kind of nylon umbrella, but flat, with reflective foil on one side used to reflect the sun's rays onto the subject's face. A combination of near 100 degree heat and that reflector had me practically cooked, with burned out retinas thrown into the bargain. A human hamburger with relish, slowly sizzling. I had a tan long before kick off.

No-one really thought Ireland would beat the Italians, but that's just what happened thanks to Ray Houghton's single goal. Mossie Keane and his merry men must have been hoarse with joy. I was back on the van after the game surrounded by an army of fans preparing to paint the 'Big Apple' even more green. Across the parking lot from the Meadowlands stadium was a race track and I got word that the Irish Tourist Board were hosting an after match party. If nothing else, the colour from a group of celebrating fans would make a great piece for the next morning. It was private I learned, but the Irish were in such high spirits that I managed to persuade the organisers to let me in with a camera. Bingo! Within a few minutes I'd bumped into Larry Mullen from U2, then the Prime Minister Albert Reynolds, then the team themselves, letting their hair down with an almighty party. What a scoop! Right place, right time, some great interviews, even better pictures, and to cap it all, there were no other television crews there. Andy Townsend turned up somewhere with a new blonde crop. 'I went in for a 'Valderrama...'he chirped (the Colombian striker with a big frizzy blonde hair-do) '....and came out with a Val Doonican.' The 'Boys In Green' just kept on delivering.

We had been using the NBC studios in the centre of Manhattan to send our stories back across the Atlantic. The day before the game we walked into the newsroom, one of the busiest in the US, to find the most odd scene. A concentrated hush had descended across the newsroom and every head appeared to be intently watching a monitor. What was so interesting, we wondered? It looked like something from a warm-up lap at the Daytona raceway. A procession of cars, not travelling very fast at all, heading up the freeway on the other side of the country in California. A news helicopter was in parallel, zooming in and out sending back live pictures. The newsroom journalists whispered their astonishment. 'OJ....' one of them said. Who or what was that? Without wishing to sound out of the loop. 'OJ Simpson...they think he's killed his wife and now they're trying to arrest him!'

He might have been a household name in the States as an actor and American football legend, but for me it was only a vaguely familiar name. Nonetheless, we bought into what was clearly a nationwide drama, live on just about every channel and watched the drama unfold. Little did I know then that the following year when the OJ Simpson trial gripped the American public, it translated across to our side of the pond too. Sky News would show live coverage of every session and that meant if I was midway through a sports presentation shift I would have to give way. 'What does the OJ trial mean for you?' was the office joke on the sports desk. 'About four hours off' was the usual reply. But it was like a real life soap opera with deadly consequences and British audiences bought into it with equal fascination. By the time the jury reached their verdict, and Simpson's lawyer had sensationally got his man off the hook, we had just about completed qualifying for the '96 Euros!

Ireland returned to New York for the final group game against Norway. Nothing like as dramatic, in fact, downright dull in contrast to the Italy sensation. It finished goalless, with Jack Charlton banned from the touchline after the Mexico row, a result that was just enough for Ireland to squeeze through to the next round of the tournament. But it was on this second visit up north that a major sports news story broke, the biggest of the entire World Cup and it caught us out when the guard was down for the only time on the trip.

The workload was heavy. Because of the time difference, five hours behind the UK, we had to record, edit and feed a story every day before midday just to be able to hit the peak bulletin of five in the afternoon back home. With training every day not starting until about ten it was an almighty rush to get everything back, factoring in travel to the feed point too. Then we'd go out and film something else in the afternoon to get ahead of ourselves for the following day. So it was pretty much non stop and I'd be lying if I said tensions in our group weren't stretched from time to time, mostly through sheer tiredness.

The press contingent sometimes sympathised with the Sky reporters and crew over the years because the demands of 24 hour news are relentless at the best of times. If you're not recording a package, there's a 'live' to be done and it could often be exhausting. Nonetheless, the Australian picture editor who travelled with us wasn't easy to work with. He had designs on management and I got the impression he thought he was better than this. But there's nothing worse than a backstabber trying to ingratiate himself with the boss at someone else's expense. We almost came to blows while up against the clock one lunchtime in front of a shocked producer at the local television station. I could see he was within a fraction of 'chinning' me, which would have been the end of his trip and probably Sky career too. Others had gone for less at a time when Sky was growing fast and egos among some of the presenters needed to be reined in.

So on the second trip to New York we would have a night out. Manhattan, and everything that comes with it, though laying off the alcohol for the most part. We were staying in a hotel close to Meadowlands, a fair way out of town, and decided to drive across the Hudson through the Lincoln Tunnel, park up and then find somewhere to eat. We ended up in a diner somewhere with a lively bar nearby. Pinball - I remember the pinball and hammering the machine with the skills I'd picked up from my parents' pub on the other side of the Atlantic. By this time, we'd had more drinks than was probably wise, considering someone had to drive home and there was some filming to be done in the morning. At this point some football fans appeared in the bar and one of them had a ball. 'Game in the street! If anyone wants to play?!' Great idea, we thought, and if someone had to get the car back across the Hudson a chance to sober up before driving home. By this time it was already close to midnight. Still, this was the city that never sleeps, so time to put it to the test.

Around a dozen of us went out, split into two teams and started a makeshift match down one of the side streets off Fifth Avenue. This went on for 20 minutes or so and with the heady buzz of booze it was helter skelter stuff. The boss, Andy Cairns, who'd worked us hard on the trip had disappeared off to bed by now and we played on. 20 minutes became half an hour, then three-quarters, and after a full hour of charging around in the New York night we all had second wind.

Central Manhattan in the middle of the night, what a place for the ultimate street football match! There was steam coming out of manhole covers scattered up and down the pitch. If there's an American equivalent of curtains twitching in the neighbourhood, I'm not sure what it would be. But gradually our little match was growing. The makeshift asphalt pitch appeared a little more crowded and I noticed some of the players were different from the ones who'd started. In fact, I didn't re-cognise half of them. This was night time New York City, and the seedy underbelly that only emerges after dark had come out to play. No idea where they came from, but it felt like every last pimp and drug-pusher had slipped out of the shadows to see what was going on. And then slip in from the sides when the ball came close. Forget six-a-side. This was was now more like fifteen, and approaching half past one in the mor-ning the rules had changed too. A new hybrid; part feet, part hands, soccer meets basketball with a bit of rollerball thrown in for good mea-sure. 20 a side by now and after a few crude tackles you got the feeling it was out of hand. Then, out of the blue, like a scene from a New York City cop film, sirens wailed on Fifth Avenue, and a couple of squad cars, blue lights flashing hurtled round the corner and slewed to a halt. Game over, and we all cut a dash for the nearest dark corner. In my case, wherever I'd left the car. The good news was I thought I'd pretty much sobered up by then and like a bat out of hell I was back on the other side of the Lincoln Tunnel faster than you could say 'Paradise by the Dashboard Light'!

But little did I know this night of long nights was still young. I got back to my hotel room around two, and there was a message on the in-house phone system. Call the office, there's a big story breaking. Nice try, I thought. A wind-up on the night we'd decided to go out and let our hair down a little. Bedtime. I was half comatose about 40 minutes later when the phone went off loudly, sending my heart pounding. It was the boss. Diego Maradona had failed a drugs test. There was a media confe-rence in Dallas later that morning and we were on a flight out of Ne-wark at seven. It was already after three, we'd have to leave in an hour, nothing was packed and my senses were scrambled. Mark Saggers, one of the presenters back at base had apparently been jumping up and down demanding to know where we'd been and why we hadn't res-ponded to the earlier messages. It was sod's law, and I stumbled blindly around trying to get my things together. It must have been a taxi to the airport because I don't remember driving and the onset of a hangover wasn't going to help. At least we had a four hour flight to try to get some sleep. But that wasn't happening either; I needed to get my head around the story. The live media conference was scheduled to start about an hour after we touched down in Texas and I would be expected to do the talking down the line. And before that, do a live insert from outside the venue. One step off the plane in Dallas and it was like walking into a blast furnace. The end of June, approaching the hottest time of the year in one of America's most scorching states and temperatures were pushing 108 degrees Fahrenheit.

I'll be honest, I felt sick. A bit too much to drink, not enough sleep, ridiculous heat and a general sense of disorientation. But I got through the 'live' without throwing up and we made our way into the building which appeared have been hastily acquired by FIFA for the day. It was instantly apparent that the media conference room was way too small for an army of media all trying to squeeze their kit into a cramped space at the back of the room. I counted around forty crews and there wasn't room to swing the proverbial cat. In fact there were so many people trying to get in that they had to us overflow rooms with an audio feed to relay the conversation from the officials who were jostling for space themselves on the front table.

I was on my hands and knees at the back because all of the elbow room above waist height was taken by jostling cameraman muttering to each other in different languages that they were getting in each other's shots. I think we all learned a few new South American expletives, and they were certainly reacquainted with a good number of ours. A media scrum was the usual way of describing it, except that this wasn't a traditional one when the person the crews were trying to film was on the move, with elbows and bits of equipment flying in all directions. It was a static press conference, so the cameras that got in first had the last laugh. That said, the sound man, squatting down somewhere with his box of tricks hooked up to the return satellite feed back at base with ease, and I could hear the studio gallery back in London even more clearly than I could when I was normally sitting a few yards away from them. It was hard to believe the leaps and bounds in satellite communications since as a boy I'd strained to hear the commentators on a crackly line from the 1970 World Cup, twenty four years earlier.

Looking back at a recording of this media conference, Sepp Blatter was in his element, telling the world how one of its greatest ever players had tested positive for the banned stimulant ephedrine and was being thrown out of the tournament. It was clear back then that he was heading for the FIFA presidency though no-one could have foreseen what a mess he would eventually make of it. I met him a few times in the following years and actually found him to be quite personable. At Sky we had the advantage of being seen abroad, and Blatter and his communications people kept an eye on that we were saying when a big story broke.

In the week following the millennium I had the chance to travel to Brazil to follow Manchester Utd in the season that they controversially pulled out of the FA Cup to take part in FIFA's Club World Cup instead. Of course Blatter was there, holding court in Rio, including a bash that had been arranged by the British Ambassador in the fabulous Copacabana Palace Hotel just off the famous beach. The United team who'd been slaughtered in the British press for bunking off from their bread and butter domestic commitments duly pressed the flesh and probably stroked Blatter's ego. It was all very low key for a tournament that was about as meaningless as they come. Though one thing that made it worthwhile was seeing Utd being taken to the cleaners by Vasco de Gama in a match they barely looked bothered about. It was my first and only look at the old, fabled Maracana before they knocked it down and built a new one for the 2014 World Cup. Legend has it that 200,000 fans once watched a match there, and you could see how. More circular than oval shaped like a traditional stadium, it was pretty much vast terraces everywhere and even for our game with 70 or 80,000 inside there was plenty of room for more. Squint, and you could almost transport the scene back into the grainy black and white world of old archive with enormous crowds marvelling at the sight of Pelé and Garrincha in their pomp.

The story for us here though was not the football as much as United's decision to walk out on the FA Cup, and negative headlines followed them right through the tournament. I bumped into Gary Lineker one night walking down the Copacabana strip and he said there was a large English gathering in a nightclub further down the road called 'Help!'. 'And you'll need it!' he chuckled referring to the hordes of hookers who appeared to be all over Rio. United's then chairman Martin Edwards was soon accused by one of the tabloids in a big front page 'splash' of spending the night with a prostitute in his hotel. Safe to say the trip did not go well on the public relations front. I have no idea whether Blatter attended the 'Help!' party but I do remember having what amounted to a surprise personal chat at the Ambassador's reception. 'I need to visit my mother soon,' he said candidly, 'because she's about to die'. I'm not sure what I'd done to gain his confidence but it was quite disarming and he came across as anything but the defiant controller of a corrupt organisation from his later years as FIFA President.

It was a couple of years before Ireland's tribulations at the '94 World Cup campaign came to light with the ticket fiasco. But on the field they'd gained plenty of new friends by reaching the second round before the predictable defeat by a Denis Bergkamp inspired Netherlands in Orlando. For the bigger football nations, certainly the leading European ones it felt like a military operation in keeping their players locked away from the media outside of the usual press conferences. And more than a quarter of a century on from USA '94 at the time of writing this, even the smaller qualifiers now keep a tight rein on their players. But back then Ireland were a breath of fresh air and who could blame them for having an old school mentality when it came to relaxing between games? Roy Keane might have been the serious one demanding a hyper professional attitude, but by my experience they gave it their all out there and returned home with heads held high.

One afternoon though captured the fun and sense of perspective for me. We had wheels, the ones that I'd driven Gary Kelly back and forth to the local television station. As we sat post training in the hotel lobby discussing the plans for the rest of the afternoon, John Aldridge and Ronnie Whelan came wandering past looking to make the most of some free time before dinner. 'Hi lads', they said, 'What are you up to for the rest the day?' I told them we were thinking of driving into Church Street in Orlando, the place where the bars were and where most of the fans gathered around the matches. 'Can we come too?' came the reply. 'Just don't tell Jack!' And with that the pair of them hopped into the back of the hire car and we drove into town. I'm not sure what the boss would have made of it if he'd found out, given Big Jack's volatility on the trip, but he never did, and two of Ireland's top players casually sat at the bar of one of the Church Street brasseries without even being recognised. No booze, naturally!

Chapter 6
White Riot
France 1998

After the Euros on home soil in 1996, France '98 was the World Cup that really brought the greatest show on earth to our doorstep. Everyone wanted to go. Easy to get to, and for fans for whom the travel experience was as rewarding as the event, it was simply unmissable. One of the most attractive countries on the planet, and wide open spaces to explore.

I'd spent an academic year in France in the early 80's and got a taste for the club game there. I was studying (sort of) in Nice, and sometimes went along to watch them. I could identify with them. Not very good, always at the lower end of the top division or the one below, and generally up against it. Sounded a lot like Birmingham City so I was right at home. Their biggest game of the season, doubling the gate, was for the visit of the then all conquering Saint Etienne, in the years when Paris St Germain were still relative newcomers without a history. Two of the French greats, Michel Platini and Jean Tigana wore the green of Saint Etienne that night but l'OGC Nice in their proud red and black stripes held their vaunted visitors to a 1-1 draw. A teenage lad by the name of Daniel Bravo was their new poster boy, the Trevor Francis of Nice, and he went on to play for the next twenty years, more than 550 games, winning the Euros with France in '84.

Two stadium visits during that academic year, '80-'81 were eventful to say the least. A long train ride to Munich to see Liverpool in the European Cup we'll come to later, but closer by I nearly ended up in serious hot water at the football stadium in San Remo, just across the French/ Italian border about half an hour from Monaco. A rock gig, on the pitch, but nothing that you could accuse of being bloated 'stadium rock' .This was The Clash, on the 'Sandinista' tour, urgent, vital and right up the street of a bunch of contrary English students. We saw some great gigs that year - Talking Heads who I loved, played in the old marquee-covered amphitheatre on the seafront near Nice's old town, the 'Theatre De Verdure', as did the B-52s or 'B? Cinquante-Deux'?? as the old chap in the ticket kiosk had asked me with a confused look. But The Clash was the one, and five of us set off from Nice squashed into an old Morris 1100 which had seen better days and previously been driven all the way down through France by its owner Andy. The suspension wasn't great and it backfired every five minutes but it got us there.

Andy had promised that he knew one of the English guys selling merchandise on the tour and that he would be getting us all into the changing rooms after the gig to meet the band. 'London Calling', 'White Riot', 'Train In Vain' - they played them all in front of about 15,000 fans on the pitch. Then, yep, sure enough we were suddenly in the bowels of the crumbling Stadio Communale and gathered around that affable urban guerilla (I'd learned fast since that old Vietnam news report!) Mick Jones. No sign of Joe Strummer or Topper Headon, but Jones, who's also an avid QPR fan, was on top form while Paul Simonon post-gigged his way through a few beers in a quiet corner. He was all ears while we regaled him with tales of how brutal the notorious CRS riot police were over in Nice, and we got on so well that we decided we would follow the band to the following night's gig in Florence and Mick would get us in.

That's when the wheels came off. Gone midnight, we headed back to the old banger parked in the street outside to find that an old Morris 1100 was no match for a reliable Renault 'Deux Chevaux'. Nor even a Reliant Robin for the matter. The engine was stone dead and not only would we not be going to Florence, but we couldn't even get home. We wandered around looking for inspiration, or at least a phone box that might lead to a rescue by the Italian version of the RAC, if there was one, when suddenly a shiny new mini pulled up behind our stricken car. It was Andy. He had broken in to it, hot wired a start and driven back to pick us up. No idea how he thought he'd get away with it when someone reported it missing, but quick as a flash he was out of the driver's seat and before we could picture spending the rest of the year in an Italian jail, he was on his hands and knees behind the broken down Morris and unscrewing the number plates. 'We'll swap the plates over, and no-one will know!' was his outlandish plan. Uh oh.

He also hadn't bargained on an old lady in one of the houses opposite watching what was going on. Before we knew it, she'd called the Carabinieri and they were on us in a flash. I was off like a shot up the road, with one of the others panting breathlessly behind me. But there was no escape and within seconds we'd been collared. I had a sub machine gun wedged under my armpit and a police officer barking instructions in a language I didn't understand. First panicked thoughts, the prison cell in 'Midnight Express'. We're not in Turkey but I bet it'll be just as bad in Italy! They walked us back to the scene of the crime, and to our astonishment Andy was already explaining that yes, the old English car was his, and he had the papers to prove it. By a stroke of luck, they thought that THIS was the car he'd been attempting to steal, with its number plates already half off, and were none the wiser about the stolen mini parked right behind. Lucky escape. We even got the old rust bucket going later in the night and managed to drive back to France. But I did wonder what the owner of the Mini must have thought when they eventually found it, mysteriously transported hundreds of yards during the night!

A few months earlier I'd also landed with a British friend in the back of a CRS van after a drunken night celebrating the election victory of President Mitterand. Jean-Marie Le Pen, the far right candidate, was well beaten, and half of Nice was out celebrating. 'Let's let some car tyres down!' was someone's bright idea, and a few too many shots of Pernod precluded discretion being the better part of valour. 'We haven't touched a drop!' was the slurred response from my Welsh friend Dave to the inquiring French police officer who'd been watching it all unfold, upon which he held up his hands to reveal fingers guiltily blackened. Vive La Revolution it wasn't. But so culpably comical, they let us off and we staggered off into the night laughing.

The far right in the south of France was well established at that time. Illegal immigrants from North Africa were a major issue for the authorities and I saw the response to it over and over again. I was in a bar one night just off the Promenade Des Anglais when the police burst in and demanded everyone stand up against a wall and show their papers. On another occasion I was strolling along in the same area carrying a kit bag after a game of football with some locals when a police car slewed across the pavement and screeched to a halt in front of me. They wanted to know if I had drugs and made me empty my bag. I think they probably regretted it after having to finger through some stinking kit. The far right problem was also exacerbated by a militant student group from Corsica who really did not like the French, or anyone else for that matter. The Corsicans were a thorn in the side of the authorities at the best of times, a nasty, brooding bunch with a persistent grudge against the French, probably because they'd ruled them since the mid 18th century. The promise of Corsican honour or threat of revenge might have sounded antiquated to us, but it was part of their make up, and the arrival of some noisy British students in their halls of residence didn't go down well. You could always tell who the Corsicans were because their rooms had the Corsican 'freedom' sticker pressed proudly onto their doors, head height and central. An image of what looked like the head of a warrior figure on a blue background with a bandana tied around. It was meant to be intimidating.

They had already made it known to some of the French students in the halls that they weren't happy with the British contingent disturbing their studies by playing music, and one night there was a major escalation. Steve was a teaching student from Portsmouth Poly, a nihilistic post-punk rocker with a semi mohawk and shambling demeanour who inadvertently wound the Corsicans up.

One evening after we'd all disappeared to bed, Steve and another of our group were flat out and stoned in his room when three masked Corsicans burst in and beat him up with wooden batons. A truly cowardly attack; the walls were spattered with blood, and Steve needed multiple stitches to his head. He declined to press charges, probably because he might have been deported for drug possession. Nonetheless everyone was shocked and even more appalled. But we didn't expect what came next. The Corsicans had an in-house committee, a kind of self regulating hierarchy, and the senior students were not impressed by the actions of the renegade trio, mostly because Corsican 'honour' had been called into question. The head of this hierarchy suggested we have the opportunity for 'revenge', as was their way, and bizarrely he offered us what amounted to a kind of ancient 'duel', or in other words, a fight, three on three to settle our differences, like modern day 'Musketeers'. Er, no thanks, 'd'Artagnan' and his chums belonged in a different age, not Nice 1981! A friend of ours, Philippe from Marseille promised he would send some friends from the 'rough-house' port city down the coast to sort them out. We politely declined, though I would come to see what Marseille was like from its dark side during the World Cup. The offending Corsican students got a dressing down from their own, and suitably humiliated, we never heard a peep from them for the rest of the academic year.

Throughout the 90s, Sky was the outsider, the underdog that I always associated with so strongly when it came to covering World Cups, up against the traditional terrestrial rights-holding powers, the BBC and ITV. But where we could compete and beat them was in our coverage around the event; the news, the colour, and relaying the sheer joy of being there via established 24 hour news coverage, which the BBC did not dip into until the winter of '97. Anything with a nod to what we might expect at France '98 we were 'all over', and a few months before the start of the tournament I had the opportunity to do a security story when Manchester Utd played a European game in Monaco. This was the time when English fans could still travel freely into Europe, post Heysel ban, but pre legislation that would later prevent many from travelling abroad because of banning orders.

The trip threw up an excellent fans story, but for years afterwards I could only think of a personal 'own goal' that nearly derailed the whole thing before we even got there. And I still laugh about it even now. Simon Oliver was my cameraman, not much into football, but a good operator and serious about his filming. As was always the way, I would do some homework on the trip out, making notes and sorting myself out so that we could hit the ground running as soon as we arrived. The two of us were sitting in adjacent seats on the flight out from Heathrow to Nice and it was my day to be the fool, the journalist who doesn't have a pen. Naturally, I asked Simon if he had one and could I borrow it? He's bound to, I thought and it'll be fine. To my surprise he was a little reticent which I thought a bit odd. It's a pen, and you're sitting next to me. I'm hardly going to run away with it! But it was a nice pen, a 'Parker' and he explained that it had 'sentimental value' so he was quite attached to it and I needed to make sure I looked after it. Fair enough, I thought. But hang on, I'm six inches away, in plain sight, and have no plans to steal it! (exaggerated shrug emoji).

I'm not sure whether this unleashed some kind of weird karma of which I knew nothing, but given his reluctance to let me use it, what happened next would have been a stretch to make up. I needed to nip to the loo, so popped the pen into my shirt top pocket, squeezed past the person in the aisle seat and made my way to the cubicle at the front of the plane.

Just don't drop the pen. Hand to chest, and yes, thankfully it was still there.

A quick pee, and I'd carry on with my notes, about which I was in mid-thought. I leaned forward to flush the handle, the move that prompts that familiar pressurised 'whooooosh!' ,and as I did so, to my horror, the pen shot out of my breast pocket and straight down the toilet. Shiiiit! No! Get it back. Hand down the pan? Would it still be there? What would I say to the stewardess? Christ. It was probably falling to earth at that very moment of panic. Worse still, I'd now have so explain it. 'Simon, really sorry, but I've….lost your pen. I dropped it down the kha-zi.' Needless to say he wasn't best pleased. But given the big build up, what were the odds!? Really!! It was almost as if some external forces were at play, even if I still chuckle about it many years later. Toilet humour with a twist.

Later that day I bumped into Angus Deayton, a big Man United fan at their pre-match training session. An extremely random meeting because he was a big name, in an unlikely place and he was chatting away for England. Though the joker in me couldn't help thinking 'Have I Got News For You?!…I've dropped your precious pen down the bog.' At least the story that followed turned out to be a good one. Organisation at the Monaco stadium was a shambles and I met scores of United fans who told me that they'd turned up without tickets and were simply able to walk into the ground without being challenged. It was a security angle that took the story out of the sport section and into the main news bulletin, and set the agenda for what would be a damaging World Cup for both the French hosts and, especially, England.

The FA based themselves way out in Western France, the seaside town of La Baule in southern Brittany with its long stretch of sand and gaggle of cockle pickers every time the tide was low. As always with England hotels, it was a fortress, with the players locked away in seclusion, and the monotony only broken by daily sessions at their nearby training headquarters. Sometimes I wondered whether the siege mentality that often set in during a World Cup was counter productive. The FA's response was always that if free access was given to the media it would get out of hand. But the Brazilians seemed to manage it well enough and they were overrun by even bigger numbers. Over the years some players would complain about the hardships of isolation over a period of more than a month. What harm would letting them out do from time to time? Other countries allowed it. I was in La Baule one night looking for somewhere to eat and bumped into three members of the Norway squad who were also staying close by. Tore Andre Flo, his brother Jostein and their cousin Havard were out together having a meal and nobody bothered them. Though when I mentioned it to some of the Norwegian media in our seafront hotel, they were all desperate to know if they had been drinking. If they were, it didn't have an adverse affect because they beat Brazil and got through their group unbeaten, at Scotland's expense.

Then again, Norway were not England when it came to the traditional media circus and the tabloid led thirst for every last drop of information to come out of the camp. France '98 came well before the 'WAGs' phenomenon, the wives and girlfriends who hit centre stage in Germany eight years later. But in La Baule, the FA wanted the players to be content and agreed to let their other halves visit the camp for a few days early in the tournament. We may not have had the rights-holding kudos of the terrestrial channels, but times had been changed by the satellite revolution and the FA had Sky installed at their hotels and training bases for all of the next few major tournaments, including this one, presumably to give the players and staff access to English content, and, to keep abreast of all the news, including what we were saying about them.

That meant they were watching us and it was usually empowering, but also made us targets for the odd wind-up. Alan Shearer was always straight in his interviews. A bit dull if the truth be told and I'd spoken to him on the end of a microphone since he was 17, when he first broke through at Southampton. But a couple of years after France '98 at the ill-fated Euros in Belgium he played the funny man. Either that, or hotel lockdown, cabin fever, had finally taken its toll. I was interviewing Peter Beardsley live outside the front of the team hotel when Shearer, who had the channel on in his room decided it was time for a prank. 'Peeeeee -terrr' came the lonely call from his balcony window, like Juliet pining for Romeo, while the little man wondered what the hell was going on. 'Peeeeee-terrrrr....' And so it went on, echoing down the street while we tried to talk about morale in the camp and how England had managed to go 2-0 up against Portugal and lose 3-2. Then a change of tack: 'Boorrrr-iiiinnngg!'....'Peeeeet-errrrrr'. My only regret was not engaging and making him come down. Shearer, stand-up comedian. Who knew?!

The late Ray Clemence dropped by our picturesque live position by the harbour most mornings to give us camp updates. These were the days before Sky Sports News and all of the media conferences at the training base were taken live by Sky News. The arrival of the wives and girl-friends into camp was good news, because it brought all the focus on to the new golden boy David Beckham and his 'Spice Girl' girlfriend Victoria Adams. Posh'n'Becks's every move filled most of the tabloids, so when she arrived in camp it was open season. And as good fortune would have it, as soon as she turned up, Beckham was put up for inter-view in the daily media conference. He was still young, at 23 but looked although he'd been through some media coaching, a quiet guy who ap-peared to be able to handle all the attention with a shy smile and ready charm. I was in the front row, and because we were taking the confe-rence 'live' got to ask the first few questions. When Becks was put up, a few of the non sports hacks were usually hanging around, hoping for something that would fill the pages nearer the front of the tabloids. I was straight in, and through a combination of nervousness and over eager curiosity managed to both mess it up and draw one of the best blushes of Becks' career. 'Now that Victoria's come over for a few days,' I asked, 'what have you been up to, apart from... the obvious?!' Oof! Not as clumsy as 'better than having your hands chopped off' but a ham -fisted hand grenade that drew guffaws from the assembled gallery and an embarrassed smile from the (crimson) golden boy, over a muffled and hasty...'Just relaxin'!' Next question!

England's opening group game was against Tunisia in Marseille. The distance from base was such that we had to fly down, and were there a couple of days in advance. It was to be one of the most eventful matches I ever attended and ended up being front and centre in the news agenda before and after. From my college days at Nice I knew Marseille had a reputation for being one of the roughest cities in France, principally because of its port status and proximity to the North African countries. Drug smuggling and crime was rife along with significant num-bers of settlers from the other side of the Mediterranean that made Marseille a multi cultural mixing pot. The football club was one of the biggest in France with a passionate fanbase and its 'ultras' had a reputation for hostility. As soon as I arrived, I made for the harbour with its fabulously colourful market stalls lining the dockside. A strong aroma of fish drifted through the air, a combination of merchants mixing 'bouillabaisse', Marseille's fish stew, and the smell of over ripe marine produce being cooked by the intense Mediterranean sun. Perfect colour for a television scene setter ahead of the game. The place was bustling with activity. Locals on bikes, car horns honking and taxi drivers shouting, competing for fares. I jumped into one to take a ride up to the Stade Velodrome, the venue for England's meeting with the Tunisians who were sure to have plenty of support in this part of France. 'Be careful...', said the driver in broken English with a hint of racist malice. 'Marseille is a divided city. There are some parts that I will not drive into' before going on to describe no-go areas where gangs of North African youths were a thorn in the side of not only taxi drivers but also the local police.

Two nights before the match, we received reports of sporadic incidents of disorder in and around the harbour with its array of bars and clubs. England fans had been arriving in Marseille over previous days and by matchday up to 30,000 would be in town. Richard Shakespeare was on the scene and in his element. He was one of the country's most prominent police on the football scene and had once infiltrated the hooligan gang at Wolves, living the life of one of their number while gathering evidence against them and eventually going to court to identify and convict the ringleaders. That, I thought, must have been tough, not to mention dangerous. Having to gain someone's confidence at a time when their guard was down, 'befriend' them and then betray them in court must have been difficult on a human level. The undercover reporter Donal MacIntyre famously did something similar, but for television, with Chelsea. A life in hiding afterwards, or at least constantly looking over his shoulder was the price he had to pay for some fascinating but risky investigating.

I first met 'Shakey' while doing some undercover work on my old patch in South Wales for the notorious Swansea - Cardiff derby which was always volatile. Then we crossed paths numerous times in the 90s at Birmingham where incidents of disorder were regular occurrences and I was often there as a fan. He was a hardened 'pro' and one of the first to use the mobile camera to film suspects at a time when legislation in the fight against hooliganism was changing and anyone caught on film could expect heavy punishments. I got to know him well and his knowledge of the scene was a more than useful source of information. One image stands out. Birmingham v Cardiff at St Andrew's in 1995 and I spotted 'Shakey' crouching down behind a wall ducking rocks and stones being hurled over from the street outside and into the away section car park. Every now and then he would pop up from behind his cover and try to film the perpetrators. A man on the front line. He also told me there was a particularly troublesome small group of Aston Villa fans with right wing leanings who had a habit of causing problems abroad with England. I was out filming a 'piece to camera' on the Marseille sea front when it became apparent that I was being approached by one of them. Shaved head, Brummie accent, and a generally anti-social attitude. My instincts were always to engage in conversation, though I don't think he was too impressed when we discussed my club allegiance. Cowering down, however, was never going to happen. 'Don't walk away....' he said with a hint of menace when I made my excuses and headed for the camera position. So I did just that. Walked away, and a small part of me remembered my 11 year old self being bullied by that schoolboy and his halfwit cronies. For all I knew it could have been him.

Shakespeare was out on the streets of Marseille filming small skirmishes between groups of England fans and North Africans riding around on mopeds. But it was the following day, the eve of the match when the situation really started to escalate. Martin Brunt, Sky's crime correspondent was also on the scene with a brief to monitor what was going on while I was there principally to cover the football side. I could see through the afternoon that groups of Arabic youths had started to build up in the old town and harbour areas, and if, as I thought, these were the ones who the taxi driver had referred to the day before, the night ahead might be challenging. England fans had been arriving in numbers all the time and by late afternoon were filling most of the harbourside bars. I was working with a young cameraman named Neil Morris on his first big overseas trip. He'd never had to film in a combat zone or riot situation before, when cameras could often be targeted, so he was apprehensive.

Sure enough, by early evening we heard reports that trouble had started near the harbour and made our way down in the evening heat. As darkness fell it was becoming widespread, and police units roamed the streets and back alleys while sirens wailed in the distance. But there was something unusual about it. I noticed that the police were paying little attention to the hundreds of North African youths who were roaming around in an area of town where we'd been told in normal circumstances they would be viewed with suspicion by the law and moved along. But here they were looking oddly liberated and having the time of their lives while the police appeared to have their sights set only on containment of the English contingent. The local youths seemed to be following the police, pied-piper fashion in some kind of novel celebration of the tables being turned, a reversal of the status quo where they would normally be the ones being pressurised. Neil was nervous. But it became clear the North Africans had no interest in the news cameras. They were too busy marching round enjoying their new found sense of liberation. A distraction from the regular tensions thrown up by French politics in the melting pot of Marseille.

We overtook the crowd and police front line and found ourselves on the corner of the harbour close to where the market stalls had been. We were out in the open when a hunched figure with face covered brushed past and hurled what appeared to be a gas canister into one of the bars. It was hard to tell who was who in the chaos and confusion. Normally, cameras would be a target when held in the traditional position on the shoulder, not helped by the cameraman with his eye to the viewfinder being blind on one side if someone approached from that direction. 'Just press record! Hold the camera down by your side and put it on a wide angled setting!' was my impromptu suggestion. That way no-one would notice that they were being filmed. And with that we dropped back against the wall of one of the harbourside buildings while individuals were bouncing and fighting in front of us. We found ourselves in a prime position, right at the moment when red flares and smoke bombs were being launched back and forth down the quay. The pictures were spectacular and some of the most graphic of a violent confrontation. We moved down the quay to where sporadic one-on-one skirmishes were breaking out. One man graphically launched a white plastic chair over the head of another, and in the confusion I hadn't even seen it, but Neil's hip slung camera speculatively captured it from the waist down as the piece of furniture catapulted off the victim and down over the harbour's edge into the water.

By now Sky News had an SNG (satellite news gathering) truck parked at harbourside and the producer responsible for it was getting jumpy.

'What if they try to tip it into the harbour?' he reasoned. At this stage both I and Martin Brunt were doing live telephone reports and running commentary into the news programmes and I was itching to use the truck for proper coverage with live pictures. After all, the majority of the North Africans following the police around had been ignoring the cameras so what was the problem? But I was overruled and the chance was missed. With the adrenaline rush having long kicked in I thought he was being over cautious. The producer, citing safety issues, decided that the truck would have to move to a quieter side street, and frustratingly, as capability to do roving live coverage without the restriction of cables was still a few years away, (the technology that I went on to use at Euro 2004), it meant being stuck up near the van on the end of a cable with absolutely no view of what was going on, which in my view defeated the object. I wasn't happy, even though we'd captured some remarkable footage on tape.

The story was making major headlines not just at home but across Europe and I gave my account the next morning into Sky News' programmes. Sir Brian Hayes, the former Met Police deputy commissioner who we saw around the England camp had been hired by the FA as a security adviser, and had long had reservations about the choice of venue for this fixture. He was right. He also felt that the trouble had been instigated by North Africans provoking the England fans, though that was not how the narrative was presented. For many years the 'English disease' was given a familiar, regurgitated treatment by journalists who tended to just report the tired old lines, especially those who had never even been near a football match. Even down to archaic would be solutions like 'bring back National Service' or 'give them all the birch'. I felt there were a few inaccuracies in the telling of the Marseille story. It was always likely to be a powder keg situation given the venue, the teams involved and the complex mix of people who lived there. From what I had seen, the Arabic combatants, whose harassment by the French authorities was, by popular local opinion a source of persistent friction, were on this occasion not given the same robust treatment as the England contingent. And that despite a larger number appearing to be misbehaving. Whether that encouraged them is open to question but it appeared to give some an excuse to 'make hay' while the police were stretched in all directions. The scenes of disorder continued into the next day, matchday.

I came into contact with the UK government's Sports Minister, Tom Pendry, just after I'd broadcast one of my morning updates and felt vindicated by his observation that I had been 'balanced' in my assessment of the previous night's events, while most of the usual outlets just blamed the England fans again. A reputation is not easily shifted.

But by lunchtime trouble was flaring up again. I was on a balcony opposite the stadium and could see what appeared to be plain clothed police snatch squads down the street picking out individuals and bundling them into the back of vans. They were distinctively dressed, as if briefed to blend in like 'casuals' - polo tops and trainers, darting in quickly and decisively to grab individuals suspected of either causing trouble or being known hooligans. The match itself was predictable with England having the bulk of support in the stadium and running out 2-0 winners. But while all this was going on there was chaos in one of the nearby official 'fan zones' where the match was being shown on a big screen. Sky reporter Emma Hurd was there to keep an eye on the situation and found herself in the middle of a battleground. England fans who did not have tickets for the game came under attack from locals after the first goal went in and a scene of wild disorder ensued. Police responded with tear gas and Emma, who was in a fixed reporting position because of the aforementioned situation with the satellite truck and its cables, could not escape the clouds of gas. But instead of fleeing she battled through her live broadcast, coughing and spluttering with eyes streaming while fights broke out all around. Gripping live news television.

It was ground breaking coverage and would lead to an infamous event at the Euro 2000 tournament in Belgium and Holland two summers later when the broadcast media, in my opinion, contributed to a grotesque 'show'. By then, banning orders for British fans with records of disorder had yet to be passed through legislation so travel was still easily manageable, and when England were drawn in the same group as old foes Germany for a match in Charleroi, an old mining town in Belgium, the media were on high alert. It was a fairly charmless place, a grey industrial wasteland dotted with old mining slag heaps, but with an historic central 'square', or actually, circular plaza surrounded by old buildings and antiquated bars. With not much else to attract visiting fans it was obvious that this would be a gathering point for fans from both countries. Earlier in the afternoon I'd been out walking with my cameraman when I was collared by some Middlesbrough fans, one or two of whom thought I was a candidate for a bit of rough treatment. I got this impression when a tanked up youth grabbed me by the scruff of the neck, or at least the bit of shirt covering the top two buttons, and told me to clear off. Fortunately, some of the same group remembered me from a perilous trip to Poland from the year before, when I'd helped them navigate a way to the stadium, and they apologised for their hasty mate before moving on.

Marseille was still fresh in the memory and it seemed every television crew known to man found a balcony vantage point from which to film, many of them paying for the right to do so. It almost felt like a Roman day out at the amphitheatre, waiting for the 'entertainment' to start. All that was missing was the emperor holding court and an exaggerated thumbs down to signal the start of the show. If that sounds over hyperbolic, in the aftermath I felt embarrassed to be a journalist. The news teams hijacked the story, with little input from the sports news regulars, and with that came the usual generalisations and peddling of football fan stereotypes. The 'arena' was split in two. England fans occupied one half and the outnumbered Germans whose own right wing risk groups had been prevented from attending by, at that time, a more stringent banning policy, were on the other side. As if by clockwork, around late afternoon and with the effects of hot sun and cold beer taking hold, tensions boiled over and the cameras rolled. Plastic chairs flew through the air, accompanied by plastic 'glasses', brought in for the day in anticipation of the inevitable. With that came a robust no-nonsense response from the Belgian authorities and graphic pictures went round the world; water cannons knocking everyone in their path off their feet, including innocent bystanders.

It was, indeed a watershed moment and the last major flashpoint for England fans abroad before legislation changed the landscape. Increased police powers accelerated the introduction of banning orders and the surrender of passports around major events, preventing known trouble makers from travelling. Incidents did continue on a smaller scale, but the days of uncontrolled 'invasions' were numbered.

At France '98, the crisis was still lurching from one match to another and the travelling roadshow rolled on. By Toulouse, very much French rugby territory, the explosive cocktail from Marseille that with hindsight should have meant a different venue, felt a world away, and travelling numbers were visibly down for England's second match against Romania. I was working with a cameraman nicknamed 'Spiney', Anthony Hagen, and it was always a pleasure to work with a fellow football fan who would 'get' the story. Even though he was a Luton fan (winking emoji). For Marseille, and most of the major sporting events we would cover over the following decade and a half there would normally be an advance 'recce' of the venues, to find the best live broadcast positions with a decent view in the background, especially if we were there for a few days. Naturally, some of the best locations needed paying for and whoever owned the view could make good money over a period of a tournament; a shot at opportunism for individuals with a nice flat and balcony, or in China's case during the 2008 Beijing Olympics, commandeer an entire block of flats opposite the 'Bird's Nest' stadium and make all of the world's television channels take up space in adjacent units. No free market there! But it was a great view, and hopefully the families who had to move out on the orders of the state were well compensated.

The Marseille experience took its toll on some of the crews and the appetite for standing out on the street unprotected was waning. In Toulouse with no pre-arranged place to base ourselves we had to find somewhere suitable 'on the hoof'. I spotted a tall block of flats with balconies a couple hundred yards from the stadium and went knocking on some doors. 'Est-ce que nous pouvons prendre les photos de votre balcon, s'il vous plaît?' I enquired, in my 'should-have-done-better-at-college' French, as a middle aged lady pushed her head round the door on the fifth floor. Maybe it was the modest wad of cash that did the trick because we got the go ahead from the first one we tried, and before the couple and two kids knew what they'd let themselves in for, the satellite engineers had run every last yard of cable up the stairwells and were trudging across the threshold, pulling the cables across shiny parquet floors with dirty kit. As improvised broadcasts go, this was up there, tripping over cables in a cramped kitchen while the residents tucked into teatime 'Quiche Lorraine'. But the view was great!

In typical England fashion, Glenn Hoddle's team managed to lose to Romania 2-1, despite a goal from the new teenage golden boy Michael

Owen. And you probably could have written the script, with the winning goal coming in the final minute by a player who plied his trade IN England for Chelsea. If things weren't going wrong off the field, they usually went pear-shaped on it; there was rarely any middle ground with England. It meant that they'd probably have to settle for second place in the group which would lead to a harder second round match.

So we trudged back up to base camp at La Baule and tried to put a brave face on it. At least Hoddle had a sense of humour. Media conferences tended to turn into groundhog day at World Cups. The players secretly challenged each other to shoehorn song titles into the session when it was their turn to be hauled out in front of the media, and by the end of each one, someone, normally the overseas reporters or outsiders with an agenda, would come up with a daft question.

'If Michael Owen was The Beatles and Teddy Sheringham was The Rolling Stones' a foreign reporter piped up from the back of the room as we got down to the last couple of questions, 'which song would you be singing in the shower, 'Twist and Shout' or 'Satisfaction'?' Hoddle was in quick as a flash, 'No idea, I've always preferred The Beach Boys!'

Most media conferences were one too many at the best of times, but that one made me laugh out loud. Hoddle saw it coming, unlike Gary Neville when England played against Albania in Tirana a few years later. Quite apart from bizarrely having the opportunity to interview one of my childhood heroes Norman Wisdom on the pitch before the game (because he was a god in Albania!) the real comic moment came at the pre-match media conference in a local hotel when a random fan managed to infiltrate the gathering. In fairness, especially abroad, no-one asked who was who, but this guy not only calmly made himself at home in the back row of seats but then had the cheek to ask a question. 'Do you think Luke Cha-wick... should be starting?' he casually enquired of Neville. Chadwick, with a 'd' in the middle that was missing from the punter's 'patois' pronunciation, was the player who rival fans cruelly used to call 'Plug', because of his resemblance to the character from the Beano comic, but he'd never got remotely near an England cap. Cue silence from the top table and some confused computing of the question while a look of incredulity spread across Neville's face. 'He's not even in the squad!' came the flabbergasted reply, followed by some huffing and puffing. Most of us howled with laughter later when we realised the stranger at the back was a random 'Cockney Red' (Manchester Utd fan from London) who'd wandered down from his room to join in. And it was even funnier when the FA's resident security adviser Ray Whitworth, a former policeman who rarely had a sense of humour bundled the intruder out of the room while Neville muttered with discontent in the background. It wasn't the last time I witnessed Whitworth do that, as we'll come to in the Japan chapter.

We all headed up to Lens for England's final group match against Colombia, a town that you wouldn't ever want to go to, and if you did it was probably because you'd taken the wrong turn in search of nearby Lille, the lovely medieval city with a stunning old town. Lens was only a short distance from Calais so a magnet for throngs of day-tripping England fans, and Lille wasn't far either, though a million miles away on the charm front. Like Charleroi in Belgium it was an old mining town and there was nothing remotely French about the buildings. In fact, walking down some of the streets lined with red-bricked terraced houses it felt more like Bradford or some of the former mining towns up north. The rest was a relatively modern eyesore, having been flattened in both world wars, first from the ground and then the air. So there was something oddly familiar about thousands of England fans wandering the terraced streets, though on this day with nowhere to go before the game.

In the wake of Marseille, the authorities were running scared and all pubs and bars had been ordered to close for miles around. Nothing was open at all from the Channel ports down to Lens, though some locals with an eye for the main chance brought in supermarket sourced crates and sold them to thirsty fans on the streets. It hadn't helped that a week or so earlier a French policeman, Daniel Nivel was almost beaten to death by a gang of German thugs. He was still in a coma when England came to town and was tragically left with a permanent disability. Five German fans were later found guilty of assault and one was jailed for ten years.

England's 2-0 victory over Colombia wasn't enough to win the group and bring with it a less difficult second round tie, but from the news perspective it didn't get much better than a knockout match against Argentina next, further south in St Etienne. Either way I was glad to leave Lens behind and return to the rustic France of traditional folklore. La Baule welcomed us back in between games and we sailed on with our daily 'World Cup Report', broadcast from the harbour or the beach. I did many of the breakfast ones, then at lunchtime Kay Burley would host a half -hour show taking calls from viewers with questions which I would attempt to answer without becoming too horizontal in the Brittany sunshine. It's strange how minor detail lingers in the memory but on my leaving Sky after more than 25 years service, the long-time head of Sky News John Ryley randomly apologised for giving me a hard time, for sitting on that beach wearing shorts!

One particularly engaging lunchtime phone-in had followed the Marseille riots and by the time we arrived in St Etienne, England's unsavoury history with Argentina, on and off the field, raised the prospect of more potential hostility. The South Americans had long claimed their moral revenge for the Falklands conflict by virtue of Maradona's 'Hand of God' goal three World Cups previously. But tensions still simmered. The day before the game I was broadcasting near the stadium when a big bulldog of a man with a Millwall tattoo collared me gruffly. Uh oh. Bracing myself for some rough manhandling it came as a complete surprise when his seizure of my right forearm went from tight grip to friendly squeeze, followed by an emphatic 'We've been watchin' you!... and we like what we've been hearin'!', a bit like Arthur Mullard would have said it. It caught me quite off guard and brought an odd sense of validation for having stuck to my story on the Marseille mayhem while most of the media just trotted out the tired old lines.

It wasn't always easy to convince a newsroom from the field on how a story should be treated. The sports guy wasn't always the news guy if the news 'wires', the agencies whose content would be treated as 'gospel' did not tally with your personal observations from the field. What was never questioned was that the wires were actually just a bit of copy written by a single person often not filing first hand. Especially in small agency offices. But because it was the 'official' wires, it must be true. That could be frustrating. A classic example cropped up the year after France '98 when England played an eventful Euro qualifier against Poland in Warsaw. Organised hooliganism was becoming widespread in Poland and Eastern Europe and the visit of the 'originals' from England threw up the prospect of disorder. England fans did their regular thing, gather in a bar and sang, usually about the IRA, or 'Ten German Bombers' being shot down by the RAF, to the tune of 'Ten Green Bottles'. I came across a remarkable scene in the old town, an outdoor open sided marquee type bar, with around 50 local youths spread around on separate tables, just sitting in silence and waiting. No talking at all, just listening. It looked like a scene from 'Reach For The Skies' or 'Battle of Britain' where the fighter pilots sat nervously around their 'mess' waiting for the call to be scrambled. What sounded like a distant chant rose up from a nearby alley, and to a man they stiffened as if to make their move, before sinking back down. False alarm. But by kick off time there was chaos inside the stadium and out.

While the match was being played, Polish fans shot flares into the England section behind the goal and the England fans responded by hurling plastic seats back. I even spotted one plastic chair with metal legs that had been flung so high that it was hanging 50 feet up from a section of black netting that separated the two groups of fans. I had long left my seat in the press box to investigate outside while a squadron of fully armoured riot police marched around in columns without appearing to be doing much. Enter Ashley, a larger than life England fan who ran a bar in Prague and who I would come across numerous times at European matches over the next few years. He'd been standing next to a woman whose coat caught fire after being hit by one of the flares and came to the rescue by using a bottle of Coca-Cola to extinguish the flames. We arranged to meet in a bar later that night where a number of England fans, he said, had been recuperating after receiving beatings earlier in the day. We filmed an interview with one whose head had been shaved, exposing a nine inch gash on the back of his head pulled together by vicious looking stitches. We recorded our report for the morning Sky News bulletins, good strong pictures with some graphic material only to find that the morning producers, some apparently barely aware that England had even been playing the night before, had not run the report. 'Why not?' I protested. 'Well, there's nothing in the wires about it' came the limp reply. 'Probably' I noted with a hint of sarcasm, 'because the guy in the local office had gone home at 5 o'clock'. It made a mockery of even being there. It wasn't the first time this had happened and I complained strongly to the Head of News Nick Pollard, whose recognition of sport's place in the news agenda was usually a breath of fresh air. Small consolation, but he was less than pleased that the material had been carelessly overlooked.

Back in St Etienne, the 'Stade Geoffroy Guichard' was slightly out of town, and those without tickets found bars in the centre to watch on television, although some premises, fearing a reprise of Marseille did not open. Many fans wandered about aimlessly. One, an ugly lump from Plymouth decided he would grab me by the throat for having the audacity to walk the streets with a camera. But out at the stadium all was calm and fans from both countries mingled freely. I felt a tap on the shoulder and there, as I turned, was a vaguely familiar face, though one I hadn't seen since my youth. It was Uri Geller, the spoon-bending phenomenon of the 70s who had mysteriously shown up at a football match in France. 'I've come to help England win' was his chat up line and before we knew it we were doing a live broadcast surrounded by a combination of the curious and the cynical, while Geller told everyone that he could influence the result. All we had to do was was join hands, make a strange humming noise while picturing positive things and England were as good as through to the World Cup quarter finals. He might even have said something about putting special crystals down near the corner flags to give England magical powers. Then again, by that stage I was probably in a trance. As it turned out, his forecast was hopelessly wide of the mark.

The good news was that 'Shakey' was in town again doing his undercover policing and we greeted each other inside the stadium as he loitered with mini video camera in hand. I had a surprise coming. A few minutes later I was grabbed from behind by a couple of men in polo shirts who I'd never seen before and dragged off down under the main stand. A mock arrest, on Shakespeare's orders. All on camera. One nil to the police! But when they'd finished laughing I was back in time to see a World Cup classic and England go a goal down to a Batistuta penalty inside the opening six minutes, prompting a scuffle on the terraces behind the goal and 'Shakey' rushing off to film some of the perpetrators. England equalised, followed by probably the most memorable goal I ever saw in the flesh. Michael Owen, 18 years old, taking off on a mazy run from the halfway line and planting the ball into the top corner of the Argentina net directly in front of the press box. Like all great moments, it remains seared onto my memory bank. I was a bit older, 30 years on from the magical Barry Bridges overhead kicked for Birmingham against Arsenal in the Cup, but the effect was the same. Frozen in time to enjoy forever. Not just the goal itself, either. I turned round in my press seat to see the English media in raptures. Many had campaigned in print for Owen to play, and I have another memory snapshot that won't be going anywhere; football writer Paul McCarthy who'd been one of those shouting loudest for Owen to be picked, standing on his seat, twirling his arms and celebrating wildly.

That's one great thing about World Cups. The nation comes to a standstill and we're all in it together. In my case, the fan with the microphone. If it was an absolute privilege to be there and do my best to convey what it was like on the ground for the people back home, I regretted missing out on the scenes of utter mayhem in towns and cities up and down the country where fans would gather on hot summer days watching on big screens. The moment where England would score (occasionally) and thousands of drinks would be flung into the air simultaneously in a rapturous shower. Extraordinary outpourings of joy. The best one I ever experienced was in Brazil, standing near waist deep in water on Copacabana Beach, when the host nation scored. Unforgettable, but we'll come to that in the 2014 chapter.

As it turned out, Owen's wonder goal was in vain. England may well have won the match had the Danish referee Kim Milton Nielsen not sent off David Beckham for what seemed nothing more than a petulant flick of the boot in the direction of the 'arch villain' Diego Simeone very early in the second half. And not just that, Sol Campbell's disallowed headed goal from a corner would probably have stood had video technology been around a couple of decades earlier. Maybe Nielsen and the FIFA collective had had enough of the England roadshow by then and were happy to see the back of them. Or Uri Geller had got his crystals in the wrong place, like Barry Fry trying to lift the fabled 'gypsy curse' at Birmingham and urinating on the halfway line instead of all four corner flags (which didn't work either!).

We lost the ensuing penalty shootout, as usual, and wouldn't win one for another 20 years. What a horrible, sinking feeling that was when David Batty's tepid penalty was beaten away by the Argentina goalkeeper. Maybe it's human nature, or just me, but I always celebrate harder when surrounded by adversaries. Probably what comes of supporting a struggling club and always having to defend the honour. And being a little contrary by nature, always seeing the other side of a story, or standing up for the underdog. But trust me, I was in a Red Square bar when that England penalty hoodoo finally ended at Russia 2018, and I more than made up for every one of the shootouts lost, as you'll discover later.

There's something hugely anti-climactic working on World Cups abroad when your nation, and the media entourage that comes with it, is knocked out. Likewise, when the host nations falls. The rug is suddenly pulled, accompanied by a collective sigh that sucks the wind out of everyone. But fortunately at France '98 Les Bleus' went nowhere, and from a relatively lukewarm response by the French public in the early rounds, which was strange, considering France's status as a major football nation, interest surged, and hysteria would kick in for the latter stages. After England's exit my cameraman Neil and I laid low for a few days in the beautiful countryside of Drome, where the Alps begin to rise, pondering England's missed opportunity and wondering whether we'd be summoned home. So my heart soared on hearing the news that we would be staying right through to the finish, and we made the long drive back up north, to Paris and the Hyatt Regency hotel at Porte Maillot just off one of the capital's busiest arteries, the Boulevard Peripherique which circles the historic centre. Not a stretch of tarmac you'd want to become intimately familiar with at the best of times, but as French patriotism suddenly flowered and Parisians bought into the idea of winning the World Cup, far too many decided it was a good idea to cruise round in circles with one hand on the horn, day and night.

In the meantime, the spectre of being non-rights holders was raised again. For England matches, we could usually find a way in through the FA or fellow broadcasters, but now that England were out it would not be so easy. FIFA were not Sky friendly when it came to access to their tournament and we would have to take our place at the back of the queue for observer tickets. France versus Italy at the Stade de France looked a long shot, one of the most over subscribed matches of the tournament and there was no way in. Italians were everywhere. They lived and breathed this and probably could have filled the media section themselves. So a view from the media room would have to do, along with the waifs and strays from far flung international places whose claim for a place in the media tribune had been kicked into touch when the tickets ran out. We listened to the roars of the crowd inside as Italy's final penalty of the quarter final shootout smashed against the crossbar and 'Les Bleus' scraped through to the semis.

The open road beckoned and from Paris we headed east towards Switzerland and Germany in search of Brazil. Vittel was the place they temporarily called home for a tilt at retaining the trophy they'd won in the Pasadena Rose Bowl four summers earlier. You'll know Vittel, not so much from its small town French charm, but from the charm-less plastic bottle with distinctive red logo that carries its famed spring water, piled up in polythene-wrapped stacks on the shelves of supermarkets the world over. Brazil were preparing for their semi final against Holland and that meant a visit to camp. Nothing was quite like a Brazil training session. Organised chaos was the best way of describing it and a sense of joy and freedom that reflected the way they played the game. Ever since witnessing this first hand I've always wondered why the big nations shut up shop and lock their players away for the duration of tournaments. It could so often breed unhappiness that manifested itself in performance. England in South Africa 2010 springs to mind. The big difference was the 'open house' attitude. Fans and media were allowed in to watch the whole thing, a far cry from the shielded approach employed by the big European nations. As we walked up towards the training camp to attempt some interviews, a small group of yellow shirted Brazilian fans were wandering along on the other side of the street. They heard our English conversation. 'Michael Owen!' one of them shouted, '...best player in the world!' to which I raised a triumphant fist in acknowledgement, if not entire agreement. All off the back of that wonder goal against Argentina, which would have been wildly celebrated by Brazilians everywhere. I don't know what it was about Argentina being unpopular. Was it their perceived cynicism and win at all costs attitude? Or just arrogance? But unpopular they were, especially among South American rivals, and I witnessed it first hand, as you'll hear later, at the excellent Russia World Cup in 2018
To see the legendary Mario Zagallo taking the Brazil training session was a strange feeling. I had been a child watching what I still consider one of the greatest teams of all time, Pelé's Brazil of Mexico '70 all those years earlier, and Zagallo was in charge way back then. Although he'd been

off around the club circuit in the intervening decades, it didn't seem possible that he could still be there. But he was, older, and a little more frail, perhaps, but still unmistakably him. The spectacle, though was made by the fans. Unlike the supporters of other nations many Brazilians based themselves near their team's camp, because they could watch them every day. There must have been upwards of 5,000 packed in around the training field, huddled together on makeshift scaffolding stands, or just hugging the touchlines. Players would come past and engage in conversation mid session. Everyone was smiling. You'd almost expect the samba to break out at any moment or the magnificent 'ching-ching' banjo rhythms of 'forro', the insanely infectious Brazilian folk music that drew me under its spell on an unforgettable night in Salvador at their home World Cup 16 years later.

It was pretty much every man for himself when it came to competing with the Brazilian media. If the players approached the game with a cheeky, creative opportunism, so it was with their reporters, and you had to do the same to keep up. 'Winging it' was the only way. Brazil were in mid session when I hit my lunchtime World Cup report from pitchside, simultaneously talking live while pushing my through a crowd of fans with camera in tow to get a better view. Stumbling and stuttering along, I had no guest and really could have done with one, so the sight of the great Roberto Carlos chatting casually to someone in front of me required a little improvisation and opportunism, in other words, an unashamed hijacking and large dollop of cheek. 'Roberto!' I bellowed like a long lost friend, though more in hope than expectation of him taking a blind bit of notice. He looked startled at the sound of an intruder, but with the camera probing keenly over my shoulder and me already halfway through a garbled greeting, the ambush was escape proof. A brief moment of panic gave way to an easy smile and he played ball beautifully, without having a clue what I was talking about.

I tried this technique numerous times with potential victims who could converse perfectly in the Queen's English but many would just pretend they hadn't heard. Prince Andrew was one of them, at Wembley, and I even used a 'Sir', to soften the difficult question that followed. But he ignored me, with his lower lip as stiff as the upper version. Princess Anne on the other hand was the opposite, happy to joust on more than one occasion when we met at horse racing events. A great sport, as was her daughter Zara during her Olympic equestrian years. Brazilians though, are just born friendly. 'Yes...I....I...want....we....win' was roughly the gist of Roberto Carlos' entire response to three or four different questions, even though I hadn't asked him if he thought they would win. No matter that it was nonsense, this was the best left back in the world and I had him 'live', in the middle of a training session before a World Cup semi final. The determination not to embarrass himself, or me, even though I very much deserved it, was enough to keep it going as long as he wanted, which was a good couple of minutes. He was like the cab driver who'd famously dropped off a guest at the BBC and accidentally been introduced live on air as the guest himself, and talking blindly about international politics without anyone noticing. A great sport! But Roberto had the last laugh when we would meet again in Japan four years later.

The real fun though was at the end of the session. The Brazilians didn't bother with a media conference, they just let it happen as soon as the players left the field, or in some cases when they were still on it, with reporters grabbing interviews whenever they could, and HOWever they could. Lots of pushing, sharp elbows and crowds of hacks chattering over each other at the same time. Some of the cameramen had ladders to get the upper hand, and some fell off them in the rush to grab a view of a Ronaldo or Ronaldinho. As for the interviews, microphones appeared to be an optional extra. Mobile phones would do, shoved and yanked backwards and forwards between reporter and player in a chaotic cacophony. The backdrop of an impromptu assault course just added to the entertainment; everyone on the move, tripping over cables and cursing loudly when the phone signal invariably dropped out in mid conversation.

The Brazilians beat the Dutch on penalties, and that left France battling it out with the surprise package Croatia in the other semi final. It's not often that I ever missed a goal at a football match, when you dash out for instance just before half time to beat the battle to get to the urinals, and a World Cup semi final wasn't the best place to add to the tally. But happen it did, although this time I was still engaging in FIFA's half-time hospitality when Davor Suker scored for the men in the red and white checked shirts straight after the break. I was still digesting the 'petit fours' and barely back in my seat when Lilian Thuram equalised for France a minute later. And when the full back, who'd never scored a goal for his country before got another, France, finally, fully embraced its tournament. The place went nuts, and I mean, nuts. I've no idea where they came from, but Paris emptied onto the streets and stayed there for the next four days. It was only a shortish drive round the 'Peripherique' from St Denis back to the hotel, but nothing moved. I'd never witnessed a major road being blocked by an impromptu party before and after an hour or two of drumming my hands on the steering wheel while horns blared from stationary cars, the vehicle in front decided enough was enough, and to hell with the consequences. There was partying to do, so the driver switched off his engine, got out of the car in the central lane, locked the doors and walked off down the middle of the carriageway blowing a horn. Incredibly he never came back, at least not while I was sitting there stranded. More and more people just started walking through the traffic, without a care in the world. It was another hour before anything that hadn't been abandoned shifted at all, and I eventually weaved my way through what was now a makeshift car park on the equivalent of the M25. It was the early hours, and Paris was party central.

From that moment on, World Cup fever well and truly kicked in. I've been to Paris many times but have never seen it as swamped as it was on the weekend of the Final. The night before we soaked up the atmosphere on the Champs Elysees with its street eateries almost spilling out on to the boulevard itself and excited chatter filling the night air. Who's that, over there? I wondered at the sight of someone vaguely familiar getting carried away in a karaoke bar. It was Robbie Earle, the former player turned pundit belting out a tune from The Commitments. An enthusiastic 'garçon' goaded me into a friendly bet that France would win. '50 Euros' says Brazil will win' I jousted' Ronaldo is too good' to which he tapped his nose as if to say 'I know something that you don't' .

The extra media seating capacity for the Final and some kindness by ITV producer Simon Moore, son of the legendary and late commentator Brian meant we were able to access the stadium as non-rights holding observers. My first World Cup Final and something I'd dreamed of since childhood. But while we waited for the showpiece to start, little did we know of the extraordinary goings on in the Brazil team camp in the hours before the match.

The first sign that something was amiss came when the official team sheet was pressed into the hand of my Sky colleague Gary Hughes (the Villa fan and future Head of Football whose education was cranked up a few notches that night five years earlier in the Second City derby against Blues!). Brazil's star player Ronaldo was not on the sheet. Surely a misprint? The media tribune was awash with rumours, and doubly so when half an hour later a reprint appeared with Ronaldo back on the list. Remarkably, the rumours and counter rumours that were only confirmed in the following days and weeks reached the gathered reporters fast.

The 21 year old star had apparently had some kind of 'fit', seizure or nervous breakdown during the afternoon. Roberto Carlos (it was claimed), found him having a convulsion and alerted medical staff. Naturally, they ruled him out of the match. But according to the player himself, hospital tests showed no adverse signs and he convinced coach Mario Zagallo to change his mind and let him play at the last minute. The rest is history. Ronaldo was a virtual passenger, not quite Charlton Heston in 'El Cid' riding around with a stick up his back holding him upright, but his influence was minimal and France won at a canter. Interestingly the whisper that Brazil's sponsors Nike, who'd been part of their travelling entourage had insisted that he play, reached us before the game had started. The rumour persisted afterwards too but was never confirmed. Had he been fit, maybe Ronaldo would have had too much for the ageing France defender Laurent Blanc, but either way he made up for it four years later by scoring twice in the 2002 Final in Japan.

It didn't take a genius to work out that Paris would be beyond crazy that night with celebrating French people, but if it was busy on the eve of the match the scenes after it were on another level. In fact, there was no room on the Champs Elysees, which was packed elbow to elbow from the Arc De Triomphe right down to the Place De La Concorde with flag waving, horn blaring revellers. A far cry from the shrugging, semi interested nation who'd poked at the tournament when it started five weeks earlier. It was so full everywhere that we gave up on a celebratory post tournament drink, and the 50 Euros I'd owed the French waiter from the night before's bet was conveniently smothered by tens of thousands of people, blocking access to any bar, let alone that one.

There was one final twist. While the streets seethed with people we retired back to our hotel and before long, gave in to the pull of sleep at the end of an epic day. Then, from deep slumber, the sound of my phone ringing sent me bolt upright, heart pounding, just as it had done in New York four years earlier for the Maradona drugs alert.

It was 4.30 in the morning and Jane on the overnight news desk at Sky was in a panic. 'You need to get down to the Champs Elysees!', she blurted, 'A car has crashed into the crowds near the Arc De Triomphe and there are reports that 50 people are dead!' Whaaaat?! Half an hour later I was on the scene trying to make head or tail of it through scrambled senses. Most of the crowds had gone, bar scattered police and dishevelled stragglers leaving an eerie silence and a scene of carnage up and down the boulevard. A car had indeed ploughed into the crowd near the monument but the wire reports had been grossly overstated. 20 people had been injured, no-one had died. Relief. Nonetheless a night of excess brought opportunists onto the streets under the cover of the crowds.

I wandered down the Champs Elysees to find two glass fronted showrooms battered by impacts with blunt instruments, and a car on its roof on the other side of the road. Thousands of cans and bottles, the remnants of a wild celebration were strewn about the place. Astonishingly by the time I'd done my second live hit, by seven in the morning it was all gone, swept away by an army of street cleaners. You would never have guessed a million people had been out the night before, and by early afternoon I was on the plane home at the end of an epic six week journey.

Chapter 7
Paranoid Android
Japan 2002

'Konnichiwa!' (Hello!), 'Arigato' (Thank you). Two words that would come to sum up FIFA's first foray into a World Cup outside of Europe and the Americas, and the only two I knew in Japanese for all of that glorious summer off 2002. All the doubters who thought Japan (but not South Korea) would not cut it as a World Cup host because of its thin football heritage could not have been more wrong. I'll say now from the outset, it was one of the best tournaments I ever attended and culturally, was the greatest experience of them all. A complete breath of fresh air. Not just the wonderful culture; everything runs on time, there's little cynicism in society, no-one is judged and there's barely any street level crime. I'd spoken to the former Spurs player Steve Perryman who'd been out there for a few years before the World Cup and he told me no-one even locked their doors, while young children could wander the streets without fear for their safety. If that sounded far fetched, and I had raised an eyebrow, he was right, it felt like stepping onto another planet.

England's journey from France '98 to the Far East had been a bumpy ride, and was rarely out of the news agenda. Glenn Hoddle's sacking on non football grounds made banner headlines, as did the arrival of the charismatic Kevin Keegan. He was made for the media as soon as he was linked with the job while still in charge of Mohamed Al-Fayed's Fulham. Everyone was talking about it. Howard Wilkinson presided over a couple of games as caretaker manager, one of which at Wembley was attended by Al-Fayed, who I collared post match below the steps of the old Twin Towers, wanting to know whether Keegan was going to be freed by Fulham to rescue his country.

The Egyptian owner of Harrods had been shamelessly mocked by some for seeking British citizenship, and the interview gave me one of my most awkward moments. A large crowd had gathered around us to listen, when out of nowhere from the back of the crowd, a growling 'Scouse' voice bellowed out '...DON'T think you're getting a passport! YA RAG 'EAD!' in full earshot of everyone. Awkward silence. Cue sharp intakes of breath from the studio gallery through my earpiece. But through the thickest of skin he laughed it off, and when the crowds had gone pulled out a giant Harrods Toblerone while I mumbled a private apology.

For all Keegan's charisma he fell short at his one major tournament, Euro 2000 and then had the 'bottle' to fall on his sword after losing at home to Germany in the opening qualifying match for Japan. Biblical rain was the backdrop for a double last stand, Keegan quitting on the same day we said goodbye to the place where England had won the World Cup 34 years earlier; the Twin Towers' last appearance before England's spiritual home was completely rebuilt. Two more caretakers stepped in, Wilkinson again, then Peter Taylor before Sven-Goran Eriksson, the FA's first ever foreign coach arrived to steady the ship and carry England though to Japan. But there was a stopping off point along the way that could never be passed over, both for its astonishing result and the stories that came with it.

The return qualifying match in Germany was arguably England's most memorable win ever beyond the '66 Final; a 5-1 thrashing of the old enemy was beyond everyone's wildest dreams. I got the greatest view, standing on the pitch directly behind the net in Munich's old Olympic Stadium where England ran riot in the second half. The surreal scoreline was matched by an aural otherworldliness whenever England added to their tally. Because the stadium had no roof and the England fans were banked up right at the far end of the stadium, when the ball hit the net right in front of me, there was the most peculiar phenomenon, a second or so of silence, a delayed acoustic reaction, before the explosion from the other end reached my ears. What I got was the sound of the ball hitting the net, that satisfying soft slap of leather on nylon, accompanied instantaneously by a joyful yelp from the goalscorer (Michael Owen x 3) and then a fraction later, the rolling sonic boom of 10,000 thunderous voices. I felt like running on the pitch and joining in the player pile-on!

It was an unforgettable night to match a fun-filled build up. England, for reasons best known to themselves had decided on a team hotel not just right in the centre of Munich but right next door to probably the noisiest bar in Bavaria, the famous Hofbrauhaus, where locals clad in traditional 'lederhosen' would stay up most of the night bellowing drinking songs, keeping the whole neighbourhood awake. Odd choice of accommodation, and apparently it was Eriksson's idea. But love them or loathe them (and they made many an enemy on Merseyside in their treatment of fans after the Hillsborough disaster), The Sun newspaper then came up with one of their more amusing ideas. Nick Parker was the news reporter I often bumped into on the road for trips like this and with tongue in cheek he decided that the choice of hotel had been a German dirty tricks campaign to stop England's players getting any sleep on the eve of the match. So here was the plan. The Sun bus, the one I'd seen parading the chesty Melinda Messenger around at the France World Cup, would come to the rescue and give the Germans a taste of their own medicine. So at half past five in the morning on the day before the match, the open top bus, complete with 'Page 3' girls and a mini brass band on board, rolled up outside the Germany team hotel and blasted out a trombone wake up call. No idea what they played, but given events on the field the following night, maybe a take on Beethoven's Fifth.

As practical jokes go, it was a good one, and it captured the imagination back home. Don't believe the stereotypes about Germans not having a sense of humour because it's not true. Germany's press officer Harald laughed hard at the media conference later that morning, though striker Carsten Jancker and goalkeeper Oliver Kahn both got woken up and had to force a smile. In fact Kahn who had to bend down and pick the ball out of his net five times, didn't appear to see the funny side at all, which amused us all the more.

The trip to Germany was one of the first to be affected by the change in legislation after the crowd incidents that marred England's Euro campaign in Belgium the year before, and would change everything in Japan. It led to fewer fans with a history of causing trouble being allowed to travel, though it had taken the best part of a quarter of a century to work out. I'd seen the seeds being sown first hand 20 years earlier in the very same place we'd just been to, Munich and the Hofbrauhaus, when Liverpool were heading towards a third European Cup success in the space of five seasons. But it was so different back then for offenders; nothing more than a slap on the wrist, a small fine, and back out onto the streets to do it all again. Which made being caught a minor occupational hazard and nothing more. I remember this trip for the matter of fact humour that came with the mischief and a sense of the camaraderie that brought groups of lads together on the road. Football travel in those days was a way of life for the diehards and while our small group had taken the train to Bavaria from Nice on our student rail cards during the college year abroad, some of the Liverpool fans we met in the Hofbrauhaus the day before the game had epic travel stories to tell. Some had made it all the way from Liverpool without tickets, for either train or match. Of those, most arrived with just the clothes they stood up in, but all wore the badge of honour of making it all the way to Munich for the princely sum of nothing.

One fan turned up at the bar with a clutch of tickets in hand; a ticket tout had been 'jumped' and relieved of his possessions. Another, bizarrely strolled around the premises taking shoe sizes; a haul of trainers, the prized footwear of choice for the emerging football 'casual' ,had somehow been liberated from a department store. Surely an exaggeration, I thought. But no, one of his mates was waiting outside with a large white plastic bin bag stuffed full of Adidas and Puma. The 'best' was saved to last. A small commotion in another part of the Hofbrauhaus revealed three or four young men busily hunched over one of the long wooden drinking tables. One of them, looking hot and bothered was wearing handcuffs, or at least, a single handcuff, with the other end that should been attached to a police officer, hanging open and loose. They'd somehow 'done a runner' and were trying to get the 'cuffs off. A few minutes later someone else appeared with a miniature hacksaw and we left them, slack-jawed, frantically sawing away. Tales like this were the stuff of terrace legend. But by Japan 2002 the landscape had changed.

Events like the above showed you could never be too careful, even when just walking the streets. The climax of England's qualifying group for Japan had an unexpected twist both on and off the field. David Beckham's dramatic free-kick in stoppage time against Greece at Old Trafford was a magic moment replayed over and over again, though I have to admit I was already looking forward to the prospect of a play-off when the golden boy bent it like Beckham so often did, into the top corner. Bizarrely my press box seat was about two away from Chris 'Lady In Red' de Burgh who was leaping around like a madman when it went in. Not that that made any difference to my loathing of the said song.

The two play-off matches for the previous Euros against Scotland at Hampden and Wembley had been fantastic occasions, especially in Glasgow, and my reasoning was that England would still make it through a two-legged play-off and the away leg would be a fantastic occasion. Not needed, as it turned out. But Beckham's heroics weren't the only thing that made the 'papers over those few days. The night before I'd been walking with some of the Sky team back to our hotel near Old Trafford from Harry Ramsden's fish'n'chip restaurant about a mile away. Not the most salubrious part of Salford, in fact, Ordsall was to be avoided at the best of times as we later found out. But I was none the wiser and made the mistake of responding to a gang of youths, no older than 14 or 15 who abused us from across the road.

Cameraman Dave Caine and I were a hundred yards or so ahead of the others and came under attack. I'd wandered into the road to see what the little gang were up to when a cavalry load of them came charging round the corner from a hidden housing estate. Dave took something over the head and one rat-like urchin launched a bottle of beer at me from point blank range. It grazed my chin and smashed on a tree behind me. The rest of our group had stopped in their tracks some way behind when they saw the number of assailants and we were on our own. So we made good our escape sharpish and called the local constabulary who were there in minutes. 'What are you doing in Ordsall?' one of the officers asked incredulously. 'It's a no-go area at night and THAT housing estate...' gesturing to the one we'd just passed '...is full of kids whose dads are lifers - they run wild!' He wasn't wrong. Charlie Sale's Daily Mail sport gossip column ran a story on our lucky escape, which might also have applied to England's travails on the field.

*

We arrived at Narita airport in Tokyo, loaded down with gear. Because we were shooting and editing our own material from the road, we had vast amounts of kit, thirteen heavy flight cases. SO heavy, it was a miracle the plane could even take off when we left Heathrow. I can still remember the look on the face of the Virgin check-in girl when we pitched up expecting to avoid the excess baggage charges. My jaw hit the floor when she demanded an extra £4,000 to carry it all. A worried call to the office followed, then relief at the thumbs up and even a nice bonus; the extra charge meant an upgrade to 'Upper Class' and an unexpected half hour in the plane's bar in the company of Led Zeppelin guitarist Jimmy Page who was on the way to Tokyo to pick up an MTV Legends award. Truly a random encounter; we even got on to football and how Robert Plant loved Wolves, which got me going on some of their peers who were fellow Blues, Jeff Lynne and Roy Wood. Very oddly, I met Jimmy again years later, on the train home from London after the aforementioned Gallipoli centenary. I nudged my son Henry to alert him to the esteemed figure sitting opposite us, only to get a vaguely irritated 'who?' shrug, when the mobile phone screen held far more of interest. Then we got talking, he'd remembered the Tokyo trip, and Jimmy, who had a son the same age just discovering the joys of vinyl, was now an obsessive attender of record fairs. He'd just been digging through crates of vinyl trying to find a rare pressing of Zep's 'Whole Lotta Love' complete with a rogue misspelling of 'Lottaaa' and two extra 'a's!

Like at all World Cups, the build up to the opening game always seemed to be the biggest, probably because it was the longest and England against Sweden in Saitama, just north of Tokyo was no different. While England had acclimatised on the South Korean island of Jeju before moving to Awaji Island near the Japanese city of Kobe, ravaged by an earthquake seven years earlier, Sweden were way down south in subtropical Miyazaki with its palm trees, beaches and giant replica Moai statues, copied from Easter Island thousands of miles away across the South Pacific. It was a great place for a World Cup piece to camera with its huge stone figures standing shoulder to shoulder against a backdrop of the ocean like a football team lining up for the anthems. I was there like a shot, even if wearing shorts again got me a minor ticking off. 'When in Rome' was always my take on these things. Sky Sports News generally had a desire for all reporters to wear a jacket, shirt and tie which to my mind made them stand out like a sore thumb in a football crowd and personally, made me feel awkward. And when there was heat like we had in Japan, it didn't look right. Sky News, on the other hand were much more relaxed and with that came more natural presentation.

Miyazaki had that South Pacific feel and its streets were filled with Philippinos who'd headed north across the water in search of prosperity. But neither they, nor the local Japanese population paid much attention to their European visitors. Sweden as always, were low key and laid back and played a warm up match in a municipal park against a local team which they won at a canter. They had a young sub who came on and caught my eye. 'Watch out for this kid,' one of the Swedish reporters told me and I could see why. I was standing behind one of the goals when he launched himself horizontally and flashed a scissor-kick that crashed against the foot of the post right in front of me. I noted the name. Zlatan Ibrahimovic. I almost door-stepped him as he left the field at the end, but even back then he had that, 'I am Zlatan!' untouchable look, and I thought better of it.

You would always hope for a great story to break in the build up to a big match and Sweden obliged with a 'belter', a self-inflicted own goal that would sit very nicely, thank you in the England camp ahead of the game. At first we knew nothing about it, an incident that had occurred during the closed part of a Sweden training session two or three days before the match. Later that afternoon I conducted some interviews with the players back at their hotel, and there was something about two of them that just seemed a little odd. First up was Olof Mellberg, the Aston Villa defender who a few months later would be involved in the calamitous, and frankly (from a Blue point of view) hilarious own goal with goalkeeper Peter Enckelman in the eventful Second City derby at St Andrew's.

The Swedes were very free and easy when it came to asking for interviews and Mellberg came wandering over when I requested a chat in the hotel lobby. But there was something not quite right about it. He stared at me in a searching way that I couldn't put my finger on, as if fishing for something that he thought I might know. He seemed quiet and a little agitated. Arsenal's Freddie Ljungberg was a smiley, jovial character normally, and he too seemed a little distant, giving answers by numbers that you might expect from many players but not from him. I carried on with my report and had already sent it back to Sky when I took a phone call from London that made everything fall into place. Either an agency or in-house camera had been filming at the training session earlier that day and had captured an extraordinary episode involving the two players I'd just interviewed. The pictures had leaked. Mellberg, a tough, uncompromising defender had caught Ljungberg with a dangerous late tackle, and the Arsenal man responded by squaring up to his teammate. A full on scuffle broke out and numerous Swedish players had to step in to separate the pair.

Now I knew why Mellberg had looked at me in that curious manner, worried that I knew about it and would ask him some difficult questions. If the Swedes were trying to keep the incident under wraps they hadn't done a very good job. I never did find out how the pictures had got out, but they emerged an awful lot quicker than the infamous Hartson - Berkovic incident at West Ham.

The Mellberg episode, or at least the vibe he gave off that day when I interviewed him reminded me of another encounter that made much bigger headlines a few years earlier. I was at Molineux in November '96 doing a piece on the Wolves - Blues league match. A familiar face stopped me on the touchline pre game. It was Hans Segers, the goalkeeper who'd been implicated in the match fixing scandal along with Bruce Grobbelaar in 1994. The case had not yet got to court. I'd never met Segers before, but he greeted me like a long lost friend. Maybe it was because, by then, my face was regularly appearing on screen. But I remember it because like the Mellberg incident there was something a little unnatural about his demeanour, though in this case it was more that I felt he was oddly animated, as if over compensating for something, in contrast to Mellberg's searching stare. I wondered why, then discovered it was only a month or two before the start of the match fixing trial from which Segers and Grobbelaar were eventually cleared of any wrongdoing.

But at the time of our meeting, my mind was drawn back to the day in May '94, before the scandal had even come to light in the tabloid media (via The Sun's sting) when Segers was playing in goal for Wimbledon on the last day of the Premiership season at Everton. I was working that day, and watching a live feed of the match at the Sky studios. Anyone who was alongside me that day will remember how I dashed into the newsroom to proclaim that Everton's winning goal looked very questionable. It was the goal that saved Everton from relegation as they fought back from 2-0 down to win 3-2 in dramatic fashion. Segers, as far I could see, looked as though he had not tried to save it and I was yelling it out to anyone who would listen. It just looked odd.

To this day I still don't know how Graham Stuart's feeble shot got past him. So you can imagine what crossed my mind when his name appeared in screaming headlines about players fixing matches. But he emerged with his reputation intact and my initial instincts were wide of the mark. Allegations that surfaced during the court case that money Segers paid into a Swiss bank account soon after the Everton match had come from a Far East match fixing syndicate were never proved. That's how history will remember it. But from a personal point of view, it will always trigger memories of that goal at Goodison and our random meeting on the touchline at Wolves. Oh, and by the way, Blues won that day 2-1!

As it turned out, Sweden shrugged off the Mellberg - Ljungberg in-house squabble and very comfortably held England to a 1-1 draw. The only surprise was the size of the Scandinavian support, with great swathes of yellow across the crowd while England seemed to be in the minority, though bolstered by good numbers of David Beckham's Japanese fan club, many wearing replica Beckham shirts. It was a typically underwhelming England start though my day was lightened when we had the opportunity to interview 'James Bond', Roger Moore who was doing the PR rounds before the game for the charity UNICEF.

Beckham, the captain, serial wearer of the '7' shirt was now so famous he could put any '007' in the shade, and the smart money(penny) suggested he'd done well just to be there at all. A broken bone in his foot, the metatarsal, a few weeks before, had the nation on tenterhooks right up until the big kick off. It was a great running story for the media with its 'will-he-won't-he-make-it-to-Japan' soap opera narrative, complete with fast-healing oxygen tents, and even the return of psychic Uri Geller (yes, him again) urging the nation to touch their television sets in unison to help David heal quicker. I think he owed everyone a better outcome this time after the pre-match mind bending at the previous World Cup in St Etienne that resulted only in Beckham being sent off against Argentina and England being knocked out!

So England - Argentina, the return was perfectly set up. It wouldn't have been an exaggeration to say England had unfinished business with their old adversaries after the France '98 fiasco and infamous 'Hand of God' goal in '86.

The venue was fascinating. Sapporo, right up in Japan's far north on the partially remote island of Hokkaido, the best part of a thousand miles away from where I'd started at Miyazaki in the sultry south. Argentina based themselves closer to Tokyo in Fukushima, which would be remembered nine years later for the earthquake and tsunami tragedy that killed thousands and triggered an accident at the nuclear power plant that hugged the Pacific coastline. Culturally, and physically it was a world away from England.

While we were there, Western type rooms were off the agenda, by choice. This was traditional Japan where chairs had no legs, sleeping was on mat covered floors, and partition walls were those thin, familiar chequered screens made of a wooden lattice covered in white translucent paper. Beautifully atmospheric. You could almost picture Sean Connery in a fluffy white bathrobe in 'You Only Live Twice'. Especially when you took your daily bath in the outside 'onsen' or hot thermal pools that bubbled straight out of the ground in the garden. Wembley High Road it wasn't. Nor was it Buenos Aires or La Bombonera, legendary home of Boca Juniors, but Argentina's football mad media were all over the area, and not for the first time arrogantly expecting to give England another bloody nose on the field.

Stuart, my cameraman was an old school Cockney, except that he was young, great fun, and straight out of traditional East End stereotypes. All foreign food should be treated with suspicion and everything had to be 'Pie, Mash, and Liquor' which was the green sauce that Pie and Mash shops would serve as a kind of gravy back home. So there wasn't much chance of Stu engaging in the local fare when our friendly hotel owner gave us a lift to a small bar out in the sticks in the Fukushima countryside.

A small group of locals squatted on the floor drinking Japanese 'saké' chatting excitedly, while on the opposite side of the room two men sat on stools at the bar gnawing on fish heads. Big ones, with eyes and teeth that made them look like museum exhibits. Pie and Mash seemed a distant dream. But if this was traditional Japan, it was sitting cheek by jowl right next to its modern hi-tech face; a state of the art sound system and karaoke machine standing shinily at the end of the bar. It was a free night for us, and that spelled trouble. Or at least it did for me. I had never engaged in karaoke before and vowed I never would, but the presence of no-one who would ever recognise me again and several bottles of booze had me reaching for the microphone. The underdog about to have his day.

I don't know what I expected to find in the list of songs, but I'd have bet 10,000 Yen there wouldn't have been any Radiohead, and trebled that for 'Paranoid Android'. Don't be ridiculous. Even Thom Yorke struggled to nail that in art school England, so my imagination was in overdrive, turbo-charged Honda overdrive, at the prospect of one of the locals putting down their Weird Fishes (see what I did there?) and diving into the most impossible, idiosyncratic bit of 'OK Computer'. It couldn't be sung by anyone else at the best of times, so I would have paid to see a Japanese attempt. I certainly wouldn't be trying it, and settled on 'Like a Rolling Stone'. Dylan, I figured had the kind of voice that would never compromise anyone else's attempt to sound in tune, and I wailed away until the small hours when the bar's owner, at around two in the morning decided the only way to get rid of us was to drive us home. Which he did. A surreal night, made all the more ridiculous by one of the fish head eating men at the bar suddenly breaking out into English half way through the evening: 'How are you?'...he ventured. 'I used to live in Hounslow'!

Argentina's media conferences in Fukushima alerted to us to a practical joker within the travelling throng. He worked on some kind of spoof television show and kept showing up at training with his blue, half-Mohican hair, and deadpan expression that was part of the act. He'd casually strolled up to Argentine striker Gabriel Batistuta who was in mid sentence in front of the press and plonked a black cat on the table in front of him, before skipping away. Good luck, indeed, I thought if he tried to pull a stunt like that at the England camp in front of Ray Whitworth, England's security man, who had amusingly removed the intruder in Tirana the year before. Sure enough, when we got to Sapporo, our Argentine friend was hovering at the back of the room for a media conference with Sol Campbell.

The session had barely started, in fact, the England press officer had just about finished the introduction when the blue haired one boldly strode up the side of the room, took a sharp right turn in front of the front row of reporters, leaned across the top table and with an exaggerated flourish, opened a large black umbrella over Campbell's head. The guy had more 'bottle' than Borat, and it was a simple but clever stunt. Once he'd got his shot for the rogue camera at the back of the room, he couldn't have cared less that he was then bundled out of the room by Mr Whitworth. My only surprise was that the act of opening an umbrella indoors also translated as a bringer of bad luck in South American superstition, not just ours. Or maybe he was just making fun of British quirks. Either way, I think Sol thought there was a leak in the roof.

I don't know what it was with gatecrashers at England media conferences, but they seemed to be attracted like bees around a honey pot. It wasn't very much later, when England were in Baku to face Azerbaijan that we had another interloper, this time with Beckham in his sights. I can't recall the exact question, but it was something about Becks and

'Golden Balls' and it must have been 'near the knuckle' because Ray Whitworth soon had him in a headlock and forcibly removed him from the premises.

England's visit to Sapporo was a major event for the local Japanese authorities and they were on high alert for an invasion of 'hooligans' .In that part of the world they had no idea what to expect, primarily because they had no equivalent. But the images from Marseille and Charleroi in recent years had gone around the world and the reputation of England's fans went before them, even though banning orders had recently come into force. Nonetheless, the Japanese police looked part mystified, part terrified, probably because they didn't know what they were actually on the lookout for. Their English counterparts would have told them that trouble makers did not wear colours and dressed in smart clothes, so there seemed to be genuine confusion and a little trepidation about who they were looking for and what these people were capable of. By the nature of their society they generally didn't have to deal with antisocial behaviour so it was all new. But it was obvious they had been heavily briefed and were determined that there would be no repeat of the ugly scenes at the previous two tournaments.

Throughout the day of the game, I broadcast live scene-setting reports from the streets for both Sky News and Sky Sports News. Midway though the afternoon I spotted a familiar face, SSN news desk man Keith James who was out there as a fan supporting England, and proudly wearing the old red top that England had worn when they won the World Cup at Wembley in 1966. Shirt-sleeved Japanese police in formal caps were dotted around the streets, and as Keith strolled past in the afternoon sun, it was a time for practical joke. 'Hooligan!' I casually called out, gesturing in his direction, to which one of the adjacent officers was on it like a flash. 'Hoo-rigan??' he responded excitedly, while making a move towards one of Keith's arms. So THIS is what they look like! A disarming smile and shake of the head back in the officer's direction defused the situation. Only joking! But it really did capture their sense of uncertainty.

The mood was relaxed by the time afternoon gave way to early evening and I watched one of the big local television stations presenting their news programme from out in one of the small squares. You could sense it was a special occasion as the two anchors, one man, one woman prepared to present the show, surrounded by multiple cameras, scurrying floor managers and a large crowd. Then, just as the intro music had run at the top of the programme and the woman was saying hello to the viewers, out of the blue - and bold as brass - a small man wandered straight out of the crowd and proceeded to stand right in front of the anchor, followed by an exaggerated bow. 'Hello' he said, 'I'm from England and I support Queens Park Rangers!' It was quite the ice breaker. The two presenters giggled with excitement and shook his hand enthusiastically. He'd clearly had one or two to drink but was in his element and had the gathering in the palm of his hand. He bowed again, and again, and they bowed back, to which he carried on bending his body forward with ever more exaggeration. Who would blink first?! Pure pantomime. I doubt the Sapporo news had been upstaged quite like it ever before. And as the show went on Mr QPR was off down the street like the pied piper, pursued by a posse of beaming Japanese onlookers trying to take his picture.

The Sapporo Dome was a thing of wonder, a space age looking indoor area but with a grass pitch that slid in and out of the structure on a giant tray. England had most of the support, a combination of the Beckham fan club and a good number who'd made the journey over from home. The story had probably written itself already. A penalty to England (overlooked down the years in that it was given away by Mauricio Pochettino who went on to manage Spurs) and dispatched by Beckham, the man who'd been sent off against the very same opposition in France four years before. To make it all the sweeter, the man who'd got Becks the red card, Diego Simeone was also playing again as he had been in St Etienne. Redemption! And a rare victory for England at World Cup Finals over one of the world's leading nations.

Stuart and I roamed all over Japan, and it was an epic adventure. Driving in Tokyo was like trying to navigate a path through the jungle, where every tree was represented by a concrete tower, intertwined by overpasses that weaved between the buildings like vines. Put it this way, without satellite navigation we would never have got anywhere. Japan didn't lead the world for gadgets and technology for nothing and the 'sat nav' was a lifesaver, even though we never understood a word of it. After a while, certain phrases became familiar, the Japanese for 'turn left' or 'straight on' which gradually lodged in the consciousness. Just following the arrow was all the language we needed, though on more than one occasion we wished we could have programmed the system with a translation for 'Where the f*** are you taking us!' It was also remarkable to see the amount of drivers whose navigation system defaulted to live television at the flick of a switch and people were cruising around with their eyes on some B-movie instead of the road.

Nothing though, could beat the efficiency of the Japanese, and if there was ever a flaw in their system it was fixed fast. On one occasion we were running late for a domestic flight. So late, in fact that there would have been zero chance of being let on board for an equivalent flight at home. We had thirteen flight cases to check in, not to mention our own personal luggage, and when we pulled up the hire car in a panic outside Tokyo's domestic terminal for a flight out, we had less than twenty minutes until take off. Not a chance of being allowed on anywhere else with all that kit, but something incredible happened. I practically threw the car keys at the hire car desk, breathlessly ran up to check-in and before we could ring the office to say we'd missed the flight, a small army of porters had emptied the car of all the gear, loaded it onto the plane and we were up in the clouds. Extraordinary, and not a word of complaint.

Whether it was his East End only diet or not I don't know, but Stuart's stomach did not survive the whole trip and he headed home with some kind of food poisoning, or culinary psychological trauma before we'd reached the end of the group stage. I'm not sure he even got as far as Kyoto on the drive south, which was a shame, because the jarring sight of a McDonald's in one of Japan's most traditional and beautiful cities might just have saved the day. In contrast I quietly despaired at the sight of a cheesy (with fries) symbol of Westernism invading Japan's cultural heritage. Ornate gardens, the Philosophers' Walk, stunning temples, the Golden Pavilion and….the 'Golden Arches', letting the side down with strawberry shakes and quarter pounders to go. Mind you, for all its fascinating culture, the shadow of the USA and its consumerism had long loomed large right across the Land of the Rising Sun.

England played Nigeria in Osaka, comfortably the least eventful match of our tournament, marked only by a biblical electrical storm during one of our live news hits that made us all happy we were wearing rubber soled shoes. Osaka was seedy and small groups of England fans sat in dimly lit bars down backstreet alleys in a rundown part of the older town. The goalless draw that followed was enough for England to qualify from the group behind the Swedes on goals scored, while Argentina suffered the disgrace of going home early. That never went down well in one of the hotbeds of the world game but gave all of us who'd been present in St Etienne four years before a wry smile.

England's second round match was in Niigata way out on the west coast of the main island of Honshu. It felt like an outpost compared to the bigger cities and along with the sea breeze there was a refreshing intimacy about the place. Sven-Goran Eriksson's far from camera shy girlfriend Nancy Dell'Olio shopped for fresh fruit in one of the local markets while we filmed our colour and there was a lightness about the England camp that suggested that they would make short work of opponents Denmark. Even the stadium felt different, situated out of town and surrounded by a patchwork of rice growing paddy fields. There were no boisterous fans to worry about in the place we chose to do our live broadcasts near the stadium, but the competition from a chorus of resident frogs, half submerged in the paddy fields was formidable. A call and response that was a match for any football fan choir; once one started to croak, the whole lot went up in a comical cacophony. As for the match, there was barely a squeak out of Denmark, and England didn't need to get out of second gear to win 3-0. Next up Brazil!

Of all the travelling fans at World Cups down the years, England fans by my experience embraced the places and their culture as much as any nation. Back south, two hours west of Kobe on the Shinkansen (bullet train) was Hiroshima, whose name had long been seared into collective consciousness by the horror of the atomic bomb that ended World War Two. A spare day between match travel drew me and many others into making the journey there.

The Shinkensen pulled into Kobe station, as always, punctual to the second, at almost the exact moment Japan were being knocked out of the World Cup in their second round match by Turkey. Crowds of commuters and travellers had packed onto the platform intently watching television monitors hanging from the rafters. Businessmen in suits carrying briefcases who had probably never before been drawn into the kind of whipped up sporting nationalism that we recognise so well. It was strangely quiet as the final whistle signalled the end of the hosts' tournament, and in a sharp, orderly shuffle, the platform throng made their way onto the train.

Such was the magnitude of what happened in Hiroshima on August 6th 1945 that I almost expected a barren wasteland, left as it had been after the events of that fateful morning. It was anything but. Stepping out of the station on a sunny summer's day, locals bustled about their business, girls stood in shop doorways with their familiar friendly calls of 'Moshi! Moshi!' (Hello!) and buses and taxis competed for space on the road that led away from the centre and out to the Peace Park. It was hard to picture how it must have looked more than half a century previously when all of the wooden buildings were razed to the ground in a cataclysmic fire storm. But directly below the point where the nuclear bomb detonated in the air stood the A-Dome building, spared the force of the bulk of the blast by its position, and still standing today as it was in the aftermath. The dome on top was still there, now missing its glass but with its metal framework still largely intact, defying the apocalyptic destruction that descended from the sky on that fateful day.

The Hiroshima Peace Park and museum is not a place you could ever visit without being profoundly affected. More than 150,000 people died either in the blast or via the radioactive fallout that followed. A walk round the museum was accompanied by near silence; a shocked, respectful hush. I remember an England fan in a blue Leicester City top ashen-faced at the sight of some of the exhibits. A child's tricycle half-melted by the inferno, a person's thumb blasted off its hand and whose nail continued to grow and curl grotesquely under radiation, a school lunchbox with incinerated contents still in situ, and the outline of a vaporised body seared into part of a stone wall. Wherever you looked, a reminder of the day hell descended to earth.

Distance and time probably prevented any of the teams based in Japan from making the trip to Hiroshima, unlike some of the England players who asked to visit the Auschwitz and Birkenau concentration camps during the build up the World Cup qualifier against Poland in Katowice two years later. The Football Association missed an opportunity to project some positive PR by organising a group visit and it was left to individual players to ask Sven-Goran Eriksson if they could make their own private visits, which was granted, but without any accompanying media.

Only a few poorly taken still photographs were released where the identity of players could barely be made out.

To visit and film there with some of the fans was as sobering as it had been at Hiroshima, though sadly I witnessed one group of fans displaying a Far Right banner posing defiantly near the entrance to Birkenau where the single gauge train track brought many victims of the holocaust to a stop on their final journey. By chance, cameraman Greg Ray and I came across a large group of people gathered around an individual near the railway track deep inside the death camp. It was a Jewish party from the north of England listening to Leon Greenman, at that time the last British survivor of Auschwitz whose Dutch wife and child were murdered on the first day they arrived there in 1943. We rolled our tapes and listened to him talk for half an hour, while a crowd steadily built around us. Greenman died a few years later, well into his nineties, but his clear-eyed testimony was unforgettable and deeply moving. The Holocaust Museum he set up in London remains to this day.

*

England's quarter final with Brazil reignited memories of 1970 and the magic of the two then superpowers going head to head at the group stage in the suffocating heat of Guadalajara, Mexico. World champions against favourites, live on television in the days when World Cup matches and the FA Cup Final were the only games beamed direct into the nation's living rooms. Truly a special occasion and at the time, almost certainly the most exciting television event I'd ever witnessed, alongside the moon landings of the previous summer.

England's team was weaker than it had been four years earlier and Brazil were at the peak of their powers, led by one of the greatest players of all time, Pelé. It's easy to forget that England's full backs that day were the largely forgotten Tommy Wright, and Terry Cooper, who was pretty much torn apart by Jairzinho who went on to score in every round of the tournament. Cooper, brilliant for Leeds in their legendary side of the early seventies, but whose name now always transports me back to his time as manager at Birmingham City in the early 90's. Promotion from the third tier and a ray of hope, followed not long after by the sack.

A string of snapshots remain seared onto my memory from the Guadalajara classic; Brazil's winning goal, smashed in by Jairzinho after Pelé's pass had put the goal at his mercy, Gordon Banks' gravity defying save from what I still think was one of the best headers I've ever seen, from Pelé, and then what should have been England's equaliser, hopelessly missed when it looked easier to score by Jeff Astle. I found that hard to fathom. Here was the guy who'd contributed to breaking my heart two years before when West Brom beat Blues 2-0 in the FA Cup semi final at Villa Park, and now he couldn't even make amends just a fraction by scoring a 'sitter' for his country.

Then there were the players from that day I came to view differently; the distant heroes from childhood who I never dreamt I would later work alongside. Bobby Moore, who had one of his best ever matches for England that day with a tackle so perfectly timed on Jairzinho that it would go down in football folklore, and Alan Mullery who became a regular Sky News football pundit during the 90s and beyond. My only problem with 'Mullers' was his place in the Fulham team, alongside Bobby, that 'fluked' its way past Blues in the 1975 FA Cup semi final replay. The game when John Mitchell scored off his backside in the final minute of extra time of the replay at Maine Road, one of the biggest disappointments of my football supporting life. I can still remember Harry Carpenter coming on screen for Sportsnight with the stomach churning opening lines 'It will be an all Cockney Cup Final!' delivered like a dagger through my heart. It was no consolation that West Ham beat them 2-0 in the Final.

Another encounter with Brazil also meant an opportunity to experience their unique training sessions again. It was four years on from Vittel in France when Roberto Carlos had played ball so valiantly with me before their semi final with Holland and I cheekily had my sights set on a second sparring session with the legendary defender. Who knows? He might even be fluent in English since we last met, I thought, but either way I wanted to know how he would handle coming face to face with England's star man David Beckham.

The media day was made more memorable by the addition of excitable Japanese fans to the flamboyant Brazilians who followed them around, but there was just a little more control off the field, probably a reflection of their change in coach in the shape of the disciplinarian, Luiz Felipe Scolari who would come to haunt England not just here, but in the Euros with Portugal two years later. The ladders, mobile phones and pushing and shoving were still there, but this time we were all behind barriers, a mix of Japanese efficiency and Brazil's relaxed, off the cuff attitude. Ronaldo, now the greatest striker in the world, came wandering along the barriers. 'A message for England, Ronaldo?' I enquired, hopefully thrusting a microphone under his nose. 'Ermmm...non capisco' he shrugged flatly. And that was that. Worth a try. But by the end of the World Cup we all DID understand that he was without doubt the biggest star in world football, and looking back, nearly two decades on, probably one of the finest strikers of all time, an absolute force of nature.

Nobody else stopped for any English, but by nature the Brazilians didn't like these orderly media arrangements. So as soon as the formal bit was over the barriers were by-passed, everyone was off again and it was just like old times. Out came the sharp elbows and impromptu mobile exchanges. There's Cafu! I tried him with a rapier-like question only to be met by a mumble and diplomatic aversion of the eyes before someone barged me out of the way.

A couple of ricochets later I landed in front of a familiar face, pushing through the crowd towards the bus. 'Roberto! It's great to see you again!' The little man focussed and after a second or two of computing, grinned broadly with a look and a nod that said 'You're not getting me this time!' I was amazed he'd remembered, and he beamed with amusement before jumping up on to the team bus. As chance would have it, a little over a year later we met again at the Bernabeu in Madrid. I'd gone to Spain to interview Beckham for his first match since joining Real Madrid, when he scored inside the first couple of minutes, and was then back again for a Champions League game when Real played Marseille. Didier Drogba was in the Marseille side not long before his move to Chelsea, as was Mido who later endured a torrid time at Spurs. I was in the changing room area waiting for Becks to emerge when his now teammate Roberto Carlos came striding down the corridor and instantly caught my eye. The beaming face gave way to a hearty laugh that roughly translated would have read 'You! Again!' And he was off into the night, chuckling wildly.

Shizuoka was not far from Mount Fuji, which with a rush of blood I decided to climb as soon as the World Cup was over. A two hour bus trip from Tokyo, a night in a small hotel next to a lake close to the mountain, and an all day dash up and down one of the world's iconic peaks. It was a bit of a cheat as there's a road that winds its way round the slopes to what they call the fifth station. It's then not far short of a vertical mile to the top trudging through ash and pumice if you'd rather not follow the laborious zig-zagging trailhead. Either way, a good four or five hour slog for most, which I managed in about three, at the price of wrecking a pair of shoes and looking, from the waist down, like I'd dropped down a particularly sooty chimney.

I didn't expect to find a lonely noodle shack perched somewhere near the rim at nearly 13,000 feet and the view from the top would have been great, had sod's law not brought a bank of clouds to obscure the outlook. Conditions that resembled those from a couple of weeks earlier for the eve of England versus Brazil. The South Americans, we figured would want it as hot as possible in Shizuoka while England were praying for rain, and as luck would have it a typhoon blew in from the west just in time.

The day before, it lashed down. English stair rods, and the timing couldn't have been better. We found a live broadcast position with a view of Fuji over my shoulder, except that you couldn't see a thing. The great mountain was shrouded in angry grey clouds and I held a picture up to the camera of what it should look like, with a bit of imagination. Long may it continue, we prayed, at least until after the match was over. No such luck. We woke the following morning to bright blue skies and the sort of day that could only hinder a team of pasty-faced Northern Europeans. Not easy for someone like Paul Scholes, a sun-shy red head who thrived in the Manchester rain.

Players' Union chairman Gordon Taylor comfortably fitted into the 'get me in the shade' category and he looked especially red in the face while trying to dodge our camera as he puffed his way up the hill to the stadium. Even back then he came under fire for his role at the PFA and being seen with one of his colleagues - Brendon Batson - on what was possibly a summer social trip made him look a little uncomfortable. A far cry from the days thirty years earlier when we used to cheer him on as he barrelled down the left wing at Birmingham in the great side that included the 'Holy Trinity' of Trevor Francis, Bob Latchford and Bob Hatton. There were few arguments that Brazil were better than England on paper. The four 'R's Ronaldo, Rivaldo, Ronaldinho and Roberto Carlos were the envy of the world, and it would take a R-olls R-oyce performance from England to topple them. We were all on our feet when Michael Owen dashed through to score the first goal, and even when a half fit Beckham lost possession allowing Rivaldo to equalise before half time, it was still 'game on'.

I remember going underneath the stand for a cup of tea at half time and was barely back in my seat when Brazil were awarded the fateful free-kick, miles out, that would settle the game. Ronaldinho was positioned in a direct line between my seat and David Seaman's goal away to our right, so when he shaped to hit the free-kick across to the players waiting on the edge of the penalty area, I distinctly remember thinking 'He's miscued that!'. From my direct line of vision to the goal it looked like a badly sliced golf shot, so you can imagine the dismay when the ball sailed over Seaman's head and into the net. A piece of Ronaldinho genius was the verdict in some quarters, but I didn't agree. I've always been inclined to follow my instincts and as soon as he struck that ball, mine was that it was a miscue. I was right in line and think I even uttered a mocking 'pah!' the moment he hit it.

Like so many previously mentioned images frozen onto the memory bank that one remains too. Even Ronaldinho's later sending off didn't help, though the other image that's stayed with me from that day is Danny Mills having a sneaky glance up to check the referee was looking in his direction, then rolling around in agony before the Brazil star was shown the red card. But truth was, even with the extra man England just wilted in the heat. It felt like a huge opportunity lost, with only Turkey and Germany who they'd demolished nine months earlier on their own patch, standing in their way.

The semi final in Saitama came and went with a mixed sense of both inevitability that Brazil would prevail against Turkey and regret that England weren't there. As had been the case at France '98, an overwhelming sense of the rug being pulled prevailed. From the broadcast news side, it's always been a common thread, largely because major media outlets lose interest when the audience's emotional investment falls by the wayside. When England were still involved, interest was always enormous, and seeing the big screen gatherings and wild celebrations from the other side of the world brought that strange feeling of having missed out on domestic World Cup mania.

While I was in Tokyo, I caught pictures of the scenes in Trafalgar Square during the England Brazil match. For all the effort the diehard travelling fans made, there was something just as compelling about the mass gatherings and frenzy whipped up back home. Over in South Korea they had both, with the joint hosts getting as far as the semis before losing to Germany. England, you felt, would have got past them too, and Turkey would also have provided a great opportunity to reach a World Cup Final.

But enough of the 'ifs and buts', England had their chance and didn't take it. As the FA entourage departed Japan, that collective wind being sucked out of sails brought an opportunity to explore one of the world's most fascinating cities. As an avid music fan and gig-goer I'd hoped to catch up with Norman Cook, AKA Fatboy Slim and Brighton supporter who'd scheduled a tour around the England games. He played gigs in Tokyo and Osaka but such were the late stage times and our non-stop schedule, it never happened.

But post England's departure, the pressure was off and I wasn't going to pass up the opportunity to catch Elvis Costello who was playing a gig at Kokaido in the Shibuya district, half an hour away on the Tokyo Metro. I didn't have a ticket but there were a few left and I figured that arriving around seven would give me time to buy one and have a drink first. I'd seen Costello numerous times over the previous couple of decades and was curious to experience the uber fandom of Western rock and pop acts that's a peculiar phenomenon in Japan. But having battled through the early evening commuter crowds pouring out of one of Tokyo's busiest stations, there was something odd about the bunker-like windowless venue where the gig was being staged. No crowds, not a soul. I must have got the wrong night. So I went inside. Still no-one, except a woman sitting in a ticket kiosk window and a couple of security types hanging around the concourse. Then, from beyond some double doors came the muffled 'boom-boom' bass assault of someone playing music.

The support act? Clearly, except that it sounded uncannily like Elvis' 'Pump It Up'. I know they like their tribute acts here, I thought, but still, that's a bit odd, before the man himself. I pulled the double doors open, and there he was, bespectacled and sweaty, Costello in full flow with The Attractions looking like he'd been on stage for hours. One of the security men stopped me as I made to step inside. There wasn't even time for a 'Moshi! Moshi!' before it dawned on me that he was playing the encore, and it was barely seven o'clock! 'Gutted' doesn't come close.

Tokyo gigs, it turned out had a ridiculously early curfew and this one had started at teatime, though that didn't explain how Fatboy Slim had been able to play his late night shows. Probably because he was an official World Cup DJ. If it was any consolation I bumped into legendary Sex Pistols manager Malcolm McLaren back at the hotel, casually having tea and cakes with a female companion. 'Ever get the feeling you've been cheated?' was a famous quote from Pistols' frontman Johnny Rotten, and after charging halfway round Tokyo for a gig that had nearly finished before I'd even got there, yes I did!

*

The Americans probably got the feeling they'd been cheated too after the handball controversy in the quarter final against Germany which they lost 1-0. Scotland's Hugh Dallas was the referee when Torsten Frings used his arm on the goal-line to stop the USA from scoring, and now Dallas was fourth official for the World Cup Final assisting the fearsome Pierluigi Collina. 'A foul can only be given if it's deliberate hand to ball and not ball to hand' was the Scotsman's defence, which would have been no defence whatsoever by the time VAR began to ruin football years later. Not only would the penalty have been given, but the player would have been sent off too. I've never agreed with the modern interpretation of accidental ball to hand, and Dallas was following the long since lost spirit of the game, but I have to agree that if the arm directly prevents a goal being scored, accidental or not, that's a penalty, and the Germans got lucky. As we built up towards the Final I bumped into a relaxed Dallas one afternoon out shopping in Akihabara. No regrets! And he was buzzing even more than the gadgets on show in Tokyo's famous electronics district!

Dallas and English linesman Phil Sharp weren't the only Brits in action on the day of the Final at Yokohama, not officially a part of Tokyo but feeling very much like a part of the same concrete urban sprawl. Aside from hooliganism, England's other great sporting export was ticket touting. I've seen them all over the world at different events, even in Beijing where (mostly) gullible Americans were buying seats for the big Olympic track and field or swimming events. They're unmistakable, and whatever the country or language barrier, the cry is always the same. 'Anybody need tickets?! Buy or sell!' No idea where they get them, and why they always seem to be English, but then again, I always wondered the same outside music gigs all over London when sometimes they'd appear to have tickets for the whole venue. I got to know a few of them, after a 'You're the bloke off the telly' greeting and sometimes they got me in to shows I'd not have had a chance of making. The other uncanny thing was that they nearly all seemed to be from Liverpool, with all respect to 'Scousers' .Londoners too but that Scouse call, 'Tickkkkets!' with the distinctive throat-clearing, rolling 'k' seemed to be omnipresent. Street wise, for sure, as I'd seen during that Liverpool invasion of Munich back in '81. Now, Yokohama was filled with the cries from English touts and punters paying eye watering prices for the chance to watch the world's biggest single sports event.

I couldn't help wondering again why it was that Germany were in yet another World Cup Final when we had simply blown them away less than a year before? They just seemed to be no more than workmanlike, and had got there through traditional efficiency, and the knack, in direct contrast to England of rarely self-imploding when the pressure was on. It always helped to finish top of the group stage. Germany invariably did that, while England had a habit of scraping through and making the road harder at the knockout stage. The match itself was a disappointment. Brazil would always have edge with that array of stars and it felt like a redressing of the balance from Ronaldo's nightmare breakdown in Paris. He scored both of the goals, and no-one could begrudge the 'selecao' their historic fifth World Cup. Japan and South Korea too could walk away with great credit. I flew home with my head still in the clouds at the top of Fuji and a bag full of colourful origami paper cranes that dropped like confetti from the rafters of the Yokohama stadium.

(top): Underdog & Newshound, St Andrew's, Birmingham. 2 (bottom) - Brazil media scrum, France '98

3 (top left) - Gridlock, Paris, as French fans celebrate reaching World Cup Final - France '98 4 (to right) - Bedlam, Paris '98 - future Sky football boss Gary Hughes on satellite truck roof. 5 (bottom) On air difference of opinion with Millwall Chairman Theo Paphitis, May 2002.

6 (top left) - Japan 2002 with Stuart Vickery. 7 - (top right) - With Roger Moore, England v Sweden, Saitama, Japan 2002. 8 (bottom right) - World Cup Final 2002, Brazil 2 Germany 0, Yokohama, Japan. 9 (bottom left) - With children Henry and Genevieve, Baden Baden, Germany

10 (top left) - Broadcasting live, England training, Baden Baden, Germany 2006. 11 (top right) - Vuvuzelas! USA training, Pretoria, South Africa 2010. 12 (bottom left) - Oh shit. Mark Loebell and stuck Sky News van, Rustenburg, South Africa 2010. 13 (bottom right) - Salvador, Brazil

(top)- Underdogs meet Newshound, Rio favela 2014. 15 (bottom left) - Face to face with fear-me Colombians, Rio favela, Brazil 2014. 16 (bottom right) - Killing Field - site of drug gangland assassinations, Rio De Janeiro favela.

17 -(top left) Underdogs in the (Birmingham) City of God, Brazil 2014. 18 (top left) - Mysterious slow motion street girl, Ouro Preto, Brazil 2014. 19 (bottom) - World Cup protest, Copacabana, Rio 2014.

-(top) Brazilians throng streets of Salvador to watch 2014 World Cup quarter-final on television reens. 21 (bottom left) - Forro and Samba, Salvador, after Brazil's quarter final victory over Colom- a. 22 (bottom right) - Costa Rican tears as the 'Ticos' beat Greece to reach quarter finals, Recife, azil 2014.

23 (top left) - Rip off! Top price tickets and no seats! Brazil 1 Germany 7, Belo Horizonte 2014. 24 (top right) - Moscow 2018 - four years later, for Millwall read Russia? 25 (bottom left) - Culture clash! Russians take a break from the opera. Volgograd 2018. 26 (bottom right) - Keep Right On, Mr Lenin - Novosibirsk, Siberia, Russia 2018.

Chapter 8
Krautrocked
Germany 2006

My own story of the 2006 World Cup began on a dramatic summer's day in Zurich, Switzerland six years earlier. In a parallel universe, the tournament would have been staged in England, 40 years on from memories of Sir Alf, Bobby Moore and Geoff Hurst. I still have souvenirs of the marketing campaign, a pair of long broken cufflinks and two hand-sized replica London taxis bearing the logo 'England 2006' splurged in large letters down the side. But complacency was rife, looking back, and no-one likes the cocky kid who swans around with an arrogant sense of entitlement. Especially when it was alleged by the Germans that the FA had some years earlier promised that we would back their bid in return for their support for a future English bid.

The assertion that football was 'coming home' at last, as The Lightning Seeds had also promised at Euro '96 was presumptuous. The German fans' own tongue-in-cheek version of that song, 'fußball's coming home' always left us looking a bit daft, I thought, and also crushed the myth that they don't have a sense of humour. A good many people at home believed the narrative and the only shame was that Sir Bobby Charlton's standing in the game as a great statesman probably deserved better. But the truth was, many of FIFA's international delegates did not share England's vision, or much less, back the bid. In fact, the vote was only marginally better for the FA than the disastrous campaign to stage 2018 when a significantly stronger bid was left in a humiliating heap. Five votes in the first round was enough to see off Morocco but was no match for Europe's preferred German bid and the emotional pull of going to Africa for the first time. Up against the Germans and South Africa in round two, the FA pulled in a paltry two votes to 11 apiece from both of the others. But here's where it got messy - and I was right in the middle of it. One of those votes came from the Oceania delegate, New Zealand's Charlie Dempsey, an elderly Scotsman by birth who soon found himself at the centre of a corruption scandal that reverberated around the world.

Zurich didn't cover itself in glory from the moment I touched down on Swiss soil to find my suitcase had been lost. Great start, I thought, having to scurry around the shops paying a small fortune for replacement clothes. You need to take out a mortgage there just to buy a pair of pants. But if that was an inconvenience, there was no dressing up Dempsey's naked exposé of the canvassing process. As we waited for news of the final count, I got a tap on the shoulder from one of the correspondents out there - Mihir Bose (who went to become the BBC Sports Editor) telling me that he'd been tipped off by one of the South American delegates that someone had refused to vote in the final round and that Germany had won by that single vote. I relayed the exclusive on Sky News and half an hour later FIFA President Sepp Blatter confirmed it, theatrically opening the result envelope in that faux dramatic way when we already knew the outcome. But why would someone abstain? It didn't take long for Dempsey to make it known to me that it was him. The significance was that Dempsey had been instructed by his own Association (Oceania) to switch his vote to South Africa for the final round and had he done so the result would have been 12-12 leaving Blatter, who favoured South Africa, to make the casting vote and change the entire outcome. But Dempsey refused and we wanted to know why.

England's demise was quickly overshadowed, and as the hall was awash with gossip and rumour I caught Dempsey among the crowds of dignitaries and delegates looking for an answer. He was instantly candid. The build up to the vote had already been dogged by allegations of corruption, and Dempsey claimed he'd been put under intolerable pressure to vote in a certain way. He said he felt threatened and wanted no part of it. I remember him telling me 'I had notes pushed under my hotel door' which, on the face of it, just sounded like canvassing. But something had triggered his stance and with corruption at the top of the game already being widely condemned, it all sounded plausible. South Africa, however understandably felt hard done by as it was no secret that his key vote should have gone to them. Before the hour was out, I took a phone call from a Durban radio station where Sky News was widely viewed, relaying what the New Zealand delegate had told me.

Dempsey soon resigned from FIFA's executive committee and that was effectively it - until years later, long after Dempsey had died in 2008. The wider FIFA corruption scandal that went on to bring down President Sepp Blatter and delegates like Trinidad's Jack Warner and Brazil's Ricardo Teixeira had already been played out when a former head of the German football federation, using unexplained payments from a connected Swiss court case as evidence, alleged that Dempsey had been paid a quarter of a million dollars not to vote for South Africa on that dramatic day. You can imagine my reaction when I looked back on the events of that interview with a man who it appeared had blown FIFA's murky practices wide open. The German newspaper 'Bild' ran the story with additional claims in a book by British investigative journalist Andrew Jennings that Dempsey had been paid the bribe via a briefcase full of cash delivered to his Zurich hotel room later that day. Dempsey, of course was no longer around to defend himself and nothing was proven. But the stink around the whole affair lingered. At least South Africa, as we'll come to, got the next World Cup.

England's 'golden generation' will forever wonder if they could have gone all the way in Germany. On paper there probably wasn't a better team, but as usual self-destruction would bring everything crashing down. No-one could put their finger on it but it was telling, much later, to hear Steven Gerrard, Frank Lampard and Rio Ferdinand during an impromptu discussion on BT Sport, talking about club cliques and rivalries bringing an atmosphere of disharmony. Qualification was never in doubt, but the signs of fragility surfaced in Belfast, where no-one should ever underestimate Northern Ireland.

It was my first time there and with a brief to provide background colour I took the opportunity to drive and film around many of the city's famous, make that INfamous landmarks via a taxi driver. Never mind a tour guide, a local taxi driver will always understand the beating heart of a city better than anyone else, a thousand stories shared between back seat and front when guards are down, and then retold by the driver. The ultimate gossip chamber. My chauffeur had been around at the height of the troubles and took me to all the places I'd seen on the news when I was growing up; Sandy Row and the Lower Shankill with their paramilitary murals, the Peace Wall, the Falls Road. All places that became darkly familiar through their constant place in the news agenda.

The perception back in 2005 was that Northern Ireland's following was largely Protestant. Slowly changing, but still largely the preserve of the Loyalists and nothing I saw contradicted that. Union flags flying from buildings all around Windsor Park; I even saw one young lad on the day of the match walking through the Lower Shankill with an England shirt alongside his dad's Northern Ireland green.

Now, where to find some local characters who would tell me who was going to win? The 1st Shankill Northern Ireland Supporters' Club looked hostile from the outside and was probably not the sort of place you'd have bowled into rolling a television camera a few decades earlier. But that was all done with now, right? It'll be fine, I figured, but swallowed hard nonetheless as I pushed open the old doors and wandered inside with camera in tow. There's a wonderful scene in the black comedy 'An American Werewolf In London' where the two lost American students walk into 'The Slaughtered Lamb' on the Yorkshire Moors. The hum of conversation changes in an instant. Heads turn in unison and the pub falls silent. Pin drop silent. That's exactly how it was here, and my blood ran cold as scores of eyes all turned toward us with a suspicious glare. I was waiting for the bit from the same movie scene when the scary loo-king bloke at the dart board turns and breaks the silence, pointing an accusing finger: 'You! Made! Me! Miss!!' I probably squeaked 'Er, hi, we're from Sky....' as a peace offering, but either way I breathed a sigh of relief when someone beckoned us forward.

I wanted a character and got one. In fact, they all were and had probably seen it all before in a hushed 'if-I-told-you-I'd-have-to-kill-you' kind of way. If you were to describe the forthright Ulsterman stereotype you'd probably come up with the Reverend Ian Paisley, barking out answers and jabbing a finger as he did so. But believe me, Paisley had nothing on old Davy Colwell. A bespectacled, white-haired fog horn of a man whose forthright delivery could have blown away any evangelist. He'd had a few drinks too, which heightened the effect. In fact, there's only one way to do it justice and that's to have a look on YouTube, and hope there are subtitles. Just search 'Old man can predict the future! Northern Ireland vs England' and wear ear plugs. To cap it all, Nostradamus he WAS, too. '1-0!!...for Northern Ireland!!!' he bellowed, twice, at the top his voice while slapping me around the cheeks, and cackling wildly. Underdog 1 Newshound 0. And with tails between legs, it was England heading back home to the doghouse the following night.

The next morning I was up early relaying the night's events on Sky Sports News. I'd bought a local newspaper with the story splashed across both front and back pages. As I was waiting to go live, compromised by a lack of sleep that could so easily catch you out when the mouth operates a fraction of a second ahead of the brain, instead of the other way round, a gaggle of young lads, probably 11 or 12 years old came skipping by on their way to school, all full of the night's drama. I imagined them in 30 years time, telling their own kids about the night mighty England with all their stars were turned over by 'our wee country' at Windsor Park. It would have made a great interview, but the boys were nearly late for school and couldn't stop so I gave them the newspaper and told them to hang on to it, like the cuttings I'd kept of Trevor Francis from his 'Superboy' days as a 16 year old at Birmingham. I'd known Trevor for years and a few days before Blues' famous Carling Cup Final victory over Arsenal in 2011, I passed the cuttings on to him so that he might show his own kids. I'd kept them pressed in a small black memories box for 40 years and was reluctant to let them go, but when the man himself asked if he could keep them while we sat together in the Wembley changing rooms how could I say no? It was all worth it when the underdogs went on to pull off a sensational victory in the Final, every bit as unexpected as Northern Ireland upsetting the odds against England.

*

That was a rare defeat for England under Eriksson, and his record in qualifying matches was good. In fact only Sir Alf Ramsey had a better overall record, but it was ever thus with England. Blow away all of the lesser opposition in qualifying campaigns and then blow it when the big boys came around in the actual tournaments. Time and time again. I liked Sven as a person too, he was an anglophile and Sky News watcher from wherever he was overseas, and always personable when we met around media conferences. However, as a coach and leader, something was missing; organised, yes, but a great man manager, no, especially when the situation demanded it. That Brazil defeat in Shizuoka could so easily have been a famous victory with a bit more dynamic leadership from the dugout.

It was telling that the man who would later lead England to a World Cup semi final, Gareth Southgate, himself no great dynamic leader, came up with his classic quote about Sven during the penalty shootout defeat in Germany that we'll get to in this chapter. 'We needed Churchill, but we got Iain Duncan-Smith', which might equally have been 'Uncle Arthur' aka Sergeant 'Wilson' limply trying to rouse the troops instead of Captain Mainwaring in 'Dad's Army'. Brutal put down, though probably a touch unfair, because the whole England roadshow came with excess baggage at the best of times; expectation, entitlement, whatever you want to call it.

There was an inevitability when something always seemed to go wrong. I remember an exchange with the esteemed British based Italian journalist Giancarlo Galavotti in his hushed Godfather like tones that captured it well. It was in South Africa at the 2010 World Cup when England captain Rio Ferdinand had been injured in training before a ball had even been kicked in anger. 'With England...' he declared, slowly shaking his head, 'there's always a....DIS-ASTER', lingering on that last word with a withering disdain that summed it up perfectly.

If it wasn't on the field, it was off it. Sven's love life was all over the tabloids and every trip seemed to have its dramas. One qualifying match in Slovakia in between his two World Cups (actually a Euro qualifier) was a rolling soap opera that had everything. Bratislava, in the years after Slovakia had 'Czeched' out from its neighbouring big brother in '93, had a reputation for being one of Europe's cheapest cities, and with that came an invasion of England fans. It was only a few months after the Japan World Cup when increased police powers had appeared to herald the dawn of a new type of travelling England fan. Scenes like Marseille and Charleroi seemed to be in the past, but by late 2002 banning orders were starting to expire and Slovakia, where England had never played before was accessible, cheap and attractive. Part of the joy of football travel was the getting there, and fans trying to save money would concoct all kinds of routes by air and road before arriving at the destination.

Birmingham's Carling Cup success fulfilled a lifetime ambition to see my own club in Europe and the first game, against Maribor in Slovenia was a good example. Some fans flew into Austria, some into Italy, and some direct to the Slovenian capital Ljubljana, while I went via Zagreb in Croatia and drove up to Maribor via a stop at the lovely Lake Bled about an hour's drive from Maribor. It was a similar scenario for Bratislava. No direct flights here, and many England fans flew to Vienna, Prague and Budapest before hitting the road. Around 4,000 England fans had tickets, but another 1,500 or more travelled with the intention of buying one on the streets.

We flew into Vienna, only an hour or so's drive from Bratislava and the first signs that something was brewing came at the Austria-Slovakia border. I could sense that we were about to be searched as our hire car pulled up to the border barriers. I pressed the record button on our news camera, which was lying flat on my lap in the front passenger seat, pointing at the driver's side window. One of the guards instructed us to wind down the window, ducking his head down to our level, neck cocked at 90 degrees and peering straight down the camera lens. It felt like the scene on the train from 'The Great Escape' (the theme tune for which had already become a persistent irritation, instigated by the ever present England and Sheffield Wednesday brass band), where Richard Attenborough and David McCallum have to present their papers to the Gestapo and let their guard drop at the vital moment.

There were only two of us in the vehicle but he instantly wanted our passports, and set about checking our names against a long list on an old fashioned clipboard. He made a call, then ducked down again to return the passports before waving us through. The names on his sheets were clearly those on the England banned list but it came as a surprise to me that anyone on it would have got this far anyway. But some still tried and it was only when police forces insisted on passports being handed in to local stations in the UK around tournaments or individual overseas matches that the system couldn't be circumnavigated. By the eve of the match in Bratislava, 16 England fans had been stopped at airports but it looked likely that other 'risk individuals' currently not on banned lists were heading for Slovakia.

There was something 'agricultural' about the stadium in Bratislava and the security around it. Wembley it wasn't. We made our way to a media conference with the Slovakian coach and I could barely believe my eyes to see a battered old car merrily driving around the pitch, an already muddy pitch at that, quickly being turned into a ploughed field, barely even fit for a harvest of potatoes. I knew only too well how the groundsmen at English stadiums would blow a gasket if anyone so much as put a size nine shoe onto one of their precious playing surfaces. So this was the most bizarre sight, and by the end of the following night when the match was over, I have never seen a worse pitch. Literally, squelching mud above the ankles, leaving great furrows where it looked as if tractors had been carving up and down.

There was little hint of the chaos to come when I dropped into an old bar opposite the England team hotel. Someone called out my name. It was two of the British police I'd come to know on the football beat. Little more than a month earlier, the same pair had filmed an extraordinary disturbance on the streets of Birmingham ahead of the first Second City derby in the Premier League. It came to be known as 'The Battle of Rocky Lane' and led to dozens of dawn raids and jail sentences. Their very presence alerted us to the possibility of disturbances that evening, though it was gone midnight on the eve of the match when the alert was raised. I was sitting quietly in a bar in Bratislava's old town along with two media colleagues when my phone rang suddenly. It was the Sky Sports News producer Sue McCann in a panic. 'Skuds! Skuds!' she blurted breathlessly with a strong Scouse twang, 'Two England fans have been SHOT! Come quick!'. To which I was out of the door sharpish and racing back to the England team hotel where a small crowd was gathered at the entrance.

The FA Chief Executive Adam Crozier was there looking more than a little anxious. We recorded a hurried interview without knowing much of the circumstances before Crozier was rushed off to the local hospital where the fans were being treated. I found some supporters who had been near the incident: 'We heard the shots and it sounded like a small hand gun' one of the eyewitnesses told me. 'We went downstairs and looked out of the window and all the roads had been sealed off. I think there were four or five shots.'

Crozier returned and told us about the victims' condition, serious but thankfully not life threatening. The two men, he said had been innocent victims, in the wrong place at the wrong time after a bar was cleared of rowdy fans by the owner, and security called in. One of the men had been shot in the leg, but the other had been struck in the neck and by chance the bullet missed his vital arteries. He'd staggered back from where the incident happened and collapsed in a pool of blood on the steps of the England hotel. Confusion followed amid reports that the shots had been fired by two men on a motorcycle, apparently acting as security for the bar owner. It later emerged that the bullets had been fired into the ground and ricocheted upwards before striking the victims. Either way, it was an escalation of anything we'd seen before at football and by the time I'd pulled together a report for Sky News, it was almost getting light.

But the day was anything but over. Biblical torrents of rain put the match in doubt, and I was surprised it went ahead. Conditions were atrocious on a pitch fit only for mud wrestling. England struggled their way through the quagmire to win 2-1 but no-one remembered the match for the football. England fans clashed with riot police at one end of the ground when they went a goal down. Seats were thrown and individuals could be seen with blood streaming down their faces after baton charges by the law.

To compound another eventful night, England's black players were subjected to some blatant racism, particularly Emile Heskey. On hearing what was clearly offensive chanting by large sections of the local crowd I'd taken up a place in one of the home stands to investigate and was shocked to see, close up, one middle aged man, accompanied by what appeared to be his two young sons, no older than nine or ten, openly taunting Heskey with monkey noises. No disguise about it, on his feet, arms curled up under his armpits, and bobbing up and down like a cartoon ape. Like this was some kind of regular 'sport'. No-one batted an eyelid. I would witness it again, and just as badly, when Shaun Wright-Phillips was the victim in Madrid for an England friendly against Spain. Yet the powers that be did little to punish the culprits.

Events like Bratislava reminded everyone that a World Cup in Germany, close and accessible, was not the same as Japan. The risk of flashpoints was much greater, even with large numbers of trouble makers prevented from travelling. Maybe it was the Marseille and Charleroi factors, where the media had been front and centre in covering every movement of large numbers of travelling fans, but Sky, for one were taking no chances. The advent of corporate health and safety meant no-one could go anywhere without a proper risk assessment, and anyone with the potential to be near the line of fire had to be prepared.

It seemed a little over the top to me, but every person who was on that trip to Germany had to go through intensive safety training, and if that sounds over dramatic, you're right, because the course we attended had to be seen to be believed. Gravesend in Kent was the venue for the Metropolitan Police Specialist Training Centre, where they learned how to handle themselves in riot situations. We would have to go through exactly what they did to earn our passport to Germany. This was not a box ticking exercise. It was full on riot training and the police, who used the facility all the time, appeared to take great pleasure in giving the bane of their lives on plenty of occasions, Her Majesty's Media, a good, old fashioned hard time! Far from a classroom, it was a full on film set, complete with police 'actors' whose take on playing the role of rioters was Oscar worthy. These guys meant business and before the first morning was out, I wondered what the hell I was doing there!

It felt more like an extreme reality television show than a training course, something like the show where SAS veterans knocked minor celebrities into shape, except the people doing the training were psychopaths out to have some fun at our expense. The Gravesend venue was built to represent an urban street scene, with actual buildings and a grid of streets. I've never been on the set of EastEnders or Coronation Street, but I'd bet the Gravesend set dwarfed it. It was like a small town, designed with the kind of space that could accommodate scores of police horses charging around in a real life riot situation.

Imagine the poll tax riots, or the worst of the miners' strike. This is where the police learned their tactics. It was May, just before the World Cup started, and the south east of England was experiencing a heatwave. So the prospect of having to stand out on the 'street' wearing police armour in thirty degree heat was not enticing. I failed to convince myself that I would ever remotely be in this situation while covering a story (and I'd been in the thick of it in Marseille) but we were made to stand in a line cross a street while the police trainers played the rioters. Why, I thought, did we need to wear fire proof overalls and what I can only describe as a metal version of football shinpads that came up to just below the knee? Oh, and a fully protective helmet with visor which in the heatwave compromised the ability to breathe. It turned out we needed all of it. The lot.

Three or four 'rioters' appeared at the top of our 'street' and advanced with menace. Before we knew it, they were hurling bricks in our direction. But bricks were only the hors d'oeuvres before the cocktails. Molotov cocktails. Real glass bottles, real petrol; two of them shattered and exploded right in front of me, filling my impaired vision with a huge orange flash accompanied by a surge of heat. If you've ever lit a bonfire using a few splashes of petrol, you'll recognise that air-sucking 'whoosh' that follows when the fuel ignites. This was a bit of that, competing with the reverberating sound of breaking glass. We then broke up into teams, carrying our recording equipment, with the aim of getting close to the 'rioters' though the notion of them stopping and agreeing to an interview mid missile launch made the whole thing absurd. 'Excuse me, can I have a quick word?...KABOOM! It reminded me of my cameraman Andy on the infamous trip to Warsaw opting for the 'matey' approach to a group of England fans and being sent packing with the promise of his camera being shoved where the sun doesn't shine. At least we had some fun when the police promised to capture and kidnap any individuals who were caught on their own. One or two did, and we had to pay a ransom to get them back.

The truth though was that the hooligans' ship had now sailed, or at least the law now ruled the waves. It had been a similar story three years earlier when I covered England's potentially explosive match against Turkey in Istanbul, coming in the wake of the tragedy where two Leeds Utd fans had been stabbed to death before a European club match in the same city. We went through a bespoke Sky health and safety drill, right down to security specialists identifying what a person looks like when they are 'blading' or, in other words, shaping their body to throw a punch in your direction. Just so that you could recognise it, and duck in time, which was always useful to know. We were even issued with hard hats disguised as hip hop style baseball caps to blend in; full on Public Enemy, with a reinforced shell. As it turned out, 'Harder Than You Think' ,and 'Don't Believe The Hype' both applied, because nothing happened and we didn't need the protection. England fans were banned from travelling completely and there was nothing remotely boisterous on the Bosphorus. Overkill. And so it was with Germany, too. Despite all the precautions, the tournament passed off peacefully and we could concentrate on the football.

Aside from England's routine penalty shootout exit, Germany 2006 will be remembered for the 'WAGs' phenomenon. The 'Groundhog Day' boredom that blights every major tournament between matches barely applied here, because the 'Wives And Girlfriends' kept us all amused, especially the tabloids. If France '98 had set the ball rolling with the players' other halves turning up in camp, 'spiced' up considerably by the obsession with Posh'n'Becks, in Germany you couldn't avoid any of them. England's base camp was lovely Baden-Baden in the Black Forest, and the icing on the gateau was the sight of the WAGs all trying to outdo each other in front of the paparazzi, or plain old 'snappers' as we called the football photography fraternity.

Victoria Beckham was still the queen of the crowd by a distance, and it almost felt like she had a PR team on call ready to 'alert the media' whenever she stepped out on to the streets of the quaint old spa town. But she had plenty of fake-tanned rivals all eager to show off their shopping prowess and party pieces. Sven-Goran Eriksson, in his defence was relaxed about the whole thing, and never understood the English media's desire for ownership of other people's private lives. He felt it was no-one else's business, and was right of course, but it never stopped him being hounded by the tabloids. There was something oddly chivalrous about the story where Sven was reported to have approached the partner of his soon to be other half Nancy Dell'Olio and asked if it was okay if they eloped. An honourable affair if you will, which might have matched his polite way in media conferences, along with, less appropriately, the way he addressed his players during the half time team talk when what they really needed was a good old fashioned 'bollocking' !Gareth Southgate's image of Iain Duncan Smith really does take some shifting.

So it was with Sven's blessing, and apparently at captain Beckham's request that the wives and girlfriends were camped, at their own expense at a plush hotel in the centre of Baden-Baden while the players were lodged in a lavish hideaway halfway up a nearby mountain. It didn't take long for the show to turn into a circus. The newspapers sent out extra reporters and paparazzi and the tabloids were full of stories like £57,000 being splashed out on clothes and designer sunglasses in the space of a single hour at Baden-Baden's posh boutiques. We sat at an outside bar one evening listening to a group of WAGs on the next table talking about their shopping exploits that day. The game became 'match the WAG with the player' ,though the name-dropping gave us a few clues. 'Steven already got me one of those' was the kind of chatter, followed by handbag comparisons, and eventually, a more hushed conversation when they realised that the group behind them looked like they might be 'meeja'. Not that most of them seemed remotely interested in anything other than being seen. If it wasn't the shops and restaurants it was the nightclubs, and while their other halves were tucked up in bed, the WAGs partied hard and spent small fortunes, the grotesque details of which routinely found their way into the tabloids.

If column inches were anything to go by, the football became a sideshow and England's group games did not linger in the memory. Like Japan four years earlier, England's travelling support felt different and the opening group game against Paraguay in Frankfurt passed off quietly, although the Germans showed how far ahead they were with a stadium that could quickly convert from seating to safe standing. Unfortunately FIFA would not sanction the use of railed standing, and at the time of writing this 15 years on, the Premier League in England are only just embracing the concept.

With a match to come against the rank outsiders Trinidad and Tobago, England's 1-0 victory meant they already had one foot in the knockout stages, and the routine 2-0 victory over the Caribbean outsiders in Nuremberg confirmed it. Again, the football felt like a sideshow, staged in a city with a dark history. The Nuremberg stadium lay in the shadow of Hitler's Nazi rally grounds, a vast space into which you could fit numerous football pitches, flanked on one side by a huge open terrace reminiscent of the old British football grounds from the early part of the twentieth century, before many had roofs installed. The 'Kop' terraces, named after the mountain battleground in South Africa that we'll come to in the next chapter.

One glance at the rally grounds in Nuremberg and it was impossible not to picture Hitler standing on the steps in front of huge numbers of troops and followers in the 1930s. Halfway along the great terrace stood a huge flat-roofed concrete bunker, with a big iron door leading to the closed off interior.

It felt chilling to be standing in the very place where Hitler had presided over the early stages of one of the darkest periods in human history. Familiar only through grainy, blurred, monochrome pictures, to suddenly see it all elevated into technicolour is a shock to the senses. Old black and white newsreel archives bring a distortion of reality. The ageing of film technology makes everything look further back in time than it actually is, a phenomenon that's really brought home when you see the places first hand. My visit to Auschwitz and Birkenau felt especially anachronistic. Everything looks so modern, the huts, the sentry towers, the railway line and gas chambers, betrayed by the fuzzy old archive that brought them to the world's attention. Despite being the best part of a century on, they look as modern as the rows of 1930s semis that line the streets of Britain. With that comes a dose of reality that makes what happened there all the more sobering.

England's final group game against the Swedes in Cologne was easy to get to. A tight English-style ground, and with that a good number of travelling fans. It was here that FIFA's policy of keeping non rights holding broadcasters at the bottom of the list for media tickets started to become difficult. I remember long queues of journalists from far flung places with no affiliation to the countries involved getting in ahead of us, and that made it hard to work. Interviews from the 'mixed zone' where the players would talk to the media after the game were off limits and that was fine. But it was just the getting access to matches that was obstructive in getting our job done. Fortunately, some of the FIFA media personnel saw it the same way too and one ally, who knew me from watching Sky in South Africa quietly slipped some tickets into an envelope and we were in among the fans. Two or three rows in front was a familiar figure from the world of pop who loved his football; Noel Gallagher, Manchester City fanatic, cheering on England, and who I would come to meet hungry for news from back home on the day of the World Cup Final in Johannesburg four years later.

Aside from a spectacular goal from Joe Cole in the 2-2 draw, the match against Sweden was notable only for another of those 'disasters' that seemed to follow England around like a bad smell. Michael Owen picking up a serious injury that ruled him out of the rest of the tournament. Still, not losing meant that England won the group for once and with that came a favourable draw against one of South America's lesser lights Ecuador. Not that there's any nation in South America that doesn't bleed football. I visited Ecuador some years later and the place was a joy. I only had to mention Birmingham City to have locals excitedly talking about the late Christian 'Chucho' Benitez who played briefly for Blues and then died so tragically at the age of only 27. There's a magic about all South American countries' love affair with the beautiful game, a magic that's visible wherever you go. From the Inca Trail in Peru where you pass village dirt pitches in the most impossibly steep mountain locations, to goalposts and makeshift playing spaces in the middle of the Ecuadorian jungle where the village kids play out their fantasises.

Manchester Utd's Antonio Valencia came from the Amazon jungle town of Tena where the kids played on instinct and dreamed of the big time.

The only thing that didn't make sense to European eyes was that future stars like him were ever spotted in the middle of nowhere. I even came across a village on the banks of one of the Amazon tributaries in Peru, a place of no roads, four hours from the nearest big town by boat where the centre of the village space was a communal football pitch with makeshift goalposts, crudely tied together. Yet in one of the corners of the field, adjacent to where the village kids shinned up and down palm trees in seconds to liberate coconuts, there was a kind of bandstand with an old satellite dish and television where the locals would gather round to watch Champions League matches.

As a collective, Ecuador never seriously threatened England, and the second round match in Germany's motor city Stuttgart was settled by a single free-kick from David Beckham. Nothing else about it sticks in the memory, except for having to do endless live news crosses in the build up, prompting BBC pundit Mark Lawrenson to call me 'the hardest working man in television' whenever I saw him. Thanks Mark! The victory brought England to familiar quarter final territory, where traditionally the road always seemed to end. It had under Sven in 2002 and it had under Sven in 2004. It was about to happen again under Sven in 2006. Nothing, if not consistent. But the truth was England were getting to where their world ranking said they should get.

If you look at England's place in the world rankings over the years it's rarely ever been higher than four (third is the record high for a couple of months in 2012) and more often than not in reasonably good times it hovers between five and eight which when translated into World Cup tournament numbers equates to a place in the quarter finals. So that's a par performance isn't it? In June 2006 England actually went into their quarter final with Cristiano Ronaldo's Portugal in tenth, so they had ever so slightly over-achieved when you apply rankings logic. But it was never thus when it came to expectation and downright entitlement when you were the nation that invented the game, and therein probably lies the problem. Everybody wanted to beat England, and the longer their failures went on, the more opponents knew that they would self-implode under pressure. Enter Wayne Rooney and the third curse of the metatarsals. Beckham in Japan, Rooney himself mid tournament in Portugal 2004 and now Rooney again in 2006, the result of which, like Beckham in 2002 meant he went into the tournament not fully recovered.

Another accident, another 'disaster' waiting to happen. It was a painful day in Gelsenkirchen, not least because England were due some payback against Portugal after the Euro shootout defeat in Lisbon two summers previously. But this was England, and we should have known what was coming. I was sitting one row behind and a few seats along from an old adversary, Millwall chairman Theo Paphitis. I caught his eye and he looked awkwardly at me over his shoulder. Roughly translated: 'Oh, him again!' prompting uncomfortable memories of that exchange live on Sky News the day after the riot at the New Den.

Portugal just didn't threaten at all, and we waited for the 'golden generation' to deliver their defining moment thus far. But then it happened. Again. Rooney retaliated after a skirmish for possession with Ricardo Carvalho. Only a frustrated backward push of his boot on the Portuguese defender but Carvalho's position, lying prone on the ground meant he caught it full on middle wicket. Not exactly a stamp, more a petulant flick, but so reminiscent of Beckham against Simeone at France '98, and very sadly for England it brought the same result. A red card that would ultimately cost them the chance of winning the game before the inevitabilities of the penalty shootout.

There was more to it, though, and the sight of Rooney's club teammate at Manchester Utd Cristiano Ronaldo caught winking on camera in a way that seemed to say 'mission accomplished' moments after the red card inflamed tempers across a nation. I was ambivalent about Rooney. Although he went on to break the England goal scoring record (with the help of penalties), there is no way he fulfilled his potential in an England shirt, and this was just another frustration. As an 18 year old in Portugal two years earlier, he looked like a future world beater. Sensational. But the day after England's penalty shootout demise, his family, or at least his father, didn't cover himself in glory at Lisbon airport. Rooney was already sidelined by his metatarsal injury, but there was in my opinion something unpleasant about the way Rooney Senior spoke during an exchange with me in front of a crowd of deflated England fans waiting to fly home. I was there to gauge reaction from the fans after England's exit and had to blink hard when I noticed what appeared to be Wayne Rooney standing in the check-in queue. I looked again. A dead ringer. Naturally I approached and on closer inspection it was a slightly younger version, Wayne's then 15 or 16 year old brother Graham. My camera wasn't rolling when I jokingly suggested to Rooney Junior that he was a chip off his older sibling's block. As I did so, someone charged into me from behind, shoving and shouting something along the lines of 'What are you doin'?!! You don't have permission to talk to him! I'm gonna report you!' about five times to which the crowd in front looked as embarrassed as me at the man throwing his not inconsiderable weight around. I gladly passed on my details so that Mr Rooney could make his complaint and took the opportunity to more than set the record straight when the Head of Sky Sports Vic Wakeling asked me what had happened. Rooney Junior had burst onto the international stage with far more elegance than his father showed on that day.

There was something about the penalty shootout in Gelsenkirchen that felt rock bottom for England. You got the impression that the players were paralysed by fear. They all missed, bar one, even Gerrard and Lampard, who never missed penalties. It's always been a lottery, of course, but England looked ill-prepared and surrendered meekly. Maybe it was the fault of 'Iain Duncan Smith'. Sven-Goran Eriksson was indeed anything but an inspiration when the players need some old fashioned rabble-rousing. My eyes were fixed on him while the players shuffled around nervously before their trial from 12 yards. But all Sven could manage was a bit of feeble looking hand-clapping to encourage the troops, and the rest was a disaster.

Three successive quarter final defeats in major tournaments. An emotional David Beckham returned for one final media conference in Baden-Baden where he read out a statement to a packed room announcing his resignation as captain. There was a brief pause when he stopped reading, and instinctively I felt the need to fill the void by clapping. The whole room then joined in a round of applause. It felt right because for all England's failures, here was one man who always gave it everything. The applause finished him off; he dragged himself to his feet and exited stage right in a pool of tears. It felt like a natural parting of the ways. FA Chief Executive at the time Brian Barwick had already decided Sven-Goran Eriksson's time at the helm was up. A newspaper 'sting' months earlier had caught the Swede apparently agreeing to an invitation from a 'Fake Sheikh' to dump England and take over instead at Aston Villa. Though Barwick might have acted differently if he knew the hapless Steve McClaren was incoming next!

Sven's wandering eye was one thing, but Cristiano's winking eye was another. Once we'd got over the rug being pulled from England, we made our way south again to Munich and the Allianz Arena for the semi final, Portugal against France. The mood was one of deflation and some people had had enough. Sky Sports duo 'Keys and Gray' not long before losing their jobs after what were considered sexist remarks off camera, unsuccessfully defended as 'banter', had been presenting a daily World Cup chat show from the road. But in Munich, with England already home, they decided they would not be making the effort to walk up a modest hill to present a show overlooking the stadium, and someone else had to fill the slot instead. Their stance did not go down well. My Villa supporting friend Gary Hughes who went on to big things at Sky Sports in the following years had been producing them and was left in a compromised position.

Several thousand England fans had tickets for the Munich semi final, expecting their team to be there. Some didn't take them up, but the majority seemed to be there. Not an obvious gathering from displays of flags and banners but as soon as Cristiano Ronaldo, newly christened the 'winker', touched the ball for the first time, their presence was obvious. 'BOOOOO!' came a crescendo of displeasure that was clear to hear all over the stadium. Ronaldo went on to have a stinker and France beat them by a single goal. Small consolation for the England contingent, though you got the feeling Ronaldo would still be feted at Manchester Utd.

When David Beckham became public enemy number one for opposition fans during Premier League games after his sending off at France '98, United fans took the contrary stance and defended their man. The vocal element sang anti-England songs, and it's probably fair to say the sight of 'Manchester Utd' emblazoned across the middle red band of the cross on the flag of St George remains rare. Then again, it's far more common to see England flags carrying the name of clubs outside of the elite few, or even towns without a team at all, probably because the international stage brings a sense of the 'big time' that's missing from the humdrum of the lower leagues and footballing backwaters.

The World Cup Final in Berlin's Olympic Stadium again raised the spectre of Germany's Nazi past. Like Nuremberg and its rally grounds, the Olympic Stadium will always be remembered for the black American athlete Jesse Owens winning four gold medals at the 1936 Games in front of a squirming Hitler. The stadium itself is an arresting sight with its large gap in the architectural circle at one end, almost as wide as the penalty area. But it was also a chink in its security armour and would come to play a part in enabling me to see at least a part of my third straight World Cup Final!

We were back in the realms of Sky being at the bottom of the list for match tickets and with demand for the final sky high, there seemed little prospect of getting in. The idea of having to watch the biggest single sporting event in the world from outside the arena in the media room was gut churning. Yet, once again, we were outsiders in FIFA's world and as kick off approached there was nothing even approaching a sniff of a media ticket. One particular official had been around at several of England's matches and appeared to make it his mission to keep non-rights holders out. I think he was getting fed up with me. How could it be that Sky, which put so much money into football, I reasoned, were considered persona non grata at World Cups? The official was only doing his job, but I tried to reason that we could not do ours if we were not allowed to watch the match. But as kick-off ticked closer the answer was the same. 'Sorry, you'll have to watch from the (nearly empty) media room'. We were welcome to the cold comfort of some lukewarm coffee from the urn on the table in the corner. Great.

While the world's media had gathered inside the stadium I had to go outside to our street position to do a short live broadcast just before kick-off. It was a good ten minute walk back to the media centre and while I was en route back, the game had already started. As I made my way down a near deserted street parallel to the stadium, cursing that I wasn't inside, there was a distinct commotion from within. Something's happened! It wasn't a goal, too quiet for that. The crowd noise was one I couldn't identify, lost in translation amid a foreign exhalation of both joy and indignation, depending on loyalties. Either way, it sounded odd and I couldn't work it out. Thirty seconds later there was a more familiar roar, with extra volume, the sound of a goal being celebrated, though nothing quite like the 'YESSSS!!' that always accompanies the ball hitting the back of the net from British crowds. In South America it's a distinctive 'GOHHLLLLL' sound that rises from the throng whenever one of their teams score. France and Italy? An aural minestrone cooked up somewhere between the two.

I scrabbled around for my phone and tried to get online. Now it made sense. France had been awarded an early penalty, and Zinedine Zidane had scored it. The crowd sounds now fitted the action, though it only increased the despair that I wasn't inside watching it. By the time Italy equalised inside 20 minutes I was already back in the media room and as half time came round it was time to go for broke. My Sky colleague Nick Collins was in the same boat and we decided, amid the half time comings and goings of people around the security entrances that we should have one last attempt to defy our excluders and get inside.

Our FIFA friend was nowhere to be seen, so I approached one of the operatives guarding the gate explaining our plight and wondering if we might, just for a few minutes, be kindly allowed to pass through and have a quick peak through the wide open gap at the end of the stadium before coming back outside for the start of the second half. No harm in that, right? A long shot, I thought, but worth a go. I must have spun a winning yarn because to my surprise he waved us through, pointing the way round to the viewing gap while crowds of people provided a nicely timed bit of camouflage.

As soon as his attention was diverted elsewhere, we turned sharply to the right and ducked into the throng who were making their way back towards the stadium. Media entrance this way, indicated a large yellow arrow, and before anyone had rumbled us, we were through the door and bounding up the concrete stairs towards the media tribune. It was packed, and as the whistle blew for the start of the second half there wasn't a seat to be had. Now what?! I felt like a fugitive from The Great Escape, especially when I spotted the 'gestapo' who'd denied us entry all day, standing at the back of the tribune. 'Oh shit!' I thought, ducking down my head. But there was no way I was leaving, and Nick and I both slid down into a sitting position on the steps, notes on our knees, pretending to be busy. It probably wasn't the best idea to seek eye contact with the FIFA enforcer, but curiosity got the better of me and when I did, he was looking straight at us with a dismayed look that said 'How the hell did they get in here!??' How would it look, I thought, to be dragged out of the World Cup Final by the collar, fully expecting a team of heavies to come down and escort us out.

The eye-balling continued, but my confidence was growing the longer he took no action and I probably even managed a half grin back in his direction. 'I'm just doing my job' was the studied look, and with notes scattered all over the steps, I think he gave up. I wasn't the only one who missed Zidane's headbutt on Materazzi during extra time. The ball was miles away from where the incident happened and most of us were looking in the opposite direction. So we all gasped at the sight of the great man being shown a red card.

Italy's five perfect penalties in the Final's climax came as a surprise because their record in shootouts was almost as bad as England's. But all the media talk was about Zidane and his extraordinary assault that cost France dear. The following day I wanted to hear from Sepp Blatter so decided to go for the old-fashioned 'doorstep' at the plush FIFA hotel a few yards away from the Brandenburg Gate. I'd met the FIFA President several times before and always found him to be approachable, so seeing him reclined in a large velvet armchair among a group of other 'bigwigs' did not put me off. I didn't expect him to make any comment on Zidane at all and was surprised when he asked where my camera was and that he would come to chat if we waited outside. 20 minutes waiting came and went, and that was when sod's law struck again. A parking attendant was showing too much interest in our car and by the time we'd rushed off to move it, Blatter had been out, gone back in and disappeared.

What would I have confronted him with? A bit like the rogue radio caller to Bobby Moore that prompted his 'I never 'ad it in the first place, mate' riposte from the Bogota bracelet saga, you're probably thinking something along the lines of ....'where DID you stash the loot from those FIFA slush funds?!' As I write this he's just been cleared along with Michel Platini of corruption charges. But in 2006 the wider scandal was still years from hitting the headlines and all I wanted at that moment was a killer quote from the man at the top about the most famous headbutt in football history (with Dion Dublin on Robbie Savage in the 2003 Second City Derby a close second). He would have done it too, with something like 'thiiisss is the futbol...' a bit more diplomatic than his own goal about wanting to see women play in tighter shorts (exasperated shrug emoji)!

I actually found Blatter to be quite a personable, even vulnerable guy when his guard was down. Or maybe he was just being nice because I know they used to sit in the FIFA offices in Switzerland in the 90s and watch us on Sky News in the days when you couldn't get rolling sports news on television anywhere else. I even felt a bit sorry for him at the height of the corruption scandal when that media conference gatecrasher gleefully ran up to the top table and showered Blatter with a bagful of fake dollar bills. Easy target. But the man in the spotlight just couldn't control a clutch of shady delegates whose dark days of disgrace would soon be illuminated for the world to see.

Chapter 9
White Man in Hammersmith Palais
South Africa 2010

South Africa 2010 felt like a landmark and a true home from home. Africa's first World Cup, arriving four years later than it might have done had it not been for that voting fiasco in Zurich a decade earlier. There's something about the old colonies that makes them feel more British than Britain. 'England Expects' blares the maritime message on the old waterfront in Cape Town, Queen Victoria stares down from her statue in Port Elizabeth and from Durban, right down through the KwaZulu-Natal coast to small towns like Margate and Ramsgate it feels like a slice of the old country, with better weather. From Sky's early days it had a big following there, expats and longtime colonials eager to keep up with the news from home, watching every move we broadcast from halfway across the globe.

Locals too, who just wanted to hear us talking about English football on their satellite links. Not just in South Africa either. I once received a heartfelt letter from Nigeria begging me for help in predicting the English results. Mohammed worked at a local university and just needed me to sort out the scores so that he could win the pools and make his fortune. One day a carefully packaged parcel arrived from Nigeria in the post room. Inside was a bespoke brief case, handmade from goatskin leather and painstakingly embroidered with my name and the Sky News logo, perfectly dyed right down to the exact shade of blue. There was just one problem. The goat from which it had been extracted was barely dead, and within a couple weeks the smell and mould were such a health hazard that it had to go. Still, his wobbly handwritten note was straight from the heart and it wasn't easy to tell him that I didn't have control over the results. But what an image of 60s and 70s Britain that conjured up. We all did the pools, and I can still picture the inky page and small boxes where we placed the small 'x' trying to predict the 'score draws'.

South Africa's problem was the perception that it was not a safe place to visit. Stories of muggings and killings were rife from Johannesburg to Cape Town and all places in between. With that came a charm offensive from South Africa Tourism and I was invited to visit the country the summer before the tournament, coinciding with FIFA's traditional Confederations Cup and, as it happened, rugby's 2009 Lions Tour. I went to two of the Tests and it opened my eyes to the visceral nature of rugby fandom within the country's minority white largely Boer population, while football remained the preserve of the blacks.

The decisive Lions Test match against the Springboks in Pretoria was astonishing. This wasn't the rugby we got at home, the honourable sporting affair played and watched by gentlemen. It was hostile, and more like a lairy night of football at St Andrew's or The Den than anything you'd find at Twickenham. The crowd roared, snarled and turned on their own coach until a dramatic long range penalty won the match for the 'Boks in the dying minutes - and with it the series. That stadium, Loftus Versfeld in Pretoria, was also earmarked for the football World Cup along with another famous rugby stadium, Ellis Park in Jo'burg. and I hoped they would bring the kind of passion that I'd just witnessed.

By chance my trip took me to Sun City, famous for its golf course and casinos - and it was there that I stumbled on an exclusive story about England and their training base plans for the following year. Sitting in a deserted bar at the luxurious Palace of the Lost City hotel, the barman asked where I was from and casually mentioned that he'd heard that England would be staying in a brand new, still only half-built 'resort' (as they're all known round there) about half an hour's drive away. He had of course, told the wrong person if it was a secret, and the next day I was there to have a look, opposite a game reserve, in an enclave known as Phokeng not far from the old mining city of Rustenburg. If I needed any confirmation that this was the place that England's new coach Fabio Capello would be setting up camp, it came from a group of contractors on what was still little more than a building site, a million miles away from the lavish sporting complex that it turned into 12 months later.

That very morning the FA had made a site visit, and a few enthusiastic visual descriptions later established that Trevor Brooking had been there along with security guru Ray Whitworth and others. The criticism of England when they failed at major tournaments was that the FA always went for ridiculously over the top accommodation instead of 'keeping it real' and attacking the job at hand. This, it turned out was no different, and if anything, was worse, without even considering what it must have been costing. Isolated, over comfortable, and lacking stimulation for the players. Other countries had apparently been interested but England being England insisted on first refusal. On top of that, the traditional local tribespeople of the Royal Bafokeng Nation also wanted England to come and when they had a head tribesman known as the Phokeng King there was indeed (ahem) 'no phokeng way' the FA could refuse! Juvenile very probably, but the joke rolled on.

The downside of all of the above episode was that my trip was not officially a working one and a minor in house diplomatic incident was thrown up. It was essentially a recreational visit laid on by South Africa Tourism for what we would now, in the world of Instagram probably describe as 'influencers'. Not that I had any of that. Another Sky News team on a logistical recce, and one from Sky Sports News were also in the country at the time, and because I had delivered some content when I wasn't expected to it was considered in some quarters that I had 'muddied the waters'. I only saw it as a bit of initiative. What kind of journalist ignores a story when it falls in their lap? The Head of Sky News had no problem with it. But another management voice felt undermined so the story only half saw the light, which was frustrating.

The Confederations Cup was essentially a trial run for some of the World Cup venues and a chance for some of the nations to get a feel for the place. Bloemfontein in the old Orange Free State (they've since dropped the Orange) will never sit comfortably in my memory for what happened to England there during the World Cup, as we'll come to, and I don't think I've ever been colder at a football match than the night USA beat Spain in the Confederation Cup semis. This was all conquering España, already European champions and on course to win the next two major tournaments too. Seeing them seize up against the Americans probably gives you an idea of just how cold it was.

South Africa's 'Highveld' lies on a plateau at an elevation of around 5,000 feet and on winter nights, chilly is not the word. That first night I was there the wind was whipping across the plateau from the Drakensberg mountains. No wonder the Spanish boys from warmer climes didn't fancy it. But that's not to say it wasn't a great introduction to South African football fandom. The English game is widely followed there, and most fans have a Premier League team even if that's mostly the usual suspects. Numerous fans came over to chat to the bloke from faraway

Sky News. It reminded me of England's trip to Malta, another Sky viewing hotbed where I was as fair game for a 'photo op' as the England players themselves. It also brought me an early introduction to the 'vuvuzela', the horn-cum-trumpet that went on to plague the World Cup with its nauseating cacophony. As I had as a boy in Birmingham, I think I spent most of the match transfixed watching the Bloemfontein Celtic fans behind one of the goals, all dressed up in green and white, rhythmically swaying en masse to a club song. Unmistakably Africa, and the World Cup was all the better for finally heading here.

England's opening World Cup match against USA just happened to be in Rustenburg, in the newly renovated stadium only a short drive from England's base which looked very different to the day I saw it as a building site the previous June. Even though it was close to a large city, the setting was rural, where you could leave an area of modest conurbation and suddenly be out on those wide open African plains. Our hotel base was on the other side of Rustenberg, in a small settlement half an hour's drive away. The Sparkling Waters sounded idyllic and had its charms with a long drive and large colonial lawn backed by a rocky escarpment where one of the rangers-cum-groundsmen told me leopards lived but were rarely seen. I checked there was a bolt on my door, but was more concerned by a two inch gap underneath it through which any snake could have slithered and strangled me while I slept at night. Those fears weren't helped by my cameraman Paul Shears going out for a dirt track run one morning and almost stepping on one of the most poisonous specimens.

This was very definitely the most surreal World Cup yet. Next door to the hotel was a small game reserve in which we had permission to go for a run. No deadly animals we were assured, but of all of the thousands of jogs I've done since then I'm not sure there's been one like it. The BBC's Dan Roan and Andy Swiss and I running alongside a large herd of zebras which took off in a stampede at the sight of what, to them, probably looked like Three Lions on a hunt. We could just about make out the panic through the dust storm but didn't stop to admire the view in case there really were any big cats bringing up the rear.

There was memory jogging too, via Yorkshire's finest satellite engineer Mark Loebell, who, like cameraman Stuart in Japan, wanted the comforts of good, old fashioned British food. That was always easier to find in an old colony like South Africa than the Land Of The Rising Sun, but getting yourself understood with a broad Yorkshire accent in the Royal Bafokeng Nation upped the ante. 'BUTT-AH!' he fired off with indignation at breakfast to a confused waitress. Probably three or four times in a row, louder each time, while the rest of us tried to suppress laughter. 'I need some BUTT-AH!' ,now as if addressing a half-wit while miming the spreading of knife across toast. It was even funnier when she turned on her heels and went to fetch the manager. I think he ended up with just plain jam.

The day before the match brought home the joy of the African hosts in staging their first World Cup. A large group of volunteers and stewards had gathered in one of the Rustenburg stadium's stands for a security briefing when they suddenly broke into tribal song, swaying together in perfect time, as if this was an everyday thing. Magical. I'd been in the same stadium the previous summer for South Africa's Confederations Cup match against New Zealand, and such was the cost of tickets that most of the locals had been priced out. The result was a half empty stadium until the organisers realised there were more fans outside then in, opened the gates at half-time and allowed everyone in for free. I don't suppose the same happened for any of the World Cup matches.

South Africa, or 'Bafana Bafana' as the national team is known (which means 'Go, Boys!' in Zulu) had the honour of playing the opening World Cup game at Soccer City in Johannesburg, the day before England's opener. Nearly 85,000 in attendance, and the rest of the home nation glued to their television sets. Directly opposite the Royal Bafokeng Stadium in Rustenburg were the remnants of the old village that would have been the only thing around for miles before the constructors moved in across the road. They even had a new road now, or at least a new approach road, complete with freshly laid tarmac and bright new white lines leading to a large roundabout, where the investment then stopped abruptly. Beyond that a pot holed road with natural sand that lined both sides.

While we waited to film reaction to Bafana Bafana's opening match with some of the tribespeople in their homes opposite the stadium complex, the satellite truck got stuck fast in the sand and sank down to its axles. It took an age to extract, but this being South Africa, we were rescued by a pair of old cricket pads wedged between the sand and back wheels, providing the traction to escape the deepening pit. The locals barely noticed. This sort of thing happened all the time. An abandoned tractor was left rusting a few yards away, recently painted in the colours of the rainbow nation and draped in its flags. The adjacent small rustic homes couldn't have been in greater contrast to the huge stadium across the street and I entered one that didn't even have a front door to find a family sitting on the dirt floor watching the World Cup's opening match on an elaborately wired up old television set. No-one batted an eyelid that I'd just walked in. The only disappointment was that South Africa didn't quite hang on for victory against Mexico, and the dropped points in a 1-1 draw would come to cost them at the end of the group stage.

England's preparations had been the usual catastrophe (the 'DIS-ASTER' so perfectly pitched to me by Italian journalist Giancarlo Galavotti) when Rio Ferdinand pulled out of the tournament through injury on just about the first day we got to the training base. Lead story on Sky News. There was nothing quite like the British media's appetite for a sporting disaster or hard luck story. The news executives positively revelled in them, encouraged by the all too familiar vision of most of the country having a good old moan. Here we go again. It's what we do and who we are.

It happened so early in the trip that most of our kit, including the aforementioned satellite truck had yet to arrive. That meant having to pull together a report followed by a live insert on the day's sorry events with just a laptop and camera, which back in 2010 still took a bit of setting up. On top of that, while it's still daylight in Britain in June and there's no time difference, it's pitch black in the South African winter by six in the evening. So there we were having to use the car headlights in the field adjacent to the Rustenburg stadium to relay the bad news about Rio, and by the time we'd finished our sequence, the car battery had gone flat. But if a dead car in the middle of the African nowhere sounded like a nightmare, we got a pleasant surprise. South Africa, it turned out has its own version of the 'AA' right down to the familiar yellow and black logo we know so well from home, and within an hour, a rescue truck was in the middle of our field with a brand new battery to save the day.

It's fair to say we all expected England to beat the Americans, though I'd been at their training camp in Pretoria a few days before the game and spoke to their English based players, who revelled in being underdogs. Fulham's Clint Dempsey was one of them, an underrated player in the Premier League. I was there at Ellis Park twelve months earlier when he'd scored one of his team's goals in the Confederations Cup Final against Brazil. 2-0 up, only to lose 3-2. So it was no surprise to see him score against England, though nobody was quite prepared for Rob Green's howler presenting Dempsey with a gift equaliser, wiping out Gerrard's early goal. I can still see it now from my seat high up in the main stand. A tame low shot, and the goalkeeper, all knees and elbows, letting the ball squirm out of his grasp and over the line, almost in slow motion. Horrendous.

I spotted a glum looking Ant and Dec shuffling away at the end. Aside from the 'Celebrity' tag, 'Get Me Out Of Here!' was probably about right. For all the hype and expectation, it seemed to me we overlooked the simple fact that some of England's players just weren't good enough. Great for their clubs in the cut and thrust of the English game, but exposed when the stakes, and the company were high. Club versus country conflicts rarely helped, and I've long felt that club loyalties came first, certainly for the fans, and probably for many of the players too. The dropped points against the Americans added a little pressure to England's group match against Algeria in the fabulous new Green Point stadium in Cape Town. This was old colonial territory and we were all over it.

I walked up the snaking road that leads to the top of Signal Hill with its panoramic view over the stadium and waterfront. Not an ideal place to stop a satellite truck on a hair pin bend with nowhere safe to park but we managed it and found a vantage point on the grassy slope with the most magnificent backdrop. The magnificent stadium oval was directly below and the dark shadow of Robben Island loomed out of bright, sparkling seas in the distance. Cape Town is a Sky News stronghold, and after a couple of hourly broadcasts being beamed into local homes, before long we had crowds of well wishers with links to the old country slipping and sliding on the green gradient craning for a view of what was going on.

The previous June I couldn't have timed my first visit to Cape Town any worse. Heavy rain for three days. The clouds were so low I never once saw Table Mountain. What a let down. But twelve months on, and again in the South African winter, the conditions were the polar opposite. Bright sun and clear skies with winter daytime temperatures soaring up towards the mid 20s. I tried to figure out how, in the same country, at the same time of year, I could have nearly frozen to death in Bloemfontein and yet now be throwing off layers in a heatwave. The England fans down at the Waterfront bars and restaurants lapped it up. St George's cross flags lined the harbourside and we all prepared for an England victory.

But to describe the match as underwhelming was an understatement. England were awful, and the players could hardly complain about being jeered by the thousands of angry fans who'd paid four figure sums to be there. As one of those who felt that Rooney (who should have been reaching his prime at 24) never fulfilled anywhere near his potential at major tournaments, this was one of his lowest points and he should have known better than to mock the booing fans when the camera was on him at the end of the match. Fair game was how the fans (and media) saw the players, who's viewing of a different kind of game when they got back to base was not the escape from long camera lenses they were looking for. The FA laid plans for a relaxing visit to the Pilanesburg Game Reserve close to Sun City and England's base at Rustenburg. But the media would not be invited, which didn't go down well and only invited a siege mentality. Like the visit to Auschwitz a few years earlier it was another opportunity missed, a chance to ease the pressure, lighten the load and build a modicum of positive PR.

With news bulletins and column inches to fill, the 'snappers' and television camera crews were out in force, peering through the long grass, hunting down the Three Lions. The headline writers couldn't go wrong. But easy prey they weren't, despite elaborate plans to capture them on lenses longer than a giraffe's neck. Some of the hyenas in the media pack vowed they'd have the last laugh and second guessed the route they might take. My crew covered one of the lesser park entrances with a spotter near the gate and our van about half a mile down the track with the cameraman ready to pop out through the sun roof and film the approaching bus. The reporters had all been warned off, but nothing specific covered the cameramen so we sprung into action. As luck would have it, like a big cat ready to pounce on the unsuspecting impala - the players' wagon came right down our way and the plan worked like a dream. The only problem was that I really did not want to be seen. The option to go and hide in the bushes would probably have led to being eaten alive by a pack of wild dogs so wasn't an option, and as the bus drew alongside and towered over us they could see straight onto our vehicle. I thought I could hear one of the FA 'suits' Adrian Bevington bellowing his displeasure at the sight of us, but the lump on the back seat covered in a makeshift blanket did not betray my presence at the scene of the crime!

Port Elizabeth had the feel of a South African English Channel town, and the history to match with its statue of Queen Victoria and quaint bed and breakfasts around the seafront. The only thing that betrayed it was its fabulous weather and long sandy beaches juxtaposed with industrial co-nurbation at one end. But it was from here on successive days that I witnessed the contrasting fortunes of the home country and our once colonial nation whose 4,000 settlers had first come here to establish 'PE' as its known, in 1820. The afternoon before England's final crunch group game against Slovenia, South Africa played their last match against France. The French might have won both the World Cup and Euros in successive major tournaments a decade earlier, but by 2010 they were a rabble, without leadership and almost fighting among themselves. So it was no surprise to see them lose to the hosts aswell. The only sad note was that South Africa's 2-1 victory wasn't enough to get them through to the next round either.

I'll remember Bafana Bafana's exit for where I watched it, one of the most arresting backdrops from which I'd ever watched a football match, live or on screen. I'd been filming England based material in the Nelson Mandela Bay Stadium that lunchtime and decided to walk around the large lake that lies right next to the stadium. As I got to the furthest side of the water away from the football ground, I heard a vague commotion from inside one of the industrial looking buildings on the lake's edge. Without a moment's thought I walked straight in through the nearest entrance to what turned out to be a pharmaceuticals company and followed my nose. A bid odd, I thought, that there wasn't a soul around. No receptionist, no-one. Directly in front of me I came across a pair of battered double doors through which I thought I could hear the commotion again. One ham-fisted fumble with the big industrial handles later the doors were ajar and I almost jumped out of my skin. Several hundred pairs of eyes locked onto me simultaneously, pinning me back against the wall. One of those moments where you've accidentally marched into the wrong office at a sensitive moment and just wanted to melt away. The bit where you silently mouth 'Oh...er, um...sorry' and desperately try to slip back out without tripping over your own feet in embarrassment. Except I quickly realised that the collective stare had lifted up a few degrees and the whole factory was engrossed watching South Africa's match against France on a big screen directly above my head.

I slipped inside expecting someone to ask me where my pass was and tried to blend in. That's when it hit me that I stood out like a sore thumb. Every face was black. Except me. Hundreds from the shop floor and a few more serving food and drinks along one side to where I shuffled self consciously, expecting imminent expulsion. I felt like The Clash's Joe Strummer singing 'White Man In Hammersmith Palais' which always conjured up a great image of one of punk's coolest icons standing alone in an all rasta reggae crowd in early 70s London. It also reminded me of a memorably unifying image from Amnesty International's Human Rights Now! concert tour in 1988 when Bruce Springsteen, Peter Gabriel, Sting, Tracy Chapman and Youssou N'Dour had played to what looked like a sea of exclusively black faces in Abidjan, Ivory Coast. If I felt awkward, I needn't have worried. No-one spoke to me but no-one could have cared less that this 'intruder' was there. Football might have been viewed traditionally as the black man's preserve in South Africa but the beautiful game bore no prejudice, and here was a mesmerising display of partisanship in the new united rainbow nation. Every face locked onto the football while a country held its breath. Then suddenly the game was done, and even though South Africa had won, their World Cup was over, cruelly, on goal difference. I recognised that empty feeling of the rug being pulled and within moments the room was empty without as much as a murmur. Back to work. But despite being an outsider I felt I'd been a part of a unique South African experience from the inside, and it was a special privilege to have been among them, something that I would experience again, off the beaten track in Brazil four years later.

*

England's 1-0 win against Slovenia the following day you'll remember as being as uninspiring as their other two group games and even though they were through, sod's law, aka 'that'll-teach-you-not-to-blow-matches-you-should-be-winning', conspired to stop England finishing top of the group. As we sat in the media tribune pondering a winnable second round match against Ghana, you could hear the groans halfway back to Blighty when Landon Donovan scored an injury time winning goal for USA against Algeria which meant they won the group instead, and England's route instantly became harder. Not Ghana, but the old foe Germany next instead, on the Highveld of Bloemfontein. That would come with low expectations. Bitter experience taught us that England rarely did well against big teams in major tournaments.

Ah, Bloemfontein, my old friend! At least the freezing weather stayed away this time. and it was positively balmy in comparison. But I should have known better than expect anything other than another disaster when I was sitting in our hotel on the morning of the match. I casually bit into a piece of uncooked complimentary popcorn winking provocatively at me from a saucer on the hotel bar and one of my teeth exploded on impact. I now had a lower left molar with a crater that felt wider than the Grand Canyon, and quite apart from the agony had to find an emergency dentist fast.

It was often said in Britain that South Africa had the best dentists and now I'd be finding out the hard way. Fortunately Sky News had a bureau in Johannesburg with all the resources that came with that and before I knew it I was lying almost horizontal in the dentist's chair, though not with remotely as much joy as Gazza against Scotland at Wembley in Euro '96. It might have been a Sunday when everything was closed but the guy who came to my rescue was a one man army and general, which he needed to be because his wife had left him in charge of three young kids for the weekend. They buzzed around our feet while their trooper dad applied what appeared to be a series of cocktail sticks into my mouth pinning the new enamel into place. 'It will last about five years' he said as I gratefully left the surgery, but as I write this 12 years on, everything is still in place. Don't let anyone ever tell you that South Africa doesn't have the best dentists. And don't let anyone else sort out the bill. To my horror, almost two years later I took a call at Sky from a newspaper journalist in Jo'burg threatening to name and shame me for not paying the man for his heroic work. The Sky bureau chief had innocently neglected to sort out the bill, and what must have happened was the dentist going to the press to chase what he was due. I was mortified and it was quickly rectified. 'Sky Man Bites Off More Than He Can Chew' or taking the Free State too literally would probably not have been the half of it!

*

The rest of that day is history, and the best team won. But no-one will ever convince me that Frank Lampard's disallowed 'goal' would not have made it a very different game had the officials not got it so badly wrong. 2 -0 down, then 2-1....the goal to make it 2-2 would have re-energised England so much that the fading golden generation might just have reversed the 2-0 up, 3-2 down catastrophe of the then defending World Cup champions against West Germany that had so informed my football watching education, 40 years earlier in Mexico (see opening chapter). Even Rooney, who had an awful tournament, would have woken up.

The majority in the media section shrugged it off afterwards as 'would not have made any difference'. 4-1 was 4-1, but I begged to differ because the whole dynamic of the game would have changed. I will always remember the drama of the moment as it unfolded. Tellingly, not that I want to defend the incompetence of the referee and linesman, all of the eyes around us in the stands who did not have access to television replays could not be sure if the ball had crossed the line, and that alone does indicate that the officials just couldn't see properly, given their positions on the field some distance away from the goalline. When it happened in real time and before the replays had been shown, half of the English media in the press box were on their feet, myself included. Then the pause. I looked to my right where a large group of England fans were sitting. Some looked imploringly across at me, gesturing towards our television monitors with animated expressions of confusion and despair. A friend behind the goal from the far end instantly texted me. 'Did that go over?' He was five times further away than the ref. Before I had time to reply, the monitors in front of us confirmed that the ball was at least a foot over the line. In unison, we all held our heads in disbelief and frustration. The spontaneous gasp of anguish among the English media told the fans around us all they needed to know. Sepp Blatter was 20 yards away to our left. He must have been squirming. It did at least pave the way for the advent of goalline technology, and if we all take a step back to reflect, the Germans probably had good cause to reason that this was karma for the 'Russian' linesman incident from the 1966 Final. Just don't tell Geoff Hurst. He still maintains it was over the line.

Nonetheless that empty, hollow feeling after going out of another World Cup felt even worse than it had after the shootout four years earlier in Gelsenkirchen. I spent the next couple of hours on a roof overlooking the stadium standing among twisted cables and piles of pigeon sh*t, broadcasting to an audience back home who'd probably long switched off. We eventually made it back to Bloemfontein's airport late in the evening, just in time for one last kick where it hurts most. Stan Collymore was hanging around looking crestfallen too. Despite being a follower of the other club in Birmingham I liked Stan for his broadcasting honesty, calling it as he saw it. I'd once been standing on the edge of the pitch at St Andrew's when Stan was playing for either Forest or Fulham and as I was interviewing one of the players, Collymore came brushing past with a cheeky 'How'd the Villa get on?' Unfortunately for Stan his very public private life dogged him wherever he went (no pun intended!!). But there we were in the departure lounge, tired and emotional waiting for our flight back to Johannesburg. Our bags were already loaded and we were about to board when a crackly message came over the tannoy. 'Due to unforeseen circumstances, we regret to say that the flight has been cancelled.' What they neglected to mention was that the plane the German team were due to take back to Jo'burg had broken down, and as a result they would be TAKING OURS instead! With OUR luggage on board! The night the Germans stole our plane, which at 1130 in the evening was a less than amusing take on our Deutsch friends getting their towels down first on the beach. Especially after they'd just kicked sand in our faces on the football field. Our hijacked luggage was still going round and round on the baggage carousel when we eventually got back to a deserted terminal about two in the morning and then had to drive back to Rustenburg.

The silver lining was that we were here for the long haul and Germany's quarter final against Messi's Argentina, coached by Maradona, in Cape Town was a fabulous prospect. I spoke to the man who'd helped dismantle England, Thomas Müller at their pre-match media conference and his assessment of England's fate was a good one (in perfect English): 'Too many alpha males, too many chiefs, not enough Indians' which roughly translated I took to mean too many big egos, and which tallied with the Rio, Lampard and Gerrard dissection of inter club cliques years later. Trying to get anything English out of the Argentina camp in Pretoria was a challenge, but sometimes no words were needed. 'Un Diego Son Dos Pelé' declared a long light blue and white banner tied to a tree outside the camp's entrance. 'One Diego is worth two of Pelé' which was worth pausing to take in given that those two of the three greatest players that ever lived had both taken their countries all the way in the World Cup, and arguably the third member of that elite group, Lionel

Messi was now trying to do the same in South Africa. But you'd never have guessed it when Messi barely touched the ball a few days later, Maradona stood transfixed on the sidelines, and Germany took them to the cleaners. 4-0 was quite a statement and I felt privileged to be there.

*

By 2010 we hadn't yet seen the worst of Uruguay's Luis Suarez. He'd yet to sink his teeth into anyone, but that was no consolation to Ghana in their quarter final against them. Once bitten, twice shy probably covered it when Suarez stopped an almost certain winning goal with his hands, and Ghana not only missed the resulting spot-kick but lost in the penalty shootout aswell. If that was a moral robbery for African football, Cape Town, one of its most notorious cities for crime brought the 'r' word we'd been warned about in South Africa right to my door on the night of Uruguay's semi final against the Netherlands. Suarez's red card for the handball meant he couldn't play, and no doubt contributed to their 3-2 defeat.

A little like New York in the '94 World Cup on the same night Maradona failed his drugs test, we let our hair down in Cape Town after the semi final and it was between two and three in the morning by the time I got back to FIFA's media hotel, The City Lodge, close to the 'big wheel' or 'Ferris wheel' just behind the Victoria and Alfred Waterfront. Straight away I noticed in the corridor that the door to my room was slightly ajar. Had I accidentally left it open all evening? I pushed it open and was confronted by a sickening sight. My belongings were scattered all over the room. Bags and cases turned upside down and hastily shaken out on the floor, drawers open, trouser pockets emptied and the whole space ransacked. It must have been a quick, panicked hit because some things were missed. Thankfully my passport remained, but most items of any value were gone; company mobile phone and laptop, small camera, some cash, even a jacket. I trust they tried it on in front of the wardrobe mirror before doing a bunk.

Three in the morning was no time to be having to sort out a mess like this, but a few hours later I'd worked out it must have been an inside job by one of the cleaners, who probably left my door open for an accomplice to rush in and grab what they could. We'd been warned in a security briefing before leaving home that theft and robbery, often violent robbery were an occupational hazard for overseas visitors in South Africa. That was confirmed when two sleepy police officers from the local station rolled in to reception with a demeanour that suggested they had to deal with this kind of thing twice a day. A resigned weariness to their response said it all. Barely any eye contact, and what felt like a routine request to 'write down what you've lost' on a grubby sheet of A4, casually ripped out of a scruffy notebook. I felt I could have written down anything and they wouldn't have even read it. 'A natural form of taxation' was how some saw thefts in Cape Town where poverty in some of the shanty towns was an eye opener, worse than anything I would visit in the Rio favelas at the next World Cup in Brazil.

I was staying out in South Africa at the end of the tournament so the timing for losing nearly everything couldn't have been worse, and while nothing was physically recovered, by the following afternoon of the robbery I'd established through the mobile phone company that whoever stole the handset had racked up £80 in calls to Nigeria in the space of a few hours. That's going some. I was even taunted in the coming weeks with silent calls from Nigeria to my personal mobile whose number was in the address list.

It didn't end there. My credit cards were skimmed twice in separate incidents on the road. One of them had the same hallmarks I'd also had happen to me in England. A small amount paid out to a local coach company to test the card and then a whopping £2,500 to a jeweller's store in Durban. And to add some likely police corruption to the list of events, my family and I were later stopped by a patrol car out in the middle of nowhere and accused of speeding. A two hour detour to the nearest police station was the punishment, or we could just pay the officer 1,000 Rand (about £50) and be on our way. I'd been warned about these scams too and made sure the officer peering through the driver's side window could see my camera pointing in his direction. I fumbled for the nearest note in my pocket, found the equivalent of about a tenner, screwed it up, and reluctantly dropped it in his sweaty palm. 'Ok you can go' he mumbled, looking up furtively to see if anyone else was watching, and off we went into the night.

At least I got to see and go up Table Mountain this time, via the precarious looking cable car, though that was nothing compared to the helicopter views that came with chasing down the fabled Dutch vehicle convoy that had earlier been seen snaking in a long orange line across the African plains. Incredibly, a 40-plus group of Dutch adventurers had driven around 9,000 miles over two gruelling months from Amsterdam to Cape Town (and would then be heading up to the Final in Johannesburg!). An epic journey of sandstorms, swollen rivers, shot shock absorbers, burned out engines, broken romances, one divorce and even a death. All to be there for the football.

If Cape Town felt like a home from home for England, it was even more so for the Dutch. After all, they got there first in the 1650s and were only displaced by the Brits nearly 150 years later! My cameraman Paul looked like a GI in 'Apocalypse Now', harnessed in but hanging out of the side of the chopper while we flew low over the spectacular contours of Paarl and the Western Cape looking for all things orange. The helicopter hook was a wine festival out near beautiful Stellenbosch with its whitewashed churches and Cape Dutch colonial homes. We landed in clear skies and brilliant sunshine on the lawns of a vineyard. Paradise looked a lot different from the previous year when the rain here was coming in sideways, obscuring every view. Maybe it was nature's consolation, because for all our searching around the twisting mountain roads there was no sign of the orange convoy. But the Cape red wasn't half good!

If England's World Cup had been another resounding flop, and that's a 'Definitely' ,no 'Maybe' about it, bumping into Noel Gallagher and pals in one of central Johannesburg's green spaces on the morning of the Final struck a nice chord. 'There's 'im off the telly' one of his mates called out as we wandered past a group of picnic tables near a large pond. Before I knew it the Oasis star was scrolling through my mobile phone wanting to know all about the news story that had broken the night before. A bizarre and ultimately tragic tale of booze ravaged Paul Gascoigne trying to persuade the fugitive killer Raoul Moat to give himself up from a riverside hiding place in their native Northumberland, with tragicomic promises of 'fishing rods and chicken'. We laughed awkwardly at the reported images of the arch joker Gazza, wearing only a dressing gown, turning a deadly standoff into a grotesque soap. But it ultimately didn't end well when the killer turned the gun on himself. Gascoigne was a desperately sad figure himself at that time, ruined by alcoholic binges after a brilliant, yet unfulfilled career.

This World Cup Final was no different to the ones that came before, though given where we were, even more removed from the average fan who would have given anything to be there. South Africa's hardcore football fan was priced out, of that there was no doubt. I'd been to Soweto, to Mandela's house and the dusty Johannesburg streets that fans of the Kaizer Chiefs and Orlando Pirates call home. But they weren't there, the vuvuzelas were fewer and further between and swathes of corporate fans had hijacked the 'occasion'. Tickets priced at months of a working man's salary threw into focus Africa's economic place in the world. Mind you, I managed a wry smile at the sight of a Birmingham City flag draped over the side of one of the multiple tiers in Soccer City. 'Forza Blues' emblazoned across the flag of St George could hardly have looked more out of place at the biggest match in world football. But my heart soared at the sight of it. As it turned out, it was the poorest final I attended, and all I'll remember from Spain's 1-0 victory over the Dutch was English referee Howard Webb showing an extraordinary 14 yellows and one red card in a bad tempered and niggly match. High stakes, high prices, low on quality, even lower on entertainment.

Bizarrely the Birmingham City connection followed me to breakfast the following morning. The Kojak-bald figure hunched over his scrambled eggs and sausage in a Sandton hotel looked remarkably like controversial Blues director Peter Pannu, right hand man of soon to be disgraced money launderer Carson Yeung. It was. He was on club business, looking for new players. Likely story, I thought, attending a swish sporting weekend away in club time, in glamorous company.

Pannu's reign disintegrated in the post Carson Yeung scandal when the owner was locked up in Hong Kong, and though he was also much criticised in the fallout and ultimately unseated, the story he told me that day of trying to sign one of the Chilean World Cup squad, Jean Beausejour, did indeed come to pass. With a signing like that he did play his part in the club's unforgettable journey to Carling Cup glory at Wembley the following season, but the relegation that followed weeks later was also down to him and the club's crumbling hierarchy. Good riddance. Just a tragedy the other lot from Hong Kong that followed his regime were even worse.

There aren't too many ways you can juxtapose the modestly leafy urban suburb of Kings Heath in Brum and the wide open African plains, but throw in World Cup winning 1966 and, like an aroma that suddenly transports you back to a distant time and place, I can instantly feel a warm breeze blowing through swaying savanna. Of all the movies that had an impact on my formative years, that year's 'Born Free' and the preceding 'Zulu' both made deep impressions. I only have to hear the orchestral flourish and Matt Monro's opening croon to the title tune of Born Free to be transported back to the Kingsway cinema and a desperate struggle not to let anyone see my six year-old self cry. I would keep that emotion bottled up until the dam finally burst, hearing Harry Lauder sing 'Keep Right On To The End Of The Road' as my dad's coffin slipped out of view in 2004. So many memories. You won't be surprised to know the floodgates opened again when the final whistle sounded at the Carling Cup Final as Blues celebrated their most famous hour.

'Zulu' was one of those films where it always felt like we'd lose but never did, and made for endless repeat viewings. Michael Caine, Stanley Baker and a cast of thousands of Zulu Warriors. It was a coincidence but also probably a reflection of the vaunted place in British history of the heroic Battle of Rorke's Drift in 1879 that the name Zulu Warriors was adopted more than a hundred years later by the hooligan element of the club I support. Informed too by that group's multi racial make up. The guide who later took me on a tour of the battleground and knew every blade of grass on it spoke about the legacy of the Zulu Empire and had not heard of the Birmingham brotherhood when I raised it. Judging by his interest in what was a casual 'aside', it might even now make a footnote in his historical talks.

Rorke's Drift was a place I'd always wanted to visit, so as soon as I'd finished with the football in Johannesburg, I was making the three or four hour drive out of the city and down onto the evocative plains through the cinematic landscape of KwaZulu Natal. But don't ever let anyone tell you that driving out of modern day Jo'burg isn't a deeply uncomfortable experience. Cape Town had taught me that no-one and nothing is safe or respected in South Africa. Life is cheap and mine felt like a 'two bob' takeaway while I sat at endless rows of traffic lights driving through the scary southern suburbs. It probably didn't help that one of my cameramen, Garwen McLuckie who lived and grew up in

South Africa told me a story of how someone he knew was held up at some lights at gunpoint and burned alive. And how he slept inside an intruder-proof cage within his house on the coast in case of a night time break in. But it probably DID help that I was driving a borrowed, battered old pick up truck with my stuff in the back covered over with an old carpet. Nothing to see here, I hoped. But every time I stopped in a seedy looking neighbourhood my senses were in overload and I couldn't wait to put my foot to the floor at the first sign of the city limits.

Dundee was a small, depressing provincial town signalling South Africa's colonial past. Women sat in the doorways of run down old houses while youths roamed the dusty streets. A world away from the old country but here and there you'd spot a grubby Manchester Utd, Chelsea or Liverpool shirt. A petrol stop was more than enough and within half an hour I was driving down a dirt road to Fugitives' Drift Lodge, where the old Anglo-Zulu war stories came to life. Though the relatively short journey I'd just made from a dangerous city brought with it an uncomfortable modern day take on a troubled country. The historian David Rattray who ran the lodge had been murdered there by robbers three years previously. Sobering. It's hard to imagine the scale of the carnage that went on there on January 22nd 1879, but I left with a strong sense of 'selective' memory when it came to British military history. I'd grown up with a story of heroism against the odds at Rorke's Drift, so vividly depicted in the 'Zulu' movie, and that is what passed into legend, or at least selectively so from the British perspective. Sitting on the now manicured lawns next to the small outpost that was defended so bravely in the face of a relentless assault was quite an experience. There are a series of natural, terraced rock ledges a couple of hundred yards from the back of what was the small hospital building where the Brits were holed up, and you could only imagine how terrifying it must have been to see thousands of blood-thirsty warriors pouring down towards them. The name of the Zulu stabbing spear or 'assegai', I learned, had an especially gut-churning history. 'Iklwa', as it's known, in all its onomatopoeic gory, glory, elicits a kind of sickening verbal squelch when lingered over with context, and was so named because of the sound it made when being twisted and pulled from the victim's body. Nice. Eating an evening meal of hearty stew was particularly hard to stomach after a day hearing about that.

But if 11 Victoria Crosses, the most ever for a single battle, reflected an heroic rearguard action at Rorke's Drift, what about what happened earlier on the very same day, just up the track at Isandlwana? A story less told, probably for a reason, and I was drawn deep into its scarcely believable detail. The same British army, with all its Victorian might was soundly routed, but who knew? Was it lightly airbrushed from the teachings of British history because the world's most fearsome military power at the time was embarrassed to linger on defeat at the hands, literally, of an African tribe?

But happen it did, and 1,300 British regulars and colonial forces were wiped out at Isandlwana, overrun by a Zulu force more than ten times their number. To apply the theme of this book, who were the 'underdogs' here? A trained army with state of the art rifles and field guns? Or a tribe with spears (and a few captured rifles that they didn't know how to shoot straight)? What an incredible story. No wonder I saw tour guides scattered below a large lion shaped rock that marks out the battle site telling stories of one of the greatest upsets in military history. The Zulus may have had their own Empire, but up against the world's then greatest military power, the British Empire, it should have been a mismatch, and might still have been, had Lord Chelmsford and his hapless troops not made a string of terrible tactical mistakes on unfamiliar terrain that the Zulus knew like the back of their hand. All that's left now on the grassy plain are piles of white rocks, each one representing the site of a mass grave from that fateful day.

The story followed me back along the twisting dirt track and undulating countryside to Fugitives' Drift which sits just above the Buffalo River valley on the opposite bank. There, high on a slope lies the grave of two Lieutenants, Coghill and Melvill who fled the scene of slaughter right into the river itself to save the Queen's Colour (flag/banner) before being caught and butchered by the pursuing Zulus. They both received posthumous VC's but only nearly three decades later. How telling it was that only one Victoria Cross was awarded at the time for gallantry at Isandlwana on a disastrous day for Victorian Britain.

But if ever there was an underdog hero fighting overwhelming odds, saving a fleeing, drowning man under a hail of bullets, it was Private Samuel Wassall, from Birmingham (albeit Aston, though long before the

Villa historians won anything and he would ever have heard of them!). It was also telling that within months, Britain had returned to Zululand and crushed its Empire with ruthless force. The equivalent probably of what the world's current military superpower the USA might call 'shock and awe', though there's something grotesquely one-sided about an image of the then latest technology Gatling guns mowing down everything in their path.

The Zulu story wasn't the only thing the drew me down to see its landscape first hand. Not much more than a two hour drive away to the west was another battlefield site whose name resonates with football fans across the world. Spioenkop. The 'Kop' at Liverpool is probably the most famous football stand in the world, and the adapted Spion Kop name that soon spread to dozens of football terraces, mostly in Britain, all lead back to a desolate hill in KwaZulu-Natal.

Part of my youth was spent growing up on the Spion Kop terrace at Birmingham City, and I wanted to see how and where the association was made over a century before. I'd always thought that the Kop reference was down to the terraced nature of that particular hill, and that it had then found its way into the English lexicon by the impact of events that unfolded on it during the Second Boer War of 1900. But only the second part is true. There's no noticeable terracing, just a large mound with more than one peak at different heights. But the steep sides would, with some imagination, resemble the banks of terracing that then emerged in football stadiums in Britain in the early years of the 20th century. To that extent the football terraces could have been named after any hill, couldn't they? Second thoughts, the Wrekin or Scafell don't quite have the same ring.

The Liverpool connection came from large numbers of soldiers from Lancashire based regiments who lost their lives when trapped in shallow trenches at the top of the hill under heavy fire from the outnumbered Boers on surrounding high ground. Like Isandlwana two decades earlier, tactical mistakes in the field cost hundreds of British lives that day and led to another damaging defeat (before eventually winning the war). The backstory was fascinating and my guide Simon Blackburn who ran Three Trees Lodge at the base of Spion Kop read stories from horrifying eye witness accounts while we sat in the cool breeze at the top of the hill, surrounded by monuments to the dead. How two of the world's most famous future political leaders, Winston Churchill and Mahatma Gandhi had both been present on the hill during the battle. All long gone. But there was even a surviving woman from the local village tribe who was old enough to have been around when the fighting took place and could remember the shooting. She was 113 years old. How I would have loved to have met her.

The Liverpool Kop was eventually so named in honour of local men who died on the hill, and the name caught on around the country. But there's something very 'Blues' about the Spion Kop at Birmingham. It was built on a pile of rubbish. When the owners moved to the club's longstanding home St Andrew's in 1906, described back then as an urban swamp, the fastest way to build a big bank on which to lay some terracing was to invite the locals to dump their rubbish there. Which they did. Mountains of it. Lord knows what lies underneath the foundations of the modern, rebuilt, seated Kop but as I write this in 2022 it's halfway to falling down. Unsafe. Less than 30 years after it was built! If that sounds like a curse, you're halfway there. We've long blamed the gypsies who were evicted from the site when Blues moved in a few years after the battle at Spioenkop. Mind you, whatever dark forces lie in the ground, you had to admire the construction worker who, when the stadium was being redeveloped in the early 90s, scooped up a handful of 'cursed' soil and dumped it over at Villa Park. They've won nothing since!

*

I will never forget the terraces' last stand at St Andrew's before the enforcement of all seater stadiums post Hillsborough. The match itself was a minor footnote, a 2-2 draw against Bristol City in the '93-'94 season that would end in relegation, ironically on a packed open terrace at Tranmere when Blues won their last game, but still went down on the final day. Manager Barry Fry was carried from the field like a hero by invading fans. Contrary to the last. The old Spion Kop's last stand took some beating though, and still brings waves of nostalgia whenever I see old photographs of that massed bank of long terraced steps. Like those early childhood days sitting on my dad's knee on the front row of the (still surviving) Main Stand, I spent most of that last match staring at the Kop crowd. Fans turned up with hammers and chisels, liberating anything that wasn't nailed down, and just as much that was. The old Jeff Hall scoreboard in one corner where the old boys would hang the other scores at half time lost most of its numbers, bold and white on black metal plates, well before the final whistle.

But one image lingers more than any other from that day for me, like the final shot from a nostalgic documentary or a still for the ages. Almost an hour after the final whistle, when most fans had gathered their thoughts and memories and left the terrace one last time, I came across a couple at the bottom of the steps leading out of the back of the Spion Kop. Not a soul remained bar these two sitting, with heads bowed on the final step. One quietly sobbed while the other wrapped a consoling arm around a shoulder and litter blew around them in the wind. Like the words from the old anthem, 'Keep Right On...', it was the end of the road at a happy abode.

*

I still wonder what the future holds for South Africa given its economic apartheid. But there aren't many more beautiful places on the planet. I won't ever forget going for a run down a glorious Indian Ocean beach at Sodwana, not far from the Mozambique border. The tail of a stranded young whale shark swished back and fore in the surf and there was no-one there but me. Not a chance of shifting it, but I ran straight into the waves to do what I could. A white woman soon appeared in the back of an open topped Jeep, a superior colonial type assuring me that the stricken beast was already dead. A few hours later a posse of locals descended on the beach armed with pangas to dissect and harvest the corpse.

If there was one thing I'd hoped to witness on the working trip of a lifetime, it came after the football had been and gone. One of the world's greatest natural phenomena, the sardine run, where hundreds of millions of the fish migrate north in vast shoals along South Africa's east coast, attracting huge numbers of predators along the way. It should have come in June or early July, when the World Cup was in full flow.

But as nature would have it that year, it came late, very late, in August, and brought one of the most spectacular sights I'd ever seen.

The setting was Durban's main beach, just yards from teeming crowds, and I could only imagine how this might have played out had it happened when thousands of football fans might have gathered on the same stretch of sand. A hundred yards offshore, squadrons of Cape gannets drew in their wings and dropped like stones out of the sky, hurtling violently into the water in pursuit of their prey, raining seabirds onto the dark shoal just below the surface.

'Everybody out of the water!' was the signal that all wasn't well. A lifeguard dashed through the crowds in the shallows blowing his whistle with alarm. Within minutes the police were there too. The sardines had been chased into the surf by scores of sharks while local bounty hunters seemed oblivious to the dangers, risking life and limb with nets and buckets and eyes only on a fresh sardine meal or fast buck. The beach at Amity Island in 'Jaws' had nothing on this. As a pale green wave showed its underbelly, rearing up in water scarcely deeper than waist height, I caught the outline of three sharks dashing menacingly left and right across each other. An amazing sight.

The feeding frenzy caught everyone by surprise except for the anglers who snapped into action, dozens of rods baited up with cocktails of five or six fresh whole sardines, run through by vicious looking hooks. At one stage everyone seemed to have snagged a shark simultaneously. Silhouettes heaved on arching rods backlit by the sinking sun. I even had a go myself. I'd never caught a shark before, but was underwhelmed to find it felt only like a dead weight, like trying to drag in a marker buoy that was anchored to the ocean floor. Give me a sporting mackerel, twisting and fighting for its life all day long. I saw a local man with a smallish shark slung over his shoulder nose first while he clung onto its tail like a comic book bag of swag. Another struggled with a huge beast, half in, half out of the water while people whooped and splashed in the unfolding freak show. I half expected protesters to pop up with placards reminding us that we were all God's creatures and could we please return them to the water.

South Africa 2010 had been an unforgettable adventure and a new frontier for football's global tournament. But beach culture wasn't going anywhere. The old hands Brazil were next.

Chapter 10
Favelas and Forro
Brazil 2014

I'd never had cause to look for Belo Horizonte on a map. But I'd always known the notoriety of that name. Maybe it was the 'horizontal heavyweights' of boxing folklore lying flat on their backs after being knocked out. But by the end of Brazil's second staging of the World Cup in 2014, the city had flattened two of football's biggest reputations more than half a century apart. Two of the most seismic shocks in World Cup history, both played in Belo Horizonte. England, of course, from the evidence of the previous chapters would always have been candidates for one of them. Even in their first World Cup, back in 1950, they managed to come unstuck against a bunch of part-timers from the USA who barely knew the difference between a free-kick and a field goal. Against American no-hopers priced at 500 to 1 by the bookies, England's well fancied plans for world domination were laid to rest by a guy who made his living as a hearse driver. Or, if you prefer, they went down the plughole at the hands of a dishwasher. Either way, a motley crew of amateurs who ought not have been fit to lace the boots of Stanley Matthews. The press called it 'The Miracle of Belo Horizonte', and of all England's World Cup disasters it has to rank right at the top. Underdogs 1 Pedigrees 0.

Mind you, England had no World Cup pedigree before that, because they'd turned down invitations to enter the three pre-war stagings after an apparent dispute over payments to amateur players. A shame, because they might have done some damage. Might. They'd beaten the 1934 world champions Italy later that year and wiped the floor with Germany in Berlin the year before war broke out, in front of Goebbels, Goering and numerous Nazis. I'll stop there, to highlight the role that day of Stan Cullis, the first manager I came to worship at Birmingham City from those heady days in the late 60s. Three decades earlier Stan, in his Wolves playing days had been the only England player to refuse to make the Nazi salute in Berlin. The rest did, under protest, but Cullis was so insistent he wouldn't do it that he was dropped from the team. It didn't prevent a propaganda victory for the Germans though.

England's reputation was largely down to lording it against the home nations in the early years of international football, but they'd hardly played any internationals overseas by the 1930's, and when they did, it was a mixed bag. A few hammerings of France didn't look quite so good when they eventually lost to them, and plenty of other defeats followed on European soil. Spain, Hungary, the Czechs, Austria, Belgium. A few cynics suggested England's absence from the 30s tournaments was because they wouldn't ever even entertain the prospect of losing a World Cup match. They'd only go if they were allowed to win. A bit like W G Grace refusing to walk when he'd had his middle stump knocked out of the ground. A shame they couldn't have applied a bit of this kind of attitude years later to the Eurovision Song Contest with its annual humiliation. Just not turn up. Mind you, whoever chooses the UK entry deserves the pelters, trawling music's equivalent of Sunday morning pub league football after 12 pints the night before. 'Nul points' on merit.

It was 50 years after Brazil's 1950 staging of the World Cup that I was in Rio de Janeiro for Manchester United's ill fated excursion into FIFA's Club World Championship. But what a privilege to have experienced the old Maracana Stadium before they knocked it down and rebuilt it for the 2014 tournament. It looked pretty packed with 73,000 fans inside the day I was there for United's defeat by Vasco De Gama. The mind boggles at the thought of not far off three times that number, a staggering 199,000 squeezing into the old place for the decisive match (not a traditional knockout style Final because it was decided by two group stages) when Uruguay beat the hosts Brazil 2-1. Quite apart from United's controversial withdrawal from the post millennium FA Cup, they barely looked as though they wanted to be in Brazil at all, apart from the obvious pleasures of Copacabana and Ipanema beaches when they could have been freezing their you-know-whats off back in Blighty. It felt more like a low key mid season break after the climax of that incredible 1999 treble winning season seven months previously.

I can remember Sir Alex Ferguson looking uber relaxed at United's hotel, wandering around with a plastic bag full of goodies from the local shops. I was interviewing him one afternoon at a modest little training ground in the Rio suburbs when he suddenly paused mid sentence. His jaw dropped and eyes widened. I thought he was about to keel over, until I spun round to see a giant armadillo casually walking across the pitch a few yards behind us. A novel take on the stray dogs and cats that seemed to invade English pitches most weeks when we were kids. It got me thinking of the poor old Brentford goalkeeper Chic Brodie having his career ended by a canine invader when it lunged into his groin chasing a bouncing ball during a match at Colchester in 1970. Imagine 'Golden Balls' Beckham being brought down by a rampaging armadillo. Underdog 1 Best In Class 0.

I thought those sort of creatures only inhabited Brazil's Amazon, where England had to play their opening 2014 World Cup match against Italy in Manaus. A classic venue for the newshounds, but for all the piranhas pulled from the neighbouring river in the build up (metaphorical and literal from some of the fan photos I saw), England were, er... toothless, and one defeat became two when a razor sharp Luis Suarez duly sunk his own incisors into Roy Hodgson's team in the second group match against Uruguay. Two bites of the cherry and England were out before they'd finished their starters. They couldn't even score against Costa Rica in the final group game. Even worse than the debacle in South Africa four years before.

I didn't even arrive in Brazil until England were out. This World Cup was not a working one. England might have been the spiritual home of the game but Brazil was the country that lived and breathed it like no other place on earth and the chance to experience that was a once in a lifetime opportunity. I covered England's potential path with match tickets, just in case. Second round? Recife. I'd have laughed out loud if you'd told me while I waited in the virtual ticket queue that that match would turn out to be Greece v Costa Rica. International football's equivalent of Blackburn v Crewe. But that's what we got from the way results in the groups panned out and two outsiders in a city full of economic underdogs would bring a unique, eye-opening experience. Before that though, I was on a mission to spread the gospel according to Birmingham City, in a football mad country where the most unlikely clubs have far flung followings.

I persuaded the then Blues Director, Panos Pavlakis to give me a clutch of club shirts with a view to finding some under-privileged kids in a Rio favela and sow the seeds to grow some future fans. The (away) shirts were even Brazil yellow, bright enough to dull the future pain that would inevitably accompany a life sentence following one of England's great underachievers. That, or they would just cover over the Blues badge, and replace it with a Brazil one. Still, worth a try. As luck would have it, on the flight over I found myself sitting next to a schoolteacher from one of Rio's most notorious neighbourhoods, the 'Cidade De Deus' or 'City Of God' made famous by the movie of the same name with its tale of drug dealers and gun runners from 2002. I'd imagined I would have to recce some of the roughest favelas to find a suitable home for the shirts, but before I'd even touched down in Rio we'd agreed I would visit her school and she'd find some deserving boys (or girls) to take them. Result!

Some of the old stories I heard of shootouts in the streets and used needles strewn across the neighbourhood had me looking over my shoulder before I'd even reached the city limits. None of this was made up. Brazil's poorest live in the kind of poverty that Europeans can barely comprehend. With a World Cup and Olympic Games falling within two years of each other, Rio had no option but to clean up its act. That meant a programme 'pacifying' the favelas (or slums) and driving out the gangsters who feed off them. The City Of God had been through this some years earlier and the worst was now past. Murals and graffiti covered the school walls and every few yards I'd be shown an indentation where stray bullets had ricocheted into buildings. But despite all this, the kids in the classroom, probably 11 or 12 years old beamed with happiness when I was introduced to them. Big, Brazilian, sunshine smiles that belied the hardships of their upbringing. It brought special satisfaction to see them lined up proudly in their new football shirts. I only wished I'd had more. Later that afternoon I came across a police patrol hut and squad car on one of the adjacent housing estates made up of high rise tenements. One of the boys I'd seen earlier had a streak of blood across the right shoulder of his shirt. Someone had already tried to relieve him of it. Fighting over a Birmingham City shirt in Brazil. Truth really is stranger than fiction!

My first taste of Copacabana Beach, (literally, taste) was on that club trip with United just days after the worldwide party to end all parties when the calendar clicked round from 1999 to 2000. I was knocked over by a powerful wave and got a mouthful of the ocean that tasted vaguely like, well, sh** and disinfectant. Never mind all the glamour postcards pics of that stretch of sand - treated sewage entered the sea back then, and anyone unfortunate enough to leave their mouth open when trying to negotiate a big wave could vouch for it. But it didn't stop huge crowds from congregating on one of the most celebrated sandy crescents on the planet. It was instantly and unmistakably Brazil, teeming with humanity in a country where life was lived to the full but often felt cheap.

I saw someone having their chest pumped on the sand while a crowd gathered round. But within a couple of minutes, the barefoot beach football was back in full swing while the ever present sun beat down on bronzed bodies. Life here felt like a perpetual carnival. It's just the way the Brazilian people are, every day a celebration, all rhythm and smiles. No wonder the World Cup was a magnet for hedonists from all over the planet. Ronnie Biggs was dead by 2014, but when I first visited Rio, the word was that the notorious fun loving fugitive would, for a fee, hold court at his house for groups of (usually British) lads and entertain them over beers with tales of the Great Train Robbery and life on the run. Apparently the legendary Stanley Matthews who'd been part of that England team embarrassed by the USA in Belo Horizonte was even a visitor at one time. I saw cheap flyers advertising the experience like hookers' invitations to seedy bedsits slapped onto lamp posts and alleyway walls.

The Copacabana bustled with activity and hawkers selling their wares. Sand sculptures of players carved into a bank straddled the beach and its two mile long promenade. One was unmistakably Neymar, carrying the weight of Brazil's fabled number 10 shirt and on whose slender shoulders rested the hopes of a nation. Next to him a less familiar looking Frenchman with white cockerel emblazoned onto a blue top. All built on sand. Prophetically so, as it turned out, especially the hosts, because both nations would fail to live up to expectations. Spectacularly so, in Brazil's case. Beach bars cooked up calamari and cocktails, and at the southern end where the headland meets the northern end of Ipanema, a double decker bridge of temporary television studios, housing channels from around the world, bridged both sides of the Copacabana carriageway.

The British pundits were out in force, broadcasting live from some of the parasol covered bars with their glorious waterside backdrop. But not all was as idyllic as it looked. I bumped into old friend Ian Wright one afternoon on the verge of having to return home after his wife was held up at knifepoint by burglars at their house back home. So much for Rio being the place with the problems! Wrighty was one of the great characters I'd known for years through Sky, though I hadn't covered myself in glory one day when his Channel 5 chat show used to be broadcast from the same Sky News building in Osterley. I casually walked past the 'Green Room' where the guests gathered and asked a lost looking youth if he was the new script runner. It was Justin Bieber, aged about 14, waiting to go on to Wrighty's show. Oops!

Even though just about all Brazilians love their football, there was still considerable unrest in the country over the cost of staging the World Cup. Billions of dollars, it was calculated, at the expense of the poor, when Brazil invested comparatively little in healthcare and education. From what I could see, FIFA seemed to get the brunt of the blame when Brazil's fragile government ought to have been first in the firing line. Either way, the bank of Copacabana television studios were stoned by street protesters. Through the magic of pan global social media, I was able to see Gary Lineker's studio windows overlooking the strip with what appeared to be stone damage in the back of the shot, like much larger versions of impacts caused by stones thrown up from roads on to car windscreens. I went to have a look first hand the next morning from street level and was met by a trail of destruction right across the bank of windows. Every channel, every country.

But the show went on, culminating in an enormous protest march in Rio on the day of Brazil's second round match against Chile which, as we'll come to, turned into one of the greatest football watching experiences I've ever experienced, without even being in the stadium. We've seen mass protests for decades in Britain over one thing or another, nearly always ugly, but Brazilians somehow managed to make it beautiful. It could just easily have been Carnival time on the Copacabana, when Rio celebrates the world's biggest party. Glamorous costumes competed with topless women bearing anti FIFA placards and slogans that left even less to the imagination.

The backdrop to all of this was rammed home when I left Rio for another of Brazil's biggest cities, Recife - a giant 1,100 mile leap up the Atlantic coast towards the tropics (much further if brave enough to drive), and the second round match that England had long since given up rights to. Good numbers of England fans had banked on their team being there, or had no intention of going home early whatever the outcome. The city on Brazil's north east shoulder was peppered with them, or at least the expensive new Pernambuco stadium was, situated miles out of town inland from the coast. High rise blocks lined the long sandy beach, broken up by low, rocky ledges and ribbons of brown kelp, washed back and fore by the Atlantic rollers.

But this wasn't party central Rio, and I found myself in a deadly quiet beachfront hotel a few down from where the Costa Rica team were modestly accommodated. I didn't imagine England would've been in the same one if they'd been in town instead. It was so quiet I found myself in the hotel bar alone, bar two characters propping up the bar itself. Father and son, from Sweden, and if that conjures up images of friendly, open-minded liberals, you'd have got as much of a shock as I did. The father, a dark-eyed, swarthy character in his 50s looked suspiciously at me out of the corner of his eye. It didn't help that he'd clearly had a skinful of beer and I instantly regretted engaging with him. 'Hi, where are you from?' I enquired cheerily, to be met with a surly, suspicion cloaked silence, only rescued by his lad, probably mid to late teens who explained they'd come all the way from Stockholm to experience their first World Cup. All the time we chatted, his father's eyes burned holes in the side of my head, like a protective parent from the animal kingdom who might strike without warning. Utterly unnerving. It turned out they followed the Stockholm club Djurgarden, and I didn't linger on what I already knew, that the club had a reputation for having a section of fans with aggressive right-wing leanings. I had an uncomfortable drink with them, one eye plotting the fastest route to the nearest exit point, and left as soon as I could slip away with my faculties intact. I wondered what the future held for that youngster. His father just looked like a wrong 'un.

I had yet to visit Rio's infamous favelas, the shanty towns built like tongues snaking down the city's many hillsides, and it was Recife that really brought home the extent of the poverty that blights the country.

It made sense of the protests that had accompanied the early weeks of the tournament. Recife's new stadium was built a good way from the coast, and the journey to get there brought everything into focus. A half hour train ride ran along the edge of the Capibaribe River, and within minutes we were in the slums. Endless lines of houses on stilts, all makeshift walls and corrugated roofs, decorated with washing hanging out to dry in the warm air.

This, by reputation was one of Brazil's richest cities, so how could the chasm between the haves and have nots be so great? By the end of the night I'd had a closer view, an experience that brought one of the defining images of my visit. The shuttle bus that carried fans back from the stadium dropped us at the out of town railway station. As soon as we disembarked from the bus we were met by a wall of humanity, hundreds of people, mostly youngsters, but not all, from the poorest neighbourhoods, reaching out in the dark, hoping for a hand out. Police officers erected barriers to help us get through the crowds and on to the platform. I had nothing but a pen, and pushed it though the bars where someone pulled it from view. I'd never experienced anything like it. People called out, but not in desperation. There was a vibrancy and excited chatter that captured the animated nature of all Brazilians. Even the poorest. But at the same time there was something uncomfortable about being viewed as a privileged outsider. We'd simply been to a football match, but it felt like we were waiting to be shuttled off to a different planet. When we were kids at Birmingham City, nobody was ever priced out. A few coins in the pocket was always enough to get through the turnstiles, or even under them, if no-one was watching. Whatever happened to the people's game? Nobody spoke as we made our way awkwardly through the station concourse and out towards the platforms. I looked behind and had one of those snapshot moments where the image is seared onto the memory bank. The faces behind the barriers were obscured by the metal bars from my narrow angle of vision. All I could see was a forest of hands and thousands of eager, outstretched fingers.

*

If there was a footballing version of the have nots, it was little Costa Rica, and their success was the feelgood story of the tournament.

They'd got to the second round before in 1990 when they beat a hapless Scotland along the way but this was even better. The smaller nations bring a special joy to World Cups and the 'Ticos' as their countrymen call them were the greatest of underdogs. Before the game against Greece had even started, I was queueing for a pre-match hot dog (whatever happened to imaginative, native cuisine at corporate international sporting events?) when the young man in front of me, draped in a Costa Rica flag and scarf burst into tears. Lost wallet? Bad news from home? I braved an approach with the offer of a consoling shoulder and it all came out. 'I'm so proud of my country!', he sobbed, and almost got me going too. This was what it was all about.

I remembered my own involuntary breakdown at Wembley three years before, though at least mine came at the end! I sat and chatted to a local Brazilian fan who regaled me with stories in broken English about the passion of the Recife derby, the 'Classico dos Classicos', one of the oldest and most fiercely contested in the country. In return I told him about the Second City derby and all its madness. Football as the universal language, that common partisanship, whatever the place and whoever the combatants. Then there was the drama unfolding right in front of us, two neutrals seduced by the promise of underdogs about to have their day again. Costa Rica beat the Greeks amid unbearable tension in a penalty shoot-out. I saw my friend again from the hot dog queue, on the way out of the stadium. He was still crying. Tears of joy.

The great thrill of attending World Cups (or any exotic awaydays) was just the being there, soaking up the place, the people and the culture, whether you had a match ticket or not. Before leaving Recife, I ventured to the neighbouring colonial town of Olinda, a World Heritage Site, literally joined at the hip to its modern city next door, but a world away in its low rise charm and architecture. Old Portuguese churches with white-washed bell towers juxtaposed with rows of multi-coloured cottages and airy seaside villas. Beautiful.

All of Brazil's games were heavily over subscribed, which left millions of fans watching in public places. Their second round match against Chile was in Belo Horizonte and for all the massed ranks of yellow shirts in the stadium, nowhere was quite like Rio and watching on the big screen from the official fan zone on Copacabana Beach. It was an afternoon game, roasting hot and the atmosphere pure carnival. I can only guess at six figure numbers on the promenade and beach, swelled by the anti government protest marchers moving along the strip. I made for the beach in the hope of getting into the fan zone towards the left hand with its free entry and giant screen. It was packed all along the water's edge. If I wasn't weaving through crowds to get across the beach, I was stepping over bodies catching rays on the sand.

But with the crowds came the crooks and chancers hoping to use the vast numbers of bodies as cover for some of what Rio was notorious for. A commotion developed a few yards in front of me. A youth dashed through the throng, desperately pursued a few yards behind by a balding, shouting middle aged man wearing 'budgie smuggler' swimming briefs. A struggle ensued and the youth was wrestled to the sand by the chaser while onlookers watched the drama almost impassively. They writhed around in the sand before the victim reclaimed the snatched wallet and the youth struggled free through a forest of legs. He was away into the shallows and gone, probably to try it again somewhere else. This, you got the impression was a regular occurrence.

The enclosed fan zone, with its right hand fence running along the shore almost on the high water mark was rammed to capacity an hour before the game had even started. But it was to be the best thing that could have happened. The overspill headed for the open space on the beach just beyond the fence where the view of the huge screen was just as good. Not just Brazilians and Chileans but fans of every nation, especially fun seeking Americans, draped in the Stars and Stripes. Some set up beach chairs, but most just stood in the glorious sunshine, while slowly but surely the tide came in. Water lapped around my feet, then ankles while the sun beat down relentlessly. Paradise. By the time the match got to the end of normal time it was up to my knees and the occasional wave sloshed up waist high.

Fans bounced around in the water breaking into song. I half expected Brian Wilson to race past singing 'Surfin' USA'. What a surreal experience! Watching the World Cup in the place that most encapsulated the mystique of Brazilian football, the impromptu kickabout on the beach, and not just any beach, the Copacabana where the kids learned their skills and tricks. 1-1 at the end of extra time. Penalty shootout!

Barely anyone noticed that we might soon be calling for the coastguard. The beach chairs had long been swamped and a parasol floated around in a dip in the sand, freshly transformed into a tropical lagoon. Then, the unforgettable moment when Brazil won it. Chile missed the crucial kick - and all hell broke loose. The crowd roared and water flew in all directions. Someone in front of me sprung into a somersault and landed head first into the lagoon. Another bellyflopped with a slap you could have heard in Belo Horizonte. Limbs flailed and spray filled the air. Rio needed no invitation to push out the party boat. They were through to the quarter finals.

It was always my intention to visit one of the favelas and the word was that 'pacification' had made them safe. The BBC had aired a documentary about one of the best known, rising up from behind a grid of well to do tree-lined streets that run along beautiful Ipanema Beach, the next one round from Copacabana. The star of the documentary was a force of nature called Rocky Balboa, whose speciality was an extraordinary ability to carry fridges and any other domestic alliances up from street level to the shacks and crumbling concrete boxes that piled on top of each other up the hillside. On his shoulder, without help, up hundreds of narrow steps and between buildings where there wasn't room to swing a cat.

While wandering along an innocuous alleyway at the bottom of the favela I came across a mural in his honour. A gang of youths sat around it and didn't take too kindly to me instinctively taking a photo. That would cost, I learned, and I shuffled off sharpish while they muttered something that didn't sound too friendly. But if I was going to venture up those steps, now was the time, and I set off, with small camera rolling as I went. Don't display valuables was the advice I'd been given, but I braved it and put my head down when I saw three men looming into view on both sides of the narrow staircase only a few dozen steps up.

It might have been my imagination, but I knew what had once gone on in these places and in my mind, they were eyeing me up with menacing intent. 'Put the camera away' said head, 'keep going' said heart. I think I even managed a squeaked 'Hola!' (wrong language) as I squeezed through and didn't look back, while my thighs burned from the climbing. But once up and away I felt fairly safe amid a tangle of concrete, cables, water that dripped and flowed down a mucky looking gully adjacent to the steps, and pockets of people who seemed to be happier the higher I climbed. About half way up I looked to my left and found some reassurance. Two policemen were perched on a kind of crow's nest platform overlooking the sprawl below. They didn't speak (or even smile) and I got the impression they'd grown used to the sight of adventurous tourists. Though I bet they didn't dare venture up there themselves a few years before. At least not without a small army.

The reward at the top the climb was probably the most evocative football pitch (if you could call it that) I'd ever come across. But despite its incredible view over the ocean, it couldn't hide a dark past. It was barely bigger than a 5-a-side field, a dirt pitch surrounded by high netting to stop any wayward shots going over the edge and ending up all the way down at the bottom of the mountain. The goalposts had seen better days, leaning back at both ends with torn nets barely clinging to the rusty frame. But it was on the far bank of the space into which the flat surface had once been cut that the view was truly chilling. The wall of mud was full of holes. And half way along stood a single metal post, also peppered by holes. Bullet holes. This was once a place of assassination, a killing field from the days when drug lords carried out murderous retribution.

As I thought about venturing back down, a crowd of dodgy looking Colombian fans reached the top, led by a local guide. I followed them back to the firing squad post. 'Here, they kill peoples' were just about the only English words he knew. But none further needed. The arrival of a small group of the most oblivious, beaming kids you ever saw, no more than five or six years old couldn't have been more poignant. They dashed from end to end of the field shrieking with excitement, wanting me to film them while they did it. Then watched it back ten times. Not a care in the world, but I wondered how long their joyful innocence would keep them from the terrible truths of that place.

The Colombians had been in town since beating Uruguay at the Maracana in their second round match, and now they were full of how they'd be knocking out Brazil in the quarter final. 'Col-om-bia!' was the cry as they tied three large yellow, blue and red flags and banners, emblazoned with what I assumed were club 'Ultra' slogans on to the netting overlooking the favela. They invited me to follow them over the top of the mountain through dense vegetation to where the view on the other side was just as spectacular, overlooking the Lagoa where they held the rowing in the 2106 Olympics, and the mountain beyond it where the mighty statue of Christ The Redeemer stands all-embracing at the summit.

'Eng-lish! Let's go!' the loudest one yelled at me, covered from neck to knee in tattoos. 'Col-om-bia!' But if discretion's the better part of valour, I wasn't listening - and after a few minutes of them muttering and cursing battling through the undergrowth, when we got to a ledge at the top I was far from sure they weren't planning to rob me in the bushes. Up here no-one could hear you scream. Christ! I gulped inwardly, there was precious little to Redeem THIS situation, HOWEVER wide the Lord spread his loving arms over on the adjacent mountain. Drug lords and retribution more like, Colombia's calling cards. But wait, this wasn't cocaine, those were renegade reefers being rolled up by the gang as we looked over the sheer drop down to the lake. Hail, diplomacy! I told them Colombia were sure to win the World Cup, England were rubbish, Brazil had no chance, and with that left them getting high while I shuffled off sharpish from whence we came. Back out past the bullet holes. I didn't hang around, legging it down the endless steps and out of the favela.

My elaborate path to the quarters reunited me with Costa Rica, this time against the fancied Dutch, in a city to rival Rio for its colour and carnival, Salvador, 750 miles up the coast. The flying route was almost as complicated as the driving one, which would have added on an extra 300 miles. Nobody sane drove anywhere far in Brazil, you'd never get there. But the resulting demands on flights with huge numbers of football fans in the country meant having to fly all the way inland to the wide open spaces of capital Brasilia and then back out again to the coast. Salvador, and its laid back, beach state of Bahia was magnificent. If that natural, seductive Brazilian joie de vivre wasn't enough, throw in the relentless rhythm of Africa and you get the picture. The first slave markets landed here in the mid 1500s and the vibe of the people was distinctly African. Non stop drums and dancing, with a stunning backdrop of old Portuguese colonial buildings straight out of the Renaissance. No wonder the old town was also a World Heritage Site.

If watching Brazil's second round match on the Copacabana, knee deep in water was a wonderful experience, hitting the streets of Salvador's historic old town for their quarter final against Colombia was another unforgettable occasion. Being in the stadium honestly could not have bettered it. This was an authentic, no frills Brazilian experience with ordinary people in the heart of their own back yard. And boy, do they know how to have a good time. I won't forget it for as long as I live.

It was totally unexpected too because I hadn't even factored in watching the Brazil match when I flew in the day before for the Costa Rica quarter final. Salvador was utterly alive. The whole of the old town with its cobbled streets and squares was covered rooftop to rooftop by colourful streamers, glittering bunting and elaborate decorations. Groups of drummers walked the streets belting out thunderous rhythms. It felt like carnival time. 'Take off your watch' was the message from a kind hearted boutique owner when I entered his shop. Crowds, like in Rio, were the usual cover for snatch squads, so I heeded the warning and carried nothing around the town that would make me a target.

It was in one of the main squares that I got the shock of my life. 'Chris! Chris!' came a call from behind me. It was two middle-aged men from Sheffield, 'Likely Lads' types, living the football road trip dream far from home, asking me if I remembered when I'd met and interviewed them at some England match or other, years earlier. I drew a blank and went on my way, racking my brain. There was something familiar about them. But if only they'd said Liechtenstein, from more than a decade earlier, I would have remembered them in an instant. A short time after they'd wandered off I was trying to find them again. It all came back to me, they were the ones in Vaduz who pulled off one of the greatest road trip escapades, a stunt that amused me for years afterwards. Back then they said they were from Barnsley, just down the road from Sheffield, and there were three of them then, which explained the brain fog. But the 'Likely Lads' description hadn't failed me and their tale could have come straight out of an episode of the classic British sitcom.

I'd been in one of the town's restaurants to interview a larger than life chef who promised to sing the Liechtenstein national anthem, which, unbeknown to me before going there had the same tune as 'God Save The Queen'. You can imagine the confusion of the England fans when the band played it twice before the game the following day! It was one of the great awaydays. England had rarely played in a smaller place and the stadium capacity of only a few thousand was never going to be big enough to cope with demand for tickets. The stadium which was in a riverside park barely had stands, let alone any fences to keep ticketless fans out so they erected rolls of barbed wire around the perimeter. By the following afternoon, one England fan had tried to paraglide in from a nearby mountainside and landed flush in the barbed wire, like Steve McQueen getting all caught up in the motorbike scene in 'The Great Escape'. Game over. To extend the cast list from that classic, the Barnsley boys were more James Coburn, Charles Bronson and the other one in the rowing boat because they got away with it. And no tunnelling required, though the wooden hut of Stalag Luft III was centre stage!

After I'd finished with the singing chef I bumped into the three of them having a beer and plotting up at one of the restaurant's outside tables. They didn't have tickets but vowed they'd be getting in. 'See you in there' they said, cheerily. 'Oh yeah, good luck with that' I thought. But I hadn't reckoned with their cheeky masterplan. At one end of the stadium, inside the ring of wire was a small hut. The day before the game, before matchday lockdown, fans were freely able to wander around and have a look at what, for England, was the equivalent of a non-league ground. Then, just before throwing out time they made their move. All very simple. They slipped inside the unlocked shed, kept their heads down and sat tight. It might have been a freezing night but they stayed there undetected for 18 hours. I could scarcely believe my eyes when I saw them just before kick off the next day greeting me with a matter-of-fact 'told you so!'.

I went on to meet a group of 'Scousers' in similar circumstances at the 2004 Euros. They'd bragged how ticketless entry was a rite of passage where they came from, and if I needed any proof I saw it happen with my own eyes, even with a ring of steel around the stadium in Coimbra in Portugal. They got in through the unlocked exit doors. 'Don't run!' I heard one of half a dozen of them call out in a strangled shout from a sterile area in between a couple of rows of metal barriers. They disappeared out of view round a corner looking for all the world like they belonged there. A tap on the shoulder at half time confirmed the plan had worked again. In through the out door.

They had a big screen up in the historic main square in Salvador for Brazil's quarter final against Colombia, but it was so packed I headed for the side streets and alleyways in search of a more intimate experience. Nearly everyone wore Brazilian yellow. Pre-match, an all girl drumming group roamed the backstreets making an almighty racket. Whistles sounded, horns blew, and hips swayed in rhythm. One big street party. You didn't need a bar to settle into. Every few yards televisions were pushed out of open windows, perched precariously on tables and window boxes while the narrow streets filled with revellers craning for a view. Queueing for drinks? No need. Sellers pushed through the crowds with tanks of homemade 'Caipirinha' cocktails, Brazil's national drink, a sweet concoction of spirit distilled from sugar cane, lime juice and regular sugar. I found myself on a long sloping cobbled street with chairs and tables squeezed along one side and bodies crammed into doorways or just blocking the way. How unique was this as a football watching experience! I could barely see anyone who wasn't a local. I felt like an invited guest in a country where football was life and was unashamed to wear its heart on its sleeve. The beautiful game was less a choice, more an essential ingredient of Brazil's DNA, a great leveller in a country of economic extremes, a reason for being and national celebration for all.

Everyone was out on the streets. Some of the television feeds from the kit that had been dragged out into the alleyways had a few seconds delay. My street especially. When the goals went in I heard the distant roar from neighbouring streets a few seconds before. I can still see the replay of David Luiz's bending freekick that flew into the net and sent the old town into raptures. With backing like this on a wave of emotion who could stop Brazil winning the World Cup in their own back yard? But with that came the pressure and expectation that's always floored England, and the hush that followed Neymar being carried off with a back injury in the closing minutes of the 2-1 victory planted the first seeds of doubt. Here was a man crushed by the knowledge that his World Cup was over, face contorted in pain and wracked by grief.

The street party went on late into the night, enhanced, with good fortune by Salvador being the venue that weekend for a festival of its folk music culture. Think Brazilian music and what's the first thing that comes to mind? Samba and Bossa Nova. Eternal rhythm. But I was about to get an education in Bahia folk music from Brazil's north east. 'Forro' is what they call it, an addictive blend of guitars (ukulele-esque), accordion and irresistible rhythm. Wandering the old town, I came to an open-fronted building from which those joyful sounds drifted out into the streets. A live band was in full flow, a dozen strong, all dazzling costumes and infectious drumbeats. The floor filled with women in red tops, floral dresses and headscarves forming an open circle into which individuals would sashay to a kind of call and response propelled by that ukulele-like 'ching-ching' sound. Line dancing, Salvador style.

I was crossing the dancefloor when a burly, bearded character wearing a kaftan and elaborate head covering loomed up in my path. Without warning, he took my face in the palm of his hands and with a hallelujah smile planted a lingering kiss on my right cheek. I must have looked like the outsider I felt, and this was his way of saying 'welcome!' .Either that, or I'd walked straight into a recruitment drive for some underground cult. In fairness, this had happened to me before at football matches, but not with men who looked like Demis Roussos. One of those was at St Andrew's, the Carling Cup quarter final against Villa when we scored the winning goal and a big ginger bloke to my right nearly squeezed the life out of me in a spontaneous, bouncing embrace. And I remember when England fought back to equalise in the Euro 2004 quarter final against Portugal in Lisbon (before losing as usual on penalties). The beast who landed on me that day came from about four rows back and took a few layers of skin off my face. Over enthusiastic application of industrial strength sandpaper stubble. People do strange things in the heat of the moment at football matches. I'd have drawn the line at a kiss, but Brazilians could just get away with it. Entirely natural.

Costa Rica's quarter final against Holland the following night brought their romantic journey to an end, on penalties. For me, two matches on consecutive nights in entirely different environments and I came to the conclusion that the fans in the stadium who'd paid top dollar for tickets had little of the free, spontaneous fun I'd experienced on the streets the previous evening. As I walked away from the bright lights of the match into the surrounding alleyways I got another reminder of Brazil's dark underbelly. I don't speak Portuguese but this needed no translation. I'd just passed a doorway when a young boy, no older than 11 or 12 stepped furtively out of the shadows into the gloomy street light behind me. Looking back down the alley I could barely make out anything more than a silhouette. But the image was clear. He held out a hand dangling a small package. 'Cracka?' he enquired. I shook my head and carried on walking.

I'd never expected England to reach the World Cup Final, but took a punt on the semis and was surprised that I could even buy a ticket for the Belo Horizonte semi as late as a few weeks before the tournament started. It was probably the price. An eye watering 650 dollars for a 'Category One' top priced ticket which were the only ones left. My finger hovered over the 'buy now' button before coming to terms with parting with that much money for a single football match. Much more than a season ticket for many clubs outside the elite back home. But it was the World Cup, and it was Brazil. When would I ever get this chance again? I bit the bullet, made the click and hoped it would be one to remember. Little did I know just how seismic an event it would be with a sting in the tail that I could never have envisaged when I parted with that cash.

Unlike the games up the coast, Belo was drivable from Rio, about 280 miles or a six hour run by car, longer by bus. It also had another World Heritage Site within striking distance, the old Portuguese colonial town of Ouro Preto up in the mountains. I'd met a British couple in Salvador who had just been there and raved about its charm and beauty. I took the option to fly, only a relative hop from Rio which meant more time on the ground. The two hour trip from Belo Horizonte to Ouro Preto on a rickety, fume-belching bus was made up for by what lay at the end of the road. Imagine a town in England's Lake District dotted with churches, old bell towers, historic buildings, craft shops, flower boxes and cobbled streets everywhere you looked. Its beauty was complemented by an otherworldly appearance in the streets of what appeared to be a mysterious performance artist. A raven-haired girl in a crimson dress draped in a long black cloak was walking slowly and deliberately through the streets, unflinching and oblivious to all the staring eyes. Like a super slow motion funeral march. She carried a bright red bunch of roses and the dark cloak dragged behind her across the cobbles like a gothic wedding dress train. Dracula's bridesmaid. Some kind of filming stunt, right? But I couldn't for the life of me see anyone else in tow, which made it all the more mesmerising. And ever so slightly weird.

Belo Horizonte felt worlds away from this artsy fantasy, gripped by football fever for Brazil's semi final against Germany. After those two incredible experiences watching their two previous knockout matches from Copacabana beach and the streets of Salvador, this time I was inside the Mineirao Stadium for what was sure to be an intense experience. Brazil's hosting of the1950 World Cup had got them as far as the final decisive match, but defeat by Uruguay had shattered a nation. This was going to be different, right? Neymar or no Neymar. Excitement was an understatement. Brazilians thought they'd won it before they'd started, and woe betide any doubters.

It took me back to boyhood days when going to watch Blues was the only thing that mattered. Taking the number 50 bus from Kings Heath to Bradford Street near Digbeth and making that ritual procession with the crowds up the hill to St Andrew's for the big matches. This time it was by corporate shuttle bus and I left the city's smart tree lined streets behind for the journey to the edge of town. The huge stadium lies right next to an imposing lake with a finger like inlet that runs almost right up to the gates. I saw a man from the Far East outside a lakeside cafe looking very sorry for himself. 'What's up?' I enquired. He'd spent a small fortune on a hospitality ticket that turned out to be a scam. No ticket, now empty pockets. I took the stricken man's photo and relayed his heart breaking story on social media. News reports had been awash with stories of ticket corruption and organised crime. Even one of FIFA's official partners had been implicated, the English company 'Match' based near Manchester. They provided tickets, hospitality and travel for well heeled fans, and reports surfaced of one of its executives Ray Whelan being wanted for questioning in Brazil. He was later cleared of any wrongdoing but the row over ticketing was about to land right at my door, and I had never been as angry as I was that day when I made my way into the Mineirao Stadium.

Half an hour before kick-off the place was packed to the rafters, great swathes of yellow everywhere, bar a pocket of Germans away behind the goal to my right hand side. Now, I thought, a 'Category One' ticket, for 650 dollars? That's going to be somewhere around halfway up on the halfway line, or near enough. Gate A, Block 304, Row GG, Seat 25. Such was the intoxicating atmosphere inside the stadium it took a good minute or two to even contemplate going to look for my seat. I stood there just beyond the arena entrance, transfixed, letting it all wash over me. Then the first disappointment. Block 304 was further down the field than I'd imagined, about level with the left hand penalty area. I started to climb the rows. G? That should be about halfway up. It was, but GG was nowhere to be found. I kept on climbing, occasionally looking over my shoulder to check I was still in the same arena. Higher and higher, X, Y, Z, and still no GG. Altitude sickness had already kicked in by the time I saw that AA was next, then BB, and so on. Up in the Gods didn't come close. I can assure you that GG did not stand for 'Good God!!' when I realised that my row was the one at the very top. FF would probably have covered it. 'F****** Fraud!' 'Category One' !?You're having a laugh! But if I was miffed by this point, I was in danger of self combustion when I went looking for seat number 25. I struggled down the row crammed in below the roof where there was so little light I could barely make out the numbers. 15, 16, 17, 18... STOP! Beyond that a glass panel and no access around the side. Where was 25?! No, really, WHERE? Kick off was approaching. The answer, shockingly, was that it did not exist! I'd paid 650 dollars for a World Cup semi final ticket which did not have a seat attached to it. Unbelievable. Did they not count the seats before selling them!?

This was far from FIFA's finest hour and I was on the warpath. The closest steward was about 17 years old and it clearly wasn't his fault. He shrugged apologetically, probably because he didn't understand a word of my rant. Then I noticed another dozen or more people standing at the back, yellow shirted to a man, looking as confused as I was mad. They were all in the same boat. I took everyone's email address and promised I would investigate, knowing that many of the tickets had originated in England. But at that moment, nobody was going to stop me sitting anywhere I wanted. I stomped down the endless stairs, did a sharp right and found myself half way up on the halfway line. Directly in front of me, some very comfy looking seats reserved for the Host Broadcasters. Without hesitation I clambered over a low wall and sunk into the nearest one. A perfect view and nobody said a word. Not that I would have moved anyway.

Witnessing 80,000 Brazil fans bellowing their jaunty anthem before the game gave no indication of what was to come. It was so loud you couldn't hear the music, and the fans on my side of the pitch were hopelessly out of sync with the ones on the other side. Maybe that was a sign, because the players in yellow were even more incommunicado. They looked as though they'd barely ever met, let alone ever played together and fell apart from an even greater height than my non-existent seat. It was utter annihilation, unravelling in a slow motion horror show as surreal as the caped girl's slowmo procession in Ouro Preto.

In all my years watching football I'd never seen a team concede four goals in the space of seven minutes and five in the first half hour. It was over before it had got going and I reverted to my schoolboy trait of staring at the crowd. This was classic people watching. Most fell silent from shell-shock, bar one man behind me who was on his feet bellowing volleys of abuse at Brazil coach Luiz Felipe Scolari. No-one had the energy to join in, though silently I felt little sympathy for the man whose Portugal team had knocked England out of two major tournaments running on penalties. I remember going outside for a half-time drink and seeing a girl in floods of tears. A jovial 'try supporting England' was a well meaning attempt to console. But it just made her cry harder. The only thing worth hoping for in the second half was that Germany would go on to reach double figures. May as well go the whole hog. But 7-1 was still beyond belief, an 'I was there moment' ,and the trudge back along the lake in the dark to the shuttle buses was accompanied by an eerie silence.

I at least hoped the Brazilians who'd been short-changed by having to stand at the back having paid a king's ransom for a non-existent seat would come back to me so that we could chase some compensation. The seat fiasco was one thing, and paying through the nose for the privilege of seeing their team humiliated must have really rubbed it in. But I heard from none of them. Maybe they just wanted to just forget it and bury bad memories. I pressed on regardless and 'Match', to their credit, refunded every cent of my 650 dollars, though I would have slaughtered them if they hadn't. So it turned out I watched arguably the most jaw-dropping World Cup match of all time for the princely sum of nothing. I wouldn't ever pay such an obscene amount of money for a sporting event again, and if I ever needed to ask myself why, I'd remind myself of the Copacabana and Salvador. Priceless experiences both, totally free. The people's game.

Chapter 11
Red Army Blues
Russia 2018

This chapter was written before Russia's invasion of, and war against Ukraine on February 24th 2022 - but inadvertently it feels as if it somehow now sheds a little light on that fascinating, turbulent country and how we got there. Discovering this dark and mysterious land was the reason I'd wanted to go there in the first place via the excuse of a working football trip. That February date is one I'll always remember because the day before, I'd flown back from the Winter Olympics in Beijing. We'd been expecting the invasion to happen, and I'd been sitting on the runway waiting for take off for the final leg of the flight home from Singapore to London. The flight path on the seatback screen monitor showed we'd be flying close to places like Rostov-On-Don and straight over Crimea which, while charging the memory bank you're about to draw from, didn't exactly ease my apprehension.

Two and a half hours of waiting on the runway later (technical fault, yeah, right) the captain announced we would have to re-route without explaining why. It soon became apparent. A handbrake left turn, an out of the way arc wide of Ukraine and the southern Russia border. I wish I'd photographed the revised flight plan which looked like an egg-sized bump on what should have been a straightish line back to Blighty. A wide berth was an understatement. Missiles started raining down in the vacated space the very next day. Russia's hoped for place at the 2022 World Cup was an early casualty. No-one would play them in the qualifying play-offs and FIFA had little option but to throw them out. This is where the future, then, meets the past (and the present as I write this, with the crisis worsening). I'll take up the story as I'd written it before the awful conflict in Ukraine ignited......

I'd left Sky by the time Russia 2018 came around. For many travelling football fans at home there was a feeling of 'that's a tournament I'll be giving a miss!' and not just because of the stink that accompanied FIFA's vote on December 2nd 2010, when Russia and Qatar were announced as hosts for the '18 and '22 World Cups.

The night before the 2018 vote I'd been at St Andrew's for the ill-timed Second City derby between Blues and Villa, knowing full well that if anything went wrong off the field, the media would be up in arms about the Brummies wrecking England's World Cup bid, even though the die was probably already cast. The delicious irony was that my old adversary Karren Brady was heavily involved in the England bid and I could just picture her reaction when, sure enough, there was another outbreak of crowd trouble. You didn't need to be Nostradamus to see it coming, given previous chaos in what is always a tinder box fixture. And even though Karren was long gone from the club I imagined she must have been fuming at the sight of riot police trying to stop hundreds of pitch invaders at the end of Blues' dramatic League Cup quarter final win with flares being hurled from the stands to the pitch and back again.

So much for England 2018, I thought, though no-one could have foreseen just how embarrassing the voting would be the next day from an English perspective when they picked up a paltry two votes. But with long whispered allegations of corruption in FIFA's decision making process, a few crowd skirmishes was not the reason for the FA being overlooked. In fact I'd been at No 10 Downing Street a few months earlier when FIFA President Sepp Blatter was being courted by David Cameron. Blatter was in his element that day and lapped up the attention, so no surprise at the outrage when England's strong technical bid was ignored by the voting delegates and Russia romped home.

A World Cup in Russia looked about as underwhelming as it could get in the wake of the glamour of Brazil and South Africa as previous hosts, and when Russian hooligans then ran amok against England at the 2016 Euros in Marseille, a trip to Moscow for the World Cup looked about as attractive as a fortnight at Orgreave during the Miners' Strike. No wonder not many England fans were tempted to make the trip. But how wrong they would be, because this turned out to be one of the best World Cups of all, and from a personal point of view an unexpected experience of a lifetime.

Russia, or at least the Russian people, I soon concluded are misunderstood. Don't get me wrong, if anyone decided to go there and openly misbehave or challenge the system, not much good would come of it. Domestically there are plenty who do. The notorious 'Pussy Riot' girls, longtime and persistent activists disguised as rock stars were in the news when I was there, constantly challenging the authorities, and seemingly being locked up and released on a loop. The biggest issue for the ordinary Russian people is how the country is viewed around the world, nearly all of that clouded by Western takes on former Soviet politics and the Putin regime, compounded by unhelpful episodes like the shocking Salisbury poisonings. That, I discovered did the people who live there no favours, unfairly distorting Western views of them when they had nothing remotely to do with any of it.

Ever since I can remember, the word 'Russia' would conjure up images of the old Iron Curtain, the shutters coming down, an impenetrable barrier with a grey nothingness beyond. A grim, Soviet wasteland with nothing to commend it. Robotic, unsmiling people and the last place on earth you'd probably want to visit. But much of that was based on stereotypes. No-one, it seemed to me had the inclination to see past the bleak communist years and investigate a country that could boast a rich heritage and incredible history. I had absolutely no idea what it was really like beyond all those preconceived perceptions and wanted to find out the truth. A World Cup in an unexplored land? Bring it on.

In a personal post Sky world this would be where my poacher turned gamekeeper. Working for the host broadcasters, effectively a PR role for FIFA which, when you've been the news man looking to ruffle a few feathers meant 'unlearning' that and having to think in reverse. Not so easy when the news radar goes off instinctively. Great story! would be the natural reaction, but now the instincts had to be kept in check. For a start, I suddenly had access to the stadiums where I never did before. I'd barely arrived in Moscow before I was off to film some of Russia's new sporting venues and the spectacular stadiums were an indication that the Putin regime would make the most of its time in the sun. Sochi, on the Black Sea; Samara, in the middle of nowhere and close enough to Kazakhstan that I half expected Borat to be Head of Media; Kazan; Volgograd... my head was spinning as we bounced back and fore to Moscow across Russia's vast interior, though it wasn't lost on me that the furthest east of the venues, Yekaterinburg in the far west of Siberia was still only about a quarter of the way across this enormous country. I would come to experience just how huge it was by venturing much further over when the football was (almost) done, and tackling much of the 6,000 miles back to Moscow from Russia's Far East on the mystical Trans Siberian railway.

As England made their unlikely progress through the tournament it very nearly became the most bizarre place any England fan could ever be on World Cup Final day. Had England got there, to this day I don't know how I would have managed to watch it. Which was unthinkable. Sitting on a train in the Siberian wilderness I might as well have been on the moon. Small mercies then, that they never made it, but what a story it would have made in the middle of nowhere trying to keep up with the most important match in England's history! Bitter experience, you see, had taught me that something always goes wrong and I needn't worry about where I might be when the Final was on. A monumental own goal narrowly averted!

The first indication that Russia's impetuous youth were actually just the same as anywhere came via a couple of happy-go-lucky lads, hired in to work with FIFA's contractors and having the time of their lives filming around the stadiums with their high tech drone. 'Make sure you don't film anywhere where the authorities don't allow' I told them, which was most of the surrounding area, and heavily enforced by the local police who were taking no chances on any potential terrorist attack. Anyone caught breaking the rules would be in hot water. Sure enough, the obsession with their flying eye blinded these lads to the rules, and while the pictures of Sochi's stadium from out across the Black Sea were spectacular, I was soon having to field complaints from one of the local officials that they'd been all over the 'no fly zone'. Either that, or their machine was running away with them.

Picture the fabulous free kick a few days later when Cristiano Ronaldo completed his hat trick in Portugal's 3-3 draw with Spain in Sochi's opening group match. By coincidence, or karma, the two lads had been trying to simulate a ball's eye view, almost identical as it happened to the trajectory of that Ronaldo free kick; an 'arty' shot, if you will, at the very same end. But the drone shot out of control and lashed into the net, blades whirring at full tilt. And this thing was half the size of a chinook helicopter! How it didn't leave a gaping hole in the net was a miracle - and I watched on nervously while the pair of them spent an age trying to get it free from a massive tangle. It wouldn't have surprised me one bit if

Ronaldo's shot later that week had gone straight through the weakened net and out the other side. No goal!

Unfortunately the boys didn't learn their lesson. We were in Volgograd, as luck would have it, for England's opener against Tunisia a few days later, and the two young men had their eyes on the giant statue that overlooks the city from a hillside. 'Mamayev Kurgan' roughly translated as 'The Motherland Calls' is a national icon and homage to Russia's war dead from the Battle of Stalingrad (Volgograd's previous name) which went some way to deciding the destiny of World War Two or the 'Great Patriotic War' as Russians called it. I made sure another organising committee official accompanied them for what was a night shoot, knowing that the local police were on heightened security alert. It didn't end well. The two of them disappeared and despite warnings not to fly close to the statue did precisely that.

About two hours later the breathless official who was supposed to be keeping an eye on them caught me at the stadium saying things had gone wrong and would I look at the app on his phone which had a recording of the ill-fated flight. The drone appeared to be flying only a few feet from the head of the illuminated statue, a beautiful and dramatic shot with the lights of the city and stadium in the background. Then, 'BOOM!' The screen view suddenly and violently skewed sideways followed by black. End of transmission. By now the young 'pilots' were back in the hotel bar with a tangle of twisted metal at their feet. 'What happened?' I enquired incredulously. 'They shot us down' ,came the glib reply, as if this was a badge of honour. The Russian police had apparently spotted the alien airborne intruder in the 'no fly zone' and proceeded to shoot it clean out of the sky. At least, that's what the boys said. I had no proof that this was the case and wonder whether the drone wasn't just disabled by a jamming of the frequencies causing it to fall out of the sky. Either way, it was smashed to smithereens. The only surprise thereafter was that nobody from the authorities said a word more about it. Head down, and keep walking!

The news man in me was engaged to hear that my patch for the host broadcasters covering the 'colour' stories would include Volgograd, which is unashamed to show the world the enormous sacrifice that came during arguably the most brutal battle in history, Stalingrad, over the winter of 1942-43. Part of the old ruined city has been left standing, shells of buildings raked by gunfire with bullet holes left exactly as they were to remind future generations just what happened there. More than a million dead over a few months in one city, in excess of the entire American and British World War Two losses combined is beyond comprehension. If nothing else, I thought, this would be a story that needed to be retold in the build up to the England game there. But I was wrong. FIFA's 'in house' policy was broadly 'no negative stories', however they were presented, and that meant Volgograd's extraordinary history could not be revisited.

I was, at least, able to mark it in passing. A lovely elderly lady by the name of Olga had been the stadium announcer right back from its initial construction in the 1950s and was still doing it now with Rotor Volgograd in the Russian Premier League, probably the country's equivalent of Birmingham City, yo-yoing between the divisions, which made me take to her all the more. She told me a harrowing story of a young schoolfriend being blown up in the post war years by a hidden bomb buried on the hillside around the giant 'Motherland Calls' statue. The parting gift of a giant punnet of strawberries from Olga's garden only served to explode the myth of hostile, surly Russians.

The mighty Volga River flowed right past the back of the rebuilt stadium. Lord knows what lies in that river, but put it this way, 300 unexploded bombs had to be removed during construction of the original stadium in the 50s. The sandy banks on the city side still drew hardy swimmers in the beating sun and passenger boats ventured up and down the major waterway. Volgograd's first world problems in 2018? Plagues of midges and mosquitos that came off the water and created their own carnage. Trust me, I was swallowing them by the swarm on my riverside runs and it became the biggest news story leading up to the game against Tunisia.

It might have been a far cry from the football, but Russia could show the world a thing or two when it came to arts and culture, and Volgograd had a go at marrying the two, without a hint of self-consciousness. The local opera theatre, a bus ride out of town along the river put on a spectacular show celebrating the history of the World Cup. This wasn't the 'Nessun Dorma' of Italia '90, it was visually stunning too, and we were humbled to have been invited to film some of it. At one point the stage was covered wing to wing in a silk like giant white sheet through which the heads of dozens of opera singers appeared, bathed in a fluorescent blue light while the solo soprano rose highest at the back in a dazzling white spotlight like the peak of a snow covered volcano. I had to pinch myself that we were celebrating a football event. The only shame was that it appeared to pass the football family by, and the house was filled by Russian culture vultures for whom this sort of thing was the norm. And there was us feeling proud (ashamed) of the 'X Factor' or a cheesy World Cup anthem (New Order, 'World In Motion' excepted!).

I was back a couple of nights later to see a regular performance of 'Swan Lake' and it came with a sight that summed up where we were. The opera group had set up a large television screen in the ornate theatre concourse to screen the latest World Cup matches. The Russians never lost a love of traditional formality from the pre revolution days and think nothing of dressing up for the ballet or opera. Come the interval, guests in tuxedos and tails gathered round with a glass of red to watch the action. Hands down THE most unlikely setting for some football watching communion. Though I doubt Lenin would have worn the same kit. He would have been much more 'Peaky Blinders'. Flat cap, and no nonsense, brothers! St Andrew's on a raucous match night it was not!

*

It was just like old times in the official England media hotel, on a long, sunny street that led to Volgograd's understated city centre, completely rebuilt after being destroyed during the battle. I was reunited with the old England media pack, and spent the evening before the game with the ITV team, sitting alongside Glenn Hoddle reminiscing about what might have been at France '98, a 20 year gap that had passed in a flash. We'd just remembered Hoddle's aforementioned rapier sharp riposte to the bizarre Beatles question from the overseas reporter in La Baule, when Chris Waddle, working as a pundit for the BBC joined us further down the table. Hoddle and Waddle reunited, 'Diamond Lights' on the football field but not quite as pitch perfect with a microphone. Musical partners in crime? Make that serious fraud (he winked!).

I'd later seen a flyer for a Nick Cave gig in Moscow, and certainly hadn't expected his 'Red Right Hand' to have found its way to Volgograd. I happened to mention I followed Birmingham City while interviewing some hairdressers who were dying their punters' barnets red, white and blue for Russia's latest match. 'Birrr-mingg-amm??' came the excited reply from one of them, followed by a hasty shuffle through his mobile phone and a triumphant 'you-must-know-this-guy-then' look as he held it up to show me. It was Tommy Shelby, chief 'Peaky Blinder' in trademark flat cap and trench coat. 'I like Birrr-minggg-amm film!' he enthused in very broken English while I marvelled at the unlikeliness of the situation. I didn't dwell on how the Russian sub plot, and the non-sense about the Fabergé egg had ruined series three!

There were barely any England fans in the city, the fewest by a distance for any World Cup match I'd attended. But all the pre tournament fears of hostility did not put off two of life's great adventurers, Jamie Marriott and his pal Mitch. The pair of them cycled all the way from the south of England to the south of Russia, an epic 2,400 mile, puncture punctuated ride through Germany, Poland and Ukraine. We filmed with them for the final few miles, hanging out of the back of our truck, past the giant green war helmet emblazoned with a Red Army star and 'Stalingrad' in bold Cyrillic letters below it that marks entry to the city limits. Russian hospitality raised its hand here too. Jamie had been video blogging the journey, and after being let down for somewhere to stay in Volgograd, a friendly local by the name of Vitali came to the rescue with the offer of accommodation at his mother's house in the city. A nice touch, and typical of a much maligned people. To cap a positive England fan story, for a change, Jamie and Mitch were captured in ecstatic celebrations behind the goal where the thousand or so England fans went wild after Harry Kane's stoppage time winning goal.

The war museum in Volgograd, adjacent to the ruined old buildings was a fitting place to say our farewells. My only regret was not having the courage to part with my cash for a souvenir T-shirt from the official shop. Putin, for Russian nationalists was a larger than life action hero who fought for the small man. At least, that was how many of them viewed him and he prospered from their patriotism. But for outsiders like me the sight of the Russian President laser printed onto the front of a T-shirt, bare chested and muscle bound on the back of a horse was black comedy gold. Like Boris Johnson with his trousers down at a lap dancing club. The funniest thing was the state sponsored lady at the till selling them with a straight face. It would have been worth buying one just for that.

The six hour drive out of Volgograd across southern Russia to another of the World Cup venues, Rostov-On-Don could have come straight out of the American Midwest. Endless wheat fields and lonely wooden telegraph poles interrupted by the occasional truck stop, like a scene from Kerouac's 'On The Road'. You'd have been hard pressed to tell the difference between a down-home American trucker and any Andrei or Sergei hauling his load across the lower Russian heartlands. Just ordinary people, working the never-ending roads to get by.

Without warning, we hit a T-junction in the middle of nowhere. Left to Rostov, right to Moscow, about two days to the north. Putin had built some new roads for the World Cup, and the pot-holed route across country we'd just navigated gave way to smooth, black tarmac all the way to our destination. As the carriageways widened and the lanes increased, it could have been a less busy M4. Even the service stations looked the same. Except for the cabbage pasties. Russians love cabbage pasties, even though any discernible taste didn't appear to have been a priority when the idea was first cooked up!

Rostov had a reputation as a tough city, but like much of the country, felt like a place growing fast. While some of the (older) people still appeared to be unsure of what to make of their post communism freedoms, others from the younger generation had leapt boldly into the post Soviet space and were making hay in business. 'New York, New York' just down from our hotel had learned the old trick of dressing up a dish with fancy presentation while being over in about three mouthfuls. One visit was enough, thanks, while another establishment up the way had the foresight to accommodate the visiting football fans with an open air amphitheatre, a huge screen, and large open air seating areas, made for balmy summer evenings.

This wasn't the barren, grim backdrop of former times that had discouraged many English fans from travelling. South and Central Americans, in contrast had come over in numbers, and Rostov was lit up by the glare and blare of Mexicans, 10,000 plus for their group match against South Korea, all glitter and green, sombreros, drums and general racket. It was the first time I'd witnessed a World Cup where fans from the Americas appeared to outnumber their European counterparts. The backstreets were the draw for the adventurous and I was all the happier for finding the real heart of independent Rostov. The legend 'LETO MUSIC' was nailed in bold green letters above the entrance to a small basement bar. Inside an indie band played with a Union Jack pinned to the ceiling alongside an Irish leprechaun and an array of old seven inch singles stuck to the ceiling. This was a hang-out for Rostov's artistic outsiders. The band played a curious mix of what sounded to me like American underdogs 'Guided By Voices' or British contrarians 'The Mekons' with a hint of Russian folk thrown in. Utterly themselves and all the better for it. I wondered how the underground artistic community must have fared in Soviet times with so few Western artists taking the trouble, or being allowed to travel and play behind the Iron Curtain. The Beatles' music had once found its way through figurative Soviet red tape and reached the ears of the youth despite anti Western opposition from the authorities. Even all these years on, without the censorship, you could still sense that longing for inclusion. 'Back In The USSR' was much loved by the Soviet people for that reason. Paul McCartney, who eventually got to play it to a rapturous reception in Red Square in 2003 said he'd known little about the place when he wrote it, only that he saw it as a 'mystical land'. That's just how I felt too when setting off on this journey of discovery at the World Cup. It was a two-way street. People just wanted to engage.

I was sitting in a Rostov bar one night when two young lads heard me speaking English and came over to chat as best they could about anything and everything, not least having the World Cup in their home city. It was humbling to sense their joy at being included in the party, in a country where many of the people had felt like outsiders for decades. I was later in Moscow at one of the beautifully ornate metro stations not far from Red Square and came across a band in one of the entrance corridors playing Radiohead covers. In London, or New York, everyone would just walk on by, but here a crowd gathered and watched, transfixed. It felt like an occasion.

Rostov, it turned out, was also the home of Russian rap. I'd heard the stories about gangsters in these parts, but adding some rappers to the mix sounded like American cliche. However, one of the producers from the host broadcasters for whom I was working set up an interview with some of the local artists. Nick Kostin was the promoter, a Rostov man with impeccable English and a curious hybrid Russian/American accent. He brought two local rappers with him, all 'goldie-looking-chains' and backwards baseball caps. They performed in the street for us in a tumbling torrent of Russian to an accompanying boombox. One of them, I pointed out was a dead ringer for England's Jesse Lingard. He liked that. Nick, who looked like he'd hoovered up most of the narcotics this side of Ukraine was desperate to bring some major acts over to Russia. The English grime artist 'Skepta' was top of his list, and him asking me if I could help really wasn't a conversation I expected to have with anyone when heading south through the Russian agricultural heartlands! I even made the call to his people when I got back home. But the asking price of a quarter of a million pounds for a gig in Russia was many a ruble too far, even though they did casually offer AJ Tracey, an 'up and comer' back in the summer of 2018 for far less! Rap, you see, was the music of the age, and pretty much universal. Personally, I was far more intrigued by a large billboard in Moscow that proclaimed Nick Cave and the Bad Seeds were bringing their dark theatrics to the Russian capital. Somehow strangely fitting. 'Red Right Hand' indeed, I thought, while picturing the face of that Peaky Blinders fan in Volgograd.

One thing that Nick told me in Rostov, though, was troubling. 'There's no justice in Russia' he casually complained, as if it was an occupational hazard. But a day or two later I heard a desperate first hand story of corruption that brought that statement home. The Russians I had discovered were very fond of craft beer, and every town seemed to have numerous 'spit and sawdust' type bars serving the most obscure, deadly, double figure percentage proof brews from all over the globe. Barmen in aprons with trendy Shoreditch beards and the latest beers chalked up on blackboards behind the counter. Mostly in English, strangely. 'Lubricated Labrador' from Denmark was popular, though the cherry ale from Belgium really hit the sweet spot. The story, though, soon left a sour taste.

While watching one of the World Cup matches in the bar, we got talking to a local doctor called Alex who worked most of the time in Moscow. After a skinful of exotic ale, his wide-eyed introduction of 'Hi! I'm big fan of Sarah Brightman!' was about as random as it came, made all the more bizarre in broken English. 'I Lost My Heart To A Starship Trooper' was not an ear worm I would ever have wanted catapulted back into my consciousness, but the damage was already done!

His companion though, was a woman with a harrowing story. Through her mobile phone and the power of Google Translate she told us how her husband had been a business associate of a group of men who had framed him over some kind of financial deal that went wrong. One of the group was a policeman, the classic 'bent copper' who used his influence to pin the blame on the apparently innocent victim. Despite a lack of evidence, he was convicted of fraud and jailed for six years. The rest got off. But that wasn't the half of it. It had since been discovered that the presiding judge had also taken a bribe from one of the group to send him down, allegedly common practice in that part of the world. Money talked in the post Soviet void. And to cap it all, the men bragged to each other about being the one who would also take the woman as part of the deal. She fought to resist them, she told us, but was nearly destitute, and was fighting to keep her home which the men were plotting to have taken away from her via bribes to authorities over the legality of a building extension. An extraordinary, unsettling story. No justice without power or money. Nearby, down by the River Don, on an old disused red brick building, someone had randomly spray painted the graffiti slogan 'SORRY' in ten feet tall sky blue letters. In English. It never felt more appropriate.

I made my way down to Rostov's official FIFA 'fan zone' to watch England's group match against rank outsiders Panama. The occasion was enough for most of the locals to have a ball whoever was playing. Russia's matches drew vast crowds and hysteria, especially when they qualified for the knockout stage, with flag waving and chants of 'Rass-i-ya!' (at least that's how it sounded to English ears) filling the city streets around the fan zone and cars blaring horns for most of the night. But for England's match it was a fabulous people watching exercise. When it came to football, it wasn't uncommon to find Anglophiles all over the world, drawn by an undying love for an English club. I noticed a short, bearded man with a flag of St George wrapped around his shoulders watching the big screen. Naturally I approached him for a chat. Rostov, the local Premier League club was written in Cyrillic across the horizontal red cross on the flag, like the myriad of random English towns you'd often see on St George flags at England matches overseas, often ones that didn't even have a league club. He was, surprise, surprise a Manchester United fan, like millions the world over, and had come to support England by association (ironically perhaps filling the void left by the absence of English Utd fans who you'd rarely see following England in the wake of the aforementioned Beckham sending off incident at France '98).

For an early afternoon game, the crowd in the fan zone was only moderate and many of the crowd sat on the tarmac in the sun. But as soon as 'God Save The Queen' started one man in front of me stood up, raising his left arm in a salute with fist clenched around a scarf. A bit odd, I thought, in southern Russia. England fans don't do that. But his English was almost better than mine, and like our friend with the flag was (Manchester) red through and through, from the most far flung of fandom outposts, Taganrog, home of the great Russian playwright Anton Chekhov, about two hours drive away on the Sea of Azov and very close to ill-fated Mariupol, soon to be a scene of such devastation in the war against Ukraine.

By coincidence Rostov had played Manchester United in a European match the year before the World Cup, and only just gone out by a single goal over the two legs. United didn't need any travelling fans. They were already in situ! The old stadium where the home leg was played was the classic open bowl type but was by now lying empty while Rostov were about to move into the brand new World Cup stadium just across the mighty River Don from the city centre. Mexico's match against South Korea brought the local police out in force, and not just any police. This was the home of the Cossacks, master horsemen and women. The mere mention of the word would conjure up images of athletic figures bouncing on their haunches with arms folded across chests and legs flicked out alternately in feats of buttock bursting gymnastic intensity. I'm pretty sure we used to try it as kids and collapse in a heap every time.

As luck would have it, the Cossack militia put on a production at an old theatre and cultural centre that doubled as a ballet school. We went along to film a little Russian heritage and it was magnificent. In one cavernous high-ceilinged room with huge picture windows and an impossibly shiny wooden floor (no shoes allowed!), the next Nureyevs were arching and stretching, while in the auditorium across the corridor it was pure 'Fiddler On The Roof' while we watched from the wings. Matchday then brought an homage to Cossack equine tradition and on the large riverside stretch of sand adjacent to Rostov's new stadium, the police displayed their mastery in horsemanship, part drill, part pageantry, wholly engrossing.

England's final group match against Belgium was academic after the victories against Tunisia and Panama but I had extra reason for hoping that England would win it because finishing top of the group would bring them south to Rostov for their second round match. I opted for a small bar to watch it instead of the fan zone and was underwhelmed though not surprised to see them beaten by the first major side they had faced. That brought Belgium to Rostov instead for a match against Japan and after the Mexican invasion, numbers of travelling fans were considerably down, even though the match was sold out.

World Cups usually become a ticketing free-for-all once you hit the knockout stage after casual fans try to second guess their path forward. They invariably end up getting it wrong and then either have to swap tickets and rearrange travel plans or just go with the flow. A limited number are able to follow the path of their team with specific tickets which allow for entry wherever the next match is played, but for the wide-eyed and adventurous it's hit and hope. Like me in Brazil, when England's second round match in Recife turned into Costa Rica versus Greece!

But the beauty of it all is the unexpected journey, like life, and I found myself sitting on the opposite bank of the River Don while Belgium's match was being played, watching via mobile and listening to the crowd's reaction in real time in the illuminated stadium across the water, some 20 seconds or so ahead of what was being relayed to my phone. There's something fascinating about listening to the distant sound of a crowd and trying to guess by its pitch and intensity what's happened. It reminded me of the rare occasions I'd left a match at St Andrew's early. I once heard an almighty roar at the bottom of Coventry Road at the end of a night match and knew instantly that Blues had scored, probably a late equaliser.

I have little sympathy for people who leave matches early and it didn't happen very often (the early departure or especially, the late goal for us, that is!), but I do remember one occasion that stayed with me for different reasons. It was a match around the mid 90s which we were losing, and were pressing for an equaliser. There's a tendency for those wishing to rush off at the sound of the final whistle to edge towards the nearest exit point and stand there, as if on starting blocks to beat the big getaway, neck craning for the last view of the action. I rarely did it but on this occasion shared a knowing 'here we go again' nod with a man I'd never seen before a few inches closer to the exit. I don't know why I remember him so vividly but I did, and a little spookily a few months later I was shocked to see his face on the news. It was Lee Harvey, who'd been murdered in the notorious 'road rage' attack by his girlfriend Tracie Andrews.

*

I fully expected Belgium to make short work of Japan and didn't know what to make of the first muted roar that rose from the stadium across the river. Seconds later, I was astounded to see Japan score on my screen, though the game was given away a fraction beforehand by a crowd watching from an open bar on the waterfront a little further up the river. The kind of cheer that's only reserved for the underdog. The same sequence followed soon afterwards, signalling a second goal for Japan. I was thrilled to see the outsiders upsetting the odds and headed straight for the drinkers who had the slightly faster feed. But I ought to have known it wouldn't last, and no sooner had I settled in for a beer than three further, more muted roars from across the water signalled Belgium's fightback and a 3-2 victory.

I was back in Moscow for England's second round match against Colombia and was surprised to see England fans outnumbered by their South American counterparts. Outlying cities like Volgograd and Nizhny Novgorod were one thing for getting to, but Moscow was easily accessible from London and in any normal circumstance would have been overrun by English fans for a knockout World Cup tie. But the pre-tournament fears of disorder had taken their toll and it was an odd sight heading towards the Spartak Moscow stadium to see swathes of yellow shirts and comparatively few bearing the Three Lions crest. One thing never changes though. English touts get everywhere - and I smiled to myself at the sound of a Scouse accent wandering back against the flow of the crowd through a pedestrian underpass 'Anyone need tickets?! Buy or sell!'. I didn't have one, but made my way to the nearest metro station to the stadium on the off chance of picking one up without requiring a mortgage. But it quickly became apparent they were thin on the ground. The Colombians weren't selling, and rather than wait until the last minute, I decided to head back into the city centre, find a bar and dig in.

Red Square was the obvious area to find some atmosphere but if ever I was an Englishman alone, this was the night. Everywhere was packed and I found myself squeezed onto a small table surrounded by Colombians and Brazilians. Ever the contrarian, I wasn't afraid to be vocal, and was soon celebrating England's opening goal and cursing Colombia's crude physical approach. At least I wasn't the only target of the South Americans' ire. Argentina, I quickly discovered, were public enemy number one for the yellow shirted brotherhood from Colombia and Brazil. They broke out in defiant song. 'South America! United! Except Argentina!' seemed to be the sentiment. Little translation required.

By now I had to figure how I might have to make a graceful withdrawal if England finished them off. I'd already checked where the door was when Colombia won a corner in the dying moments. 'Mina! Mina!' came the cry from the throng, some of whom by now were standing on the tables. Mina was about to sign for Everton, but at that moment I'd never heard of him, only that he was the big centre half who was coming up for the corner and the Colombians sensed he was the man to save them. 'Mina! Mina!' they hollered, ever louder. I felt like Joe Strummer again in The Clash's 'White Man In Hammersmith Palais', standing out from the crowd, all alone, only this time running the gauntlet! Sure enough Mina rose to the occasion, literally, and headed the ball into the back of the England net. The place erupted. Make that 'went absolutely mental', to coin some popular football parlance when something exciting happens at a key moment. 1-1. Extra time. Time to vacate my seat and head for the crowd around the bar where I could blend in a little more easily.

It was 12 years since I'd stood outside the Schalke stadium in Gelsenkirchen on Sky News lamenting England's catalogue of defeats in penalty shootouts and honestly thought this tournament would be the one where the hoodoo had to end. But when Jordan Henderson missed against Colombia I was almost on my knees in disbelief. How could it happen again?! Especially unbearable with an army of South Americans celebrating wildly all around me. But step forward Jordan Pickford in the England goal, and when it all turned round and the rest of the bar fell silent I almost took the roof off on my own. And didn't care who knew it. Finally! The crestfallen old chap next to me didn't speak English and I didn't speak Spanish, but we understood each other, forged by a mutual respect that only sport can bring - and I was off into the night on a high.

The second round matches marked the end of my working contract, or at least the first part of it with the host broadcasters, and I headed north to the beautiful city of St Petersburg for a week, before the leftfield turn to the east (looking south) that would take me into the heart of Russia untouched by the football. I'd negotiated a deal with the travel section of one of the tabloids to write a piece on the country that in the West we knew so little about or had any inclination, as far as I could see, to explore. It also happened to be, in the days after the World Cup Final, the 100th anniversary of the murder of Russia's royal family, the death of the last Tsar precipitated by the Bolshevik revolution. And by good fortune, I would be in the very place it happened for the anniversary, Yekaterinburg on the Western side of Siberia, on my journey back towards Moscow via the fabled Trans Siberian Express train.

St Petersburg was everything I hoped it would be. Beautiful and decadent, full of magnificent buildings that had seen better days, but whose faded glamour added to their charm. In contrast the city's new football stadium, the Gazprom Arena, was among the best in the world - certainly none more dramatically positioned out at the water's edge on one of St Petersburg's islands facing The Gulf of Finland. I walked one day all the way from the old centre past miles of waterways and through city parks, before being collared at the stadium by a pair of reporters wanting me to be a 'vox pop' for Indonesian television. A first!

I soon felt just as much a fraud trying to negotiate a peek at the Mariinsky Ballet, at sixes and sevens while the St Petersburg culture crowd were formally dressed up to the nines all around me. The fan zone was more like it, just around the corner from the spectacular and magnificently named Church of the Saviour on Spilled Blood where another of the tsars was assassinated. It wasn't lost on me that the stringent security checks getting in to the fan zone would have been a darned sight tighter than when the bombs were flung at Alexander II in the same place on that fateful day in 1881.

Had England won their earlier group decider against Belgium and been the ones who ended up playing Japan in Rostov, they would also have been on course for a potential semi final where I now was in St Petersburg, but on the same day that my flight tickets would have taken me OUT of town before the game started! Just as well they'd taken a different route then, I mused. But little did I know that lightning WAS about to strike on that score anyway! At least for now I was in St Petersburg's fan zone to see England's quarter final with Sweden on the big screens. After the Man Utd contingent in Rostov, a good number of the locals were cheering for England, and I felt far less marginalised than the Colombia experience in Moscow when the defensive senses were at full stretch. No sooner had Harry Maguire's header powered into the corner of the Sweden net for the first of England's two goals, my mind was wandering forward to where I was due to be for the semi, which in all honesty, and by bitter previous experience, I hadn't expected England to reach at all.

World Cup fever was peaking again. Social media was full of the drink-flinging explosions of joy back home that I always missed by being out on the road, but there was nothing quite like being there and plotting a great adventure through the travel maze. Russia's quarter final against Croatia nearly 1,500 miles south in Sochi brought St Petersburg to a standstill. I was staying in an apartment just off the city's famous old thoroughfare Nevsky Prospect, in a street filled with restaurants and bars. 'Hey, Chris!' came a call from the street seating outside one of them as I strolled past. It was someone who'd watched me from my Sky days and would I like to join their crowd of expats and locals to watch the match at a bar party? Rude not to! 'Rass-i-ya! Rass-i-ya!' rang around the building. If anything, this felt even more partisan than watching Brazil during those never to be forgotten occasions four years earlier.

Ordinary Russians, I discovered were extremely proud people, somehow beyond blind patriotism. But it's a complicated country. If Stalin had been the man who defied the Nazis in what they call the Great Patriotic War, I'd also heard first hand from younger folk with terrible tales passed down through the generations of repression at his hands. One story, told by my translator while we rattled across Moscow on the metro was recounted with the rawness of a still open wound. A long lost grandfather, shot indiscriminately in Stalin's name. Then there were the gulags, the concentration camps and desperate hardship in the post war years. Many despised the man and I couldn't help notice on my travels that while statues of Lenin were everywhere, I didn't see a single one of Joseph Stalin. The national pride, it seemed to me emanated from an unbreakable bond, the unspoken, shared sacrifice of 26 million war dead. Simply incomprehensible numbers. It was what the giant 'Motherland Calls' statue in Volgograd represented and went way beyond everyone just knowing someone who paid the ultimate price. It seemed to underpin their DNA.

Croatia meanwhile stood between Russia and a World Cup semi final against England. Now THAT would have been an awkward one to watch alone in a bar full of Russians, even in Siberia, and I was already making contingencies. For now though, I was one of them, and it was a feverish night of one-eyed communion supporting the underdogs in their quarter final. 'Rass-i-ya!' we called out, over and over again. If their first goal took the roof off, the second, the extra time equaliser, blew the doors off too. By which time everybody was three sheets to the wind. Of course it ultimately turned out that we had something in common with the Russians. They also lost in penalty shootouts. But if England had turned the corner against Colombia, St Petersburg didn't turn inwards and wail like we so often do. There were no tears, no gnashing of teeth and no sooner had Croatia scraped through the tension of the shootout, a brass band burst into the bar where we had been watching and turned the night into a celebration. The party spilled out into the streets and Nevsky Prospect was filled with a procession of cars blaring their horns while red, white and blue tricolours billowed from the vehicles' windows. Anyone would have thought Russia had won, but their pride in going so far and so close was a wonderful way to sign off.

Because I was due to fly out to Siberia for my travel story, I found myself having to depart St Petersburg on the day of the first semi final there when Belgium were playing France. I don't know what I would have done if it had been England. Either way, the Belgians who'd largely been conspicuous by their absence for the match against Japan when I was in Rostov kept me awake most of the night in a bar just below the old apartment I was staying in. They've always been Anglophiles when it comes to their football and love a good singing session, but, boy, they went at it on the eve of the semi. It was gone five in the morning and the dawn chorus was already in full swing when they finally stopped hollering.

I'd taken the high speed train from Moscow to St Petersburg on the way up the week before, about a three hour run through pristine wooded countryside, and the flight back was a relative hop, an hour or so. I'd left myself enough time (I thought) to catch a bit of the St Petersburg semi on my mobile when I landed in Moscow, change planes and then hop onto the long flight east to Ulan Ude, a Siberian city just north of the Mongolian border, where I'd hook up with the Trans Siberian 'Tsar's Gold' train two days later. The plan was to watch England's Moscow semi final against Croatia in Siberia the next day. I had absolutely no idea who might be watching in those parts, but imagination is a wonderful thing, and being five hours ahead of Moscow time nearly 2,500 miles further east than the nearest Russian city hosting World Cup matches, in my mind I pictured a couple of insomniac farmers sitting in a deserted bar drinking fire water in front of a fuzzy television picture. This, I thought, would be one for the ages. Where were YOU when England reached the World Cup Final?! 'Your round, Igor!' But that was getting light years ahead of myself.

The reality might just as well have been a vodka bottle over the head from a great height and my plans were thrown into chaos. Ural Airways managed to make the flight from St Petersburg to Moscow so late that I missed my connection. Great. No more flights east to Ulan Ude until the next day. I shuffled around the airport looking for someone to blame for the mess, barely noticing that France had beaten Belgium to reach the final. But I wasn't the only one in a pickle. At one of the complaints desks I bumped into a short, bewildered looking England fan whose cheery demeanour belied his predicament. Mike McKiernan was a Villa fan with a travel own goal almost up there with the error of his ways. He'd lost his passport. Left it on the plane he'd just flown in on from Cyprus. If a convoluted journey to Moscow wasn't enough of a headache, he now couldn't pick up his mortgage priced semi final ticket without the passport which was probably already halfway back to Ayia Napa. Unless, that is, he could persuade the Russian authorities to let him use a different passport. That confused them no end. Add the language barrier, and he was doing well not to be carted off to Siberia for some hard labour.

What it meant for me was the nightmare of having to make my long journey east at the exact time England were playing Croatia in the city I was flying out of. I wouldn't be able to watch it at all. No! Ural Airways had a lot to answer for, especially when the airport hotel they used to put up stranded passengers turned out to be anything but. The rickety shuttle bus to the hotel was still spluttering along through backwater pot holes more than an hour after we'd left the terminal. So much for the quick transfer. It felt like we were halfway to Azerbaijan by the time we pulled into a rundown old motel in the middle of nowhere. There was a small fairground in the yard but most of the rides had rusted solid. This place would have looked grim even in the Soviet days. The following morning I abandoned the bus and battled all the way back to the airport in an old taxi whose suspension was long shot, dumped my belongings at check-in and headed into the centre of Moscow for the match that I was going to miss! At least, I consoled myself, I had a few hours to savour the atmosphere.

I bumped into Mike McKiernan again in Red Square, ticket in hand, looking even more amused by his own absent mindedness the day before. Then again, Mike was quite mad. Utterly bonkers, to the tune of a text message that read 'When the chaos is over, I will tell you about waking up in a ditch stark bollock naked next to a Polish motorway!' A different trip, but you get the picture. A couple of old media colleagues from previous road campaigns, Dan Roan and Henry Winter joined me for an impromptu podcast on the hoof against a backdrop of red and white check-shirted Croatians making all the noise. It was odd to see so few

England fans for such a major match, especially with a small group of cockerel-clad French fans lording it around Moscow's famous square with chants of 'On est le champion!' and a cultish little ditty about their new star full back Benjamin Pavard. But by the time I'd met old Blues pal and England super fan Roger Fairclough for an early afternoon beer, the major shopping tributary that runs into a corner of Red Square was swollen with vociferous, later arriving England fans. Crosses of St George were hanging off walls and lamposts for a couple of hundred yards. This was more like it. Muscovites stopped for selfies, though one smiling little boy and his mum were none the wiser when they posed in front of 'No Surrender' and 'Millwall. We Fear No Foe. No-One Likes Us' .One for the mantelpiece.

It wasn't easy having to leave this scene behind and head for the airport three hours before an England World Cup semi final. Maybe, I hoped there would be a way I could watch it while flying. In Brazil at the previous World Cup, the airlines, I recalled, promised live television on their planes. But the ones I flew on barely managed to get from A to B without the wings falling off, let alone get a ground to air signal for entertainment purposes. That was the first problem. The second was one that filled me with dread. What happens if England win tonight? I'll be onboard a train in Siberia when they're playing in the World Cup Final! How could I possibly miss that?! I'd be relying on a dustbin lid and coat hanger trying to get a satellite picture in the middle of nowhere! There wasn't anything remotely even approaching a phone signal out in that part of rural Russia, in between the stops! If nothing else, I figured with resignation, at least I'll have a tale to tell if all this comes to pass. Or I would just succumb to the wretchedness of the situation, abandon the train, watch the match at the nearest Siberian bar, then try to catch up with them at the next railroad stop, wherever that might be in the wilderness.

And with that, I found myself boarding the plane steps at the exact moment the teams were coming out onto the field at Moscow's Luzhniki Stadium. I was into my window seat as fast as I could struggle down the centre aisle, throwing my hand luggage into the overhead locker with mobile in hand, then frantically trying to find a feed of the game. Could you get the BBC overseas on mobile without restrictions? I didn't think so, but to my astonishment I clicked on the 'IPlayer' arrow and there it was. Redemption! At least until we vanished into invisibility at 30,000 feet in a few minutes' time. They'd just kicked off and I secretly ignored all the usual messages about switching off mobile devices while the hostesses, who couldn't see me as long as I hunched down below the top of seat level, carried out the routine evacuation drill.

We hadn't started to taxi towards the runway when England got an early free kick just outside the penalty area. It was just as well there was no-one sitting to my immediate left because when Kieran Trippier curled the ball into the top corner of the net I would have probably have had their eye out. 'YESSSS!!'' ,YEEAAASSSS!!' came the muted cry from deep inside, restrained enough not to give the game away I'd thought, but clearly not, judging by the startled look on the face of the woman and two young children sitting across the aisle from me. 'Excuse me, hostess, there's a lunatic on board!' would probably have covered it judging by their expressions. I'd actually hit the seat in front so hard that a head peered back over at me to see what had happened. By then I couldn't have cared less, of course and let go a few more fist pumps while the passengers around me realised what was going on. Once stirred, the one in front, a youth with the facial features that told me he came from the area to which we were heading, Russia's border with Mongolia, was instantly invested in the excitement. '1-0 to England!' I gestured glowingly while holding up my phone. He nodded approvingly, but with a look that suggested he was as far away from having any grasp of English as we were about to be from football civilisation.

A moment later, the acceleration of the plane's take-off pinned me back in my seat and we were roaring off down the runway. How long would the picture last I wondered, keeping a wary eye on the whereabouts of the nearest air hostess policing take-off electronics abuse. As we climbed through the clouds it was still there, long enough to see Harry Kane almost scoring a second England goal while I quietly spluttered with excitement in my seat. But before I'd had time to fret again about the prospect of not being able to see the final, the remainder of the semi disappeared from view too, picture frozen under a fading signal. Limbo. Now what?

Our friend in front suddenly became more animated. Every couple of minutes he'd look back over the seat with an enthusiastic nod as if he was watching the game and 'what did I think of THAT!?' I held up a finger followed by thumb and forefinger rounded out at their tip to signal '1-0'. He responded with a shake of the head, holding up TWO fingers followed by an insistent nod. '1-0', I gestured again. But he wasn't having it and repeated his assertion, 'V' fingered like an English archer at Agincourt. 'Two?' I mouthed. '2-0?' He nodded back even more vigorously. Had we scored again and his signal had lasted longer than mine? It never crossed my mind at the time that this might have been his impression of Nostradamus. His English was more limited than my Mongolian which rated at less than zero. It was agony not knowing but I had no option but to sit back with a resigned helplessness and hope for the best. The story would remain untold until we landed in Ulan Ude at six the following morning. Torture. Absolute torture.

Needless to say, I got barely any sleep. It took me back to those early boyhood days when my mum packed me off to bed without knowing the result of the evening match and I'd wake up to the score scribbled on a piece of paper on the bedside table. 'Blues 1 QPR 4' written in biro still haunts me from that League Cup semi final of 1967. And funnily enough (though it was far from amusing at the time), it was an odd experience many years later to talk about that match with a man who played in it and tore us apart, Rodney Marsh in our days together at Sky. Him and George Best on 'Soccer Saturday' .It was even more weird chatting with Besty in the Sky canteen many a Saturday lunchtime. Legends like him only existed in the exalted gallery of golden greats, frozen in time on the small screen of my childhood memory. Not wandering down a canteen counter asking for pizza and chips.

There was also the memorable episode of 70s sitcom 'The Likely Lads' when Bob and Terry were trying to AVOID the result of an England match before watching the highlights and they accidentally caught a glimpse of a headline flyer from a newspaper seller's stand that they only saw as 'England F....' They eventually locked themselves away in a deserted church to avoid any more spoilers, while resigning themselves to what the 'F' probably led to. 'England Fantastic?' 'England Flop?'. It turned out be 'England Fogged Off'! Comedy genius.

I probably woke up from my fitful slumber about an hour out from our destination in Siberia and I could wait no longer. One of the air hostesses was walking the aisle offering hot towels and a cup of tea. 'Hi. Would it be possible when you have a minute, please to ask the pilot if he knows the result of the football?' He had radio in there, right? So he must be able to find out. Ten minutes later she was back and I was wide awake in anticipation. She leaned across the seats to my left with a smile. 'It was 2 -1' she said innocently. A rush came over me. We were 2-0 up, weren't we? We're through to the World Cup Final! Oh WOW! 'England won 2-1?' I stammered hopelessly for confirmation. 'No.....2-1 for Croatia'. Silence. The smile that accompanied those words did not soften a crushing disappointment that I hadn't felt as strongly since Blues lost the 1975 FA Cup semi final replay in the dying seconds to Fulham, or Liverpool beat us in a penalty shootout in the Cardiff League Cup Final of 2001. Our friend in front was still asleep so no good taking it out on him. So much for the 2-0 update! Then again, I don't think trolling was a thing out on the Mongolian border. He was probably just predicting the outcome. Wrongly. I was tired and emotional when the plane's wheels skidded across the runway in the dawn twilight. But if there was a silver lining, it came with a solution to a quandary that made me feel just a little bit better. At least I wouldn't now be marooned on a train in the wilds of Siberia, unable to watch the biggest football match in England's history!

That was just as well because when the final came round a few days later I never saw a frame of it. Another personal World Cup journey over, I was setting out on a new odyssey. This was the Russia a long way from the football. Buryatia, Asia not Europe, with a real feel of the East. For adventure's sake, or just being a hopeless contrarian I'd initially intended to enter Russia from the other side to everyone else for the football, via Vladivostok on the country's Far East coast and then work my way back to Moscow via the greatest railway on the planet, running a quarter of the way round the world. 'Epic' doesn't cover the Trans Siberian Railway, more than 100 years old and a mind boggling 5,771 miles across the Russian interior back to the capital. A working artery through remote landscapes that's long been the lifeblood of this part of Russia, as well as a journey through its soul. In the end I joined it for the last two thirds of its vast length, and the journey back west was the experience of a lifetime. Even at hopping on point Ulan Ude with its snaking rivers and Buddhist temples, the locals told me they had big screens up in some places for the Russia World Cup games and some bars stayed open all night with kick off times this far to the east in the early hours of the morning.

But as soon as we were out of town, this felt like a different planet, let alone the same country where the world's greatest single sport event was being staged. Mile after mile of Russian 'Taiga' ,a mix of forest and grassland, punctuated by rivers, wild flowers, small communities of wooden houses, former Soviet towns and rolling agricultural land. Whoever first said 'I can't see the wood for the trees' must have been on the move around here. Russians will never struggle for a campfire. By the time I opened my cabin curtains before breakfast on the morning before the final, we were rolling down the shore of the oldest and deepest (one mile!) lake in the world, Baikal with a satisfying, rhythmic rattle of the rails.

Even in Siberia's biggest city, Irkutsk, a couple of hours ride on the other side of Baikal, everything felt pristine. I even saw one guy catching a beautiful grayling with fishing rod and line on the crystal clear River Angara, within yards of one of the city's busiest streets. In the West you'll normally only find grayling on exclusive stretches of expensive fishing rivers on country estates, not in city centres! Once out of Irkutsk there was a communication void for a day and a half while we jolted and clattered our way back west, effectively standing still in time while we caught up with the clock. If there's a train version of jet lag, this was it. There was a television of sorts in my cabin, but the closest I got to a picture was a desperately fuzzy haze through which I could just about make out some 'Fiddler On The Roof' type dancing. Which wasn't the football. Unless they had Topol on the pitch at half time. Either way, it was an odd experience waiting for my mobile to catch a signal when we approached a semblance of civilisation and then finding out that France had beaten Croatia 4-2 to become world champions.

We eventually reached Asia's junction with Europe and pulled into Yekaterinburg, the furthest east of the World Cup venues on a major anniversary in Russian history. It was 100 years to the day since the last Tsar, Nicholas II, his wife and family were executed by the Bolsheviks in this very city as the Russian Revolution reached a bloody landmark. Imagine the British Royal Family being butchered in a basement by a people's uprising. That's what it amounted to. An extraordinary and tragic story.

The Romanov family had since been made saints by the Russian Orthodox Church and you couldn't help wondering what Russia would have looked like today if they had lived on and the Soviet decades of communism had never happened.

I didn't quite know what to expect approaching the imposing, domed Church On Blood, built on the site of the house where they were executed. Huge banners carrying photographs of the young victims had been erected on the banks of steps outside to mark the anniversary while hundreds gathered inside for an emotional, candle lit vigil. Pilgrims, many with heads covered sobbed openly. I didn't feel comfortable being there. Nostalgia, it seemed was growing in Russia for this part of their remarkable history. Or maybe, for some, it had never gone away. Ironically a few hundred yards from their death site was yet another huge statue of Lenin. The man whose Bolshevik comrades were responsible for the end of a royal dynasty. As Russia grows more prosperous again in the coming decades would the countless statues of the communist revolutionary still be viewed in the same light, I wondered? (But as I add this postscript several months into the Ukraine war, what now? What you've just read was written before the invasion without any of us knowing what was around the corner. I hope it brings a sense of how proudly patriotic I found ordinary Russians, but also how deeply defensive even the most friendly of them could be about the Motherland. 'Everyone's against us' seemed to me to be an intrinsic part of their collective psyche).

As we finally pulled into Moscow at the end of an epic adventure I pondered one thing. If politics divides, football, the people's game, ultimately unites. For all the rows about how Russia got to stage the World Cup, for the fans who made the effort to be there from all over the globe, it was a blast. One of my personal favourites, and lifetime memories. It's all about places and people - and a year on I couldn't help but marvel at reports from a unique second tier Russian club match, the longest distanced domestic meeting in the world. Here were a handful of diehard underdog fans, who'd made an incredible round trip of 13,000 miles from Kaliningrad to Vladivostok and back, to watch, wait for it.... a 0-0 draw. Proper football in two unlikely backwaters. Almost as unlikely as somewhere like.... Qatar. Oh, wait...

To be continued....

BV - #0030 - 021122 - C8 - 197/132/11 - PB - 9781913984090 - Gloss Lamination